OUR GOD OUR EARTH

SHIV ASHRAM PUBLICATION

Title: Our God Our Earth

Sub Title: Behold, I Make All Things New

Genre: Religion, Science, and Spirituality

Author: Mahesh Shastri, Priest

Published by;   Shiv Ashram Inc.
                 (a non Profit Charitable Organization)
                 Shastri Family Foundation Inc
                 (a Non Profit Charitable Organization)

                 Dedicated to all humanity

Address: 195, West Nicholai St.
                 Hicksville, NY 11801
                 United States of America

Telephone: 516 - 822 2267

Website: www.godandgod.org

ISBN: 978-0-9678381-9-9
                 0-9678381-9-3

First edition: 2008

Copies: 2500

Printed in the United States of America

Library of Congress Publication Data

Cover Images: NASA, Wikimedia and Unmasking Evolution.

Authors Photo: Jay Seth

Cover designer: Paul Glantzman

Contribution: Poonam and Pramod Raghav

My God! You are the supreme indestructible reality - that is to be known. You are the ultimate treasure and ultimate refuge of this universe. You are the eternal guardian and protector of timeless righteousness. You are the Eternal Imperishable Being. You are the original Supernatural being, the most ancient Being, the Supreme Home. You are the knower and the knowable, and the highest, Ultimate Abode. O infinite God! You are the entire world, becoming endless forms.

Gita

CONTENTS

Part One
QUESTIONING

Part Two
SAINT DIWAREE

Part Three
GOD-MADE RELIGION AND MAN-MADE RELIGIONS

****

Part One

QUESTIONING

The Path...

INTRODUCTION

It was a sunny afternoon. Sunflowers were still facing towards the sun. Birds had just returned to their nests to rest, after singing the glories of their Beloved the whole morning. A few eagles, vultures, and crows were still circling the sky, perhaps in the hope of grabbing some food for their little ones. Saint Diwaree's dead body, profusely covered with dried blood, lay on the ground and his staunch devotees were stunned, as they did not know what to do because no one had ever anticipated such a dreadful event. Everybody was shocked, trying to imagine the pain he must have felt at the time of his death. Their question was - why should such a thing happen to an innocent Saint, who had led a holy life in order to have a peaceful end?

Death was already a mystery, but this frightening tragedy left their minds even more confused and brought up many new questions about renouncing worldly things with the intention of leading a holy life to please God. No human being likes enmity because we know; 'God has given us life, not to create enemies but, to do good things, and if one cannot do good things then at least he or she must not harm anyone'. Diwaree, a devoted saint, had really sacrificed his life in the service of God with his exemplary life. The question was: why did such a good man die such a horrible death?

Apart from that they also had many more questions in their minds, such as: what happens to us at the moment of death and where do we go after that? Who has made us? Who made this world with beautiful plants and animal life? What and where is God? Life is so short, yet why do people do so many bad things for money and pleasure? Why do we fight? Why does one get upset? Why do human beings forget to search for life's main purpose and get engaged in other worldly things? Why do people follow confusing paths? Why is everyone's nature different? What are the stars, sun, moon, and other planets? What is Karma? What is luck? Why is one rich and another poor and who controls its laws: human beings or a Supernatural Power? How can we get enough money to survive: through our own efforts? Why do we have to go through separation from our beloveds? What are: dreams, sleep, the mind, and the soul? A dozen questions were already in their minds, ever-since human beings had begun thinking about the purpose of existences.

We have so many religions and creeds on this earth: Christianity, Hinduism, Buddhism, Islam, Jainism, Judaism, Shintoism, Sikhism, Baha'i-ism, Taoism, Zionism, Zoroastrianism, The Reformation, Modern Disbelief and other philosophies. We have ever so many cults and hundreds of customs, traditions and numerous scriptures. Somehow, somewhere in all these beliefs the answers must be hidden and for a reason. We have so many Holy men on earth: Preachers, Priests, Sadhus, Gurus, Lamas, Imams, Rabbis, God-men and many, many other religious leaders. Someone must possess the answers to the questions posed earlier.

From the very dawn of human civilization we, human beings have been searching for answers and God. By now, someone must possess the secrets and, if not, then there may be a reason, and we must search for that reason too. Man has achieved amazing success in the scientific field, so likewise there must be someone who has achieved similar success in unfolding these mysteries.

God has definitely sent us into this world for a reason. Our existence cannot be for nothing. Life is a question and we must find the answer. We must unfold the mystery and, with determination, we must solve this puzzle whilst we are alive. To understand the aim of existence must become the focus point of our lives. Most of us already know that eating, drinking, money and pleasure cannot be the final aim of life. For some undesirable reasons I left all worldly things to become a single-minded monk - to accomplish the goal of life. Becoming a monk and renouncing all things was little challenging, but I knew that doing something worthwhile is always tough. As a monk I started living in a holy city, among saints and monks, which was a blessing and kept wondering if I could find a true soul who could lead me in the right direction of my journey.

Here starts the journey where we will walk together step by step. Please enjoy.

****

THE HUNGRY BEGGAR AND THE HUNGER FOR FAME

A beggar, named Anna Mario, was sitting in-front of the God-Bawa's House of worship. He was in great pain and starving to death. He was sitting on a wooden cart and asking every visitor for help. Not every visitor could understand his pain even when seeing his frightening condition. Most of the visitors didn't see him as he was; they saw him according to their own understanding. Flies were buzzing all over his body. Some people were uncomfortable looking at him and did not like going near him. Some people believed that he would bring them bad luck and some believed that he was a shammer and was playing on their feelings, of pity and fear, simply to make money. Most people hated him, but a few kind-hearted ones helped him. These, kind-hearted, people felt sorry for him, and couldn't see any bad in him.

Mr. Harry Kingson ordered the workers to move him away from the shrine, because a filthy beggar didn't harmonize with the beautiful, palace–like, shrine. Harry Kingson had built this impressive shrine in which he had placed a huge photo of a God-man. Though other preachers knew the God-man to be a fake, yet no one could tell him that a cheat's picture shouldn't be placed in a prayer room. Harry Kingson claimed that his business blossomed after placing his faith in that God-man.

Harry had very good relations with powerful politicians, yet nobody knew what exactly he had done to make him, within a short time, one of the richest men in town. Some people spoke of government deals, through politicians, but there was no evidence to that rumor. Many powerful politicians visited him as they thought that, maybe, he knew how to use the right people in the right places and at the right time.

Maybe, he knew that successful people did everything in a clever way, with a different thinking, which unsuccessful people couldn't understand.

Nobody knew the reason of his success. Maybe, for him, everything in the world was a business including religion, spirituality, and death. Maybe, it was because of the power of prayers or karma. Perhaps he knew that a religious organization was the best way to gain people's confidence, and thus the first step to realizing that ambition. Perhaps by donating a large amount and getting involved with a religious organization he had gained the power to change any preacher's fortune. As, many preachers admired him, in a diplomatic way, which eventually, helped him in gaining political power. Many a smart preacher's fortune changed in a short time if he pandered to Harry's insatiable appetite for admiration. He knew money could add luster to one's reputation and he used his money to protect and escalate his reputation and political power. Everyone tried to guess the reason of his financial success.

Every religious leader admired him for some reason. Though, other wealthy men in the congregation were admired, but for Harry the admiration had become a diet. The desire for admiration spread through him like an uncontrollable greed and he was determined to do anything for praise. He built shrines, hired priests, saints, famous religious men and artists. He wanted to show the world that he knew the best way to find a solution to any challenge, which nobody could even imagine.

He financed Mr. Andrew's election campaign, who then went on to become vice-president of the country. After serving in parliament for couple of years Mr. Andrew also become multi-millionaire. Any politician's campaign that Harry supported was always successful, and, just as amazingly, a God-man also flourished in this association!

The new God-man - God-Bawa - was created by Harry Kingson with the power of his money. It was very hard to establish whether the God-Bawa was a creation of Harry's money-power or Harry was the creation of God-Bawa's mysterious and miraculous powers. But they grew together by helping each other. When Harry gave a huge donation to God-Bawa to build a monastery on a large piece of land, God-Bawa and his monastery became extremely popular and people started throwing money into his organization by becoming paid members, trustees, or common devotees. With the power of money God-Bawa's voice also became very powerful. Now, the question was: how did an ordinary person became so big and famous? Is it Karma or skill of a person?

****

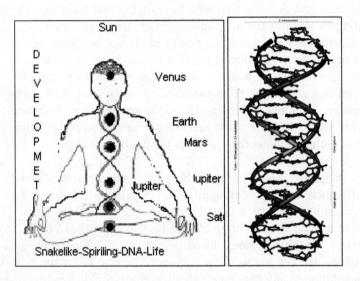

Snakelike-Spiriling-DNA-Life

Clockwise moving energy is keeping body screwed against counter clockwise moving earth.

****

Step Two...

THE MIRACLE OF MAGIC

The 'miracles of magic' work faster than anything in the world of faith, as in this world of confusion, the majority believes in 'man made magic'. It is easier to believe rather than contemplate the 'wonders of nature' or God's own miracles, which for many people, are insurmountable subjects to grasp. The mind is already occupied with day to day work and doesn't have the capacity or desire to go into the endless ocean-like depths of 'God created miracles'.

His Holiness, the God-Bawa, achieved much popularity after his association with Harry, and Harry became famous and rich with God-Bawa's support. Nobody knew the secret of their successes and their methods of achieving them. There was a time, before he became God-Bawa, when he couldn't find a solution to any of life's problems. He had had a couple of unsuccessful job interviews and even disagreements with a police officer...

He used to be an unsuccessful beggar. After that, he spent a lot of time in prayer and took to worshipping Spirits in order to ameliorate his luck. He followed every piece of advice he could get from any and everywhere. Once he spent a year, in a cemetery doing penance, as advised by his master. Another time he chanted a prayer one hundred thousand times. That took him two months with time to have food only once a day. To improve his circumstances he worshipped a dead man's skull for six months, while reading a prayer book, non-stop, for seven hours a day. While doing all these and many other things he suffered starvation and suffered many misfortunes by following the path of honesty. At that time he was penniless. No one had sympathy for his broken down trodden situation. He became very unhappy and kept crying for many days and praying from the bottom of his heart, "God! Am I not your child? You must surely be looking at me and my situation. Why can I not get the basic things in life? Am I asking you for too much? Don't I deserve a shelter over my head and enough food for my stomach? Don't I deserve a simple job and simple life.... ... " He was a poor man.

The biggest mystery was: how did he become world famous. No one understood that. It remained a secret between God-Bawa and God but for everyone else it remained a mystery. Like Harry, Bawa also realized that a clever businessman is clever only as long his secrets are not exposed. If his secrets are exposed then the clever entrepreneur has failed. A good secret is a solid foundation for any undertaking and for that reason a few honest and trustworthy people were close to him. These people too did not know the actual secrets. Some people were curious as to the reasons why a person could be worshipped by millions of followers. Was this God's decision or just a man's luck? Was this just a man's own power or were some invisible forces working from behind him? Was it the anonymous blessing of a specific spirit, or could a spirit create miracles in the life of Bawa? How could he become so rich, and why not one of them?

A miraculous incident occurred in his life, when a businessman named Hirachand was won over by him. Hirachand was astounded to meet a living being who could read his mind. The question was how could one person reach inside another's mind? What an amazing psychic? How could a beggar-like person know who he was, his name, how many family members he had, and how could he possibly know of his property, business secrets and business problems? Hirachand was totally bewildered to meet such a person; one who knew his deepest secrets, including his relationship with his wife and even the name of his mistress. He firmly believed that no one, except God, could read his mind.

After he had convinced Hirachand, Bawa had an idea. He thought 'If a person could correctly diagnose the disease and treat it then he could sell his 'medicine' for any price. The patient's first concern is the satisfactory diagnosis of his illness. Almost everyone assumed that God-Bawa had acquired his mystic powers to ward off the malefic powers of the spirits, stars and planets and could, therefore, also change the luck of those who consulted him. When asked, "Did you experience any divine powers while living in the caves?" His answer would be, "Oh! How did you know that?"

He started to claim he could help people have whatever they wanted in life, saying, "I can change your fortunes by using the same methods that I have been using for myself, Mr. Hirachand and Mr. Harry. I have lived in a sacred cave, but now I have come to the city to help those who need and deserve my blessings. I know that no doctor should stay away from his patients. Similarly leaving the holy cave I came to the city to help those who are suffering from disease and mental tension. I have learned these methods from very holy saints, who, after spending their entire lives searching to find these techniques, have passed them on to me. They have given me these powers so that I can help those who deserve it."

In the beginning, a few people, with little money, visited him but the number of visitors and amount of offerings rapidly increased. He learned that this was the easiest way to make money and reasoned that if he could get a large property then people would not look at his weaknesses, as they would with poor saints. He saw that everybody in the world has problems, but rich people have exceptional mental stress and no real peace in their lives. They are willing to offer any amount of money to a God-man who could alleviate their mental tension. They are always looking for a solution - at any price. Any God-man who could, with confidence, say, *"I can solve all your problems,"* would receive a fortune from them. From a real Saint they expected instant solutions, instant spiritual realization, and a magic touch to solve their problems, and overcome their mental barriers and blocks.

Gaining trust is important in business but appearances are also important in attracting the customers. Without an attractive and imposing personality a holy man has little acceptability and, consequently, poor market value. As in commercial enterprises a product must have attractive packaging. He started wearing the garb of holy saints. He changed his name to 'God-Miracle-Bawa', though people usually called him 'God-Bawa' or 'God'. The new attire and the new name attracted more and more new people. His new look made people believe that he was not a common holy man, but a special one. They believed that only sages with mysterious powers or superior wisdom would dress in that attire or have such a wealthy life style.

In the visitor's waiting area he kept a photo album. In the album he appeared with Presidents, Prime Ministers, Kings, Queens and many well-known rich businessmen like Mr. Harry Kingson. Many people started inviting him to their homes for blessings. Before going to their homes he would find out about their problems through rather interesting sources.

Hirachand introduced God-Bawa to Harry and revealed that God-Bawa had special powers, through which he could solve any problem; problems related to business, family, love life, children, health and much more. Then Hirachand related his own experiences with God-Bawa. At hearing this Harry became very excited and at the very first meeting he had a secret conversation with God-Bawa;

"Irrespective of the nature of the problem, whosoever comes to me shall have his or her problem solved. Nothing is impossible in the house of God. Nothing is impossible with the powers bestowed on me by the Almighty. Why fear when I am here?" whispered God-Bawa enticingly into Mr. Harry's ear.

"God-Bawa I have heard a lot about you from Hirachand, and also from my relatives. I in the short time since they accepted you, as their special master, all their wishes were fulfilled with your blessings. Now with your blessings they all are happy," said Mr. Harry in a humble manner.

What happened after that was an interesting story. How he convinced the richest man nobody knew except God-Bawa. How a person could read another's mind was a mystery. Obviously only Harry knew what was going on in his own mind. Yet the God-Bawa read his mind and told him all about his complicated problems. Since Harry had never seen or heard of a human being who could enter inside another's mind he figured that the God-Baba must be real and the one who could solve any problem.

After successfully convincing Harry he said to him, "Don't worry my son! All your problems will be solved in the next few days. This is the end of your suffering. You have been keeping a painful secret clamped within your heart. Now the good times begin. I will say special prayers for you, that only I know, and you will see a miracle in a short time," assured God-Bawa a bit enthusiastically.

Mr. Harry was agog with excitement and surprise. With folded hands humbly he said, "God-Bawa! Can we start it soon?"

With a helping expressions on his face God-Bawa replied, "Yes, tomorrow is an auspicious day. Such a fortunate time comes only once in decades. It's a great coincidence that it has come at this time. If you don't follow my instructions you shall never have a child in your life. You must arrange this prayer for ten days. Three hours in the morning and four hours in the evening. You will need to arrange certain things for the prayers. You can, if you wish, invite your friends and other family members. This is the strongest prayer to the spirit Goddess and within a year you will be blessed with a son. Success is guaranteed. This will not cost you too much, only a couple of thousand dollars. Usually, it is more than fifty thousand but for you I will grant this is as a special favor."

"That amount is nothing God-Bawa! I will do many things for you in return. A son is real wealth and cannot be compared to any amount of money," said Harry.

The next day, at around 7 a.m., the special prayer started at Harry's home to which he invited his friends. Everyday after the prayer a delicious dinner, with more than fifteen items, were served. However, the friends were not aware of the purpose of the prayers. They just assumed that it was for everyone's well being, as Mr. Harry was the chairman of a religious organization.

During those days all God-Bawa's disciples and many wealthy people came to Mr. Harry's house. They learned that Mr. Harry was a wholesale dealer of home-equipment and garments. Many wholesale buyers decided to deal with Mr. Harry, because they came to know him through a holy God-man. Harry could smell opportunity as his company was, going to become a public company shortly, and he figured that the share prices would quickly jump very high. His prayers would bring a child and big business. It was a classic example of killing two birds with one stone. The fruitful prayer sessions kept going on.

From the guests God-Bawa received a huge amount in offerings and was very happy knowing that he could never get this much in his lifetime through any honest means. The God-Bawa was confident that if he could convince a billionaire to donate his entire assets then the process would continue; more people would bring more money, which mean't more power. Anything was possible with power. All a person needed was determination and ostentatious faith.

The last day of the prayers was declared 'extraordinary blessings day'. The God-Bawa stated, "Whosoever will join the last day of prayer will definitely get something from the Divine and his or her every wish shall be fulfilled." Almost everyone was present during the final part of the ten day's ongoing prayers. He then took some cotton with a little camphor on it and said to everyone, "Now look! Look! Keep watching, The God of Fire will be manifested by the Divine powers of my prayers. Everyone, please keep watching." He then sprinkled water on a matted coil of coconut husk. When the water came into contact with the coconut husk a fire was suddenly generated without a match being struck or any other fire-starting device. Everyone sighed with surprise and then clapped. "Fire has appeared! Fire has appeared!"

"God-Bawa must be God for how else could he create fire by only chanting prayers? How...? What clearer proof can there be than this? With our own eyes we saw fire appear with prayers. If one cannot accept this, then he or she is definitely a fool," said Harry's sister and everyone agreed everyone with her.

Everyone believed that they had come to the right place, and that they did not have to go anywhere else for the truth. No more searching for God. On that day many people made up their mind to offer their lives to God-Bawa. Some became his disciples and others became followers.

The disciples declared, "Stop rushing to nowhere. Now you have understood your destiny so start walking on the right path. If you intend to follow God-Bawa tomorrow then do it today, and if you intend to do it today then do it right now or you may never be able to make it. It is now or never. Hit or miss. This is the only chance to enter the door to Nirvaan - eventual salvation."

God-Bawa's followers collected much evidence to justify the right time for God's incarnation on this earth. They collected some scientific proofs as well, such as; global warming, depletion of the ozone layer, slowing of the Earth's speed, increasing population etc. Many followers were trying hard to find even more proof to convince others that he was the real God.

They wanted other small preachers to pay obeisance to God-Bawa, so that only God-Bawa would be on top. They wanted to make one world with one philosophy, one understanding, one ruler, one religion, and one God: God-Bawa - the God of Mr. Harry - who is always right. No other God. No more confusion. All this was only possible with money, which Mr. Harry was willing to donate out of his tax deductible funds.

On the day, when he created the mysterious fire, the God-Bawa initiated many followers and from them he received good offerings. He had brought his own photos, in his bag, which was held by a close disciple. Taking the photos from the disciple one by one he autographed them in front of the followers. Then he gave one autographed photo to each disciple along with a flower. New disciples were advised to pray everyday before the autographed photo for in this way he would always remain with them. Different messages were written on those photos such as;

"Why Fear When I am Here."
"I am Here to Take Up Your Burdens."
"Give up Your Burdens I Will Carry Them for you."
"The More You Worship Me the More I Bless You.
"If You See Me I See You."

"You don't need to waste your energy, as you don't know how to carry burdens, nor do you have the strength. Wise are those who take the right decision, at the right time. Foolish are they who see proof, yet don't understand. Stubborn and ignorant are those who see every proof yet don't change their minds. Today you have made the wisest decision of your lives. A soul comes to the door of heaven after thousands of years. Unlucky are those who miss this door due to a lack of understanding. They keep churning their souls and bodies in the cycle of birth and death. Now your burdens are not your headache. Feel and realize it right now. Feel free and remain happy from now onwards. Now that you have given your life to me, I promise you I will take you to heaven. Death will be like a painless injection to you and at that moment I shall be standing right there to welcome you into my arms. After that I will grant you paradise, a place filled with happiness. I will grant you eternal life in heaven. Now, you are in safe hands. Celebrate!" was God-Bawa's sermon.

Within two years, through sheer coincidence, Mr. Harry had a daughter. Harry was very happy with his child for now at last his friends would respect him at functions and other public places. They would not think of him anymore as unlucky and condemned, with a barren wife. Moreover, no more would they look down at him with their superior airs because he had now become a father and regardless, whether it was a son or a daughter, he had an heir to his assets. Also he would not be forgotten after his death.

Harry Kingson was not sure whether he had the child through the God-Bawa's prayers or his own luck. The unanswered question that remained in his mind was; 'if it was luck then why did it not work before? The God-Bawa must have some hidden powers,' he thought. After being blessed with a child he talked very highly of God-Bawa. He never gave thought to the negative reactions that could result if someone's dreams did not come true. For many reasons he developed a blind faith in God-Bawa.

He started telling everyone that, God-Bawa could change the impossible to possible. With a matured personal appearance, an amazing and big house, a friend to rich politicians, always immaculately dressed and, having built up the image of a religious man; no one ever suspected, for a moment, that Harry would use religion to further his aims.

If on the judgment day, God were to question him as to why he had misled others he planned to answer God by saying; he had told no lies. He had got a daughter only through the God-Bawa's prayers and that was precisely what he told others. However, God-Bawa had to be questioned first. For if God-Bawa - a holy man - could lie then why couldn't he? If a holy man could tell lies: then why not a businessman? If a religious God-man could do wrong things: then why not a common ordinary man? Anyway, if God wanted to punish him, he would tell God that there are eight criminals bigger than him and that they should be punished first. Having had this little inner dialectic, he decided to keep on misguiding people telling them that 'God-Bawa could solve any problem' and thereby expanding his business.

After hearing Mr. Harry's public statements thousands upon thousands of unhappy people came to see God-Bawa with their problems. They came with problems in love, health, finance, a family member's anger, children and so on. Everybody had a problem but only the chosen could enter his palace. God-Bawa had his own way of selecting them. By telling them what their problems were he gained their confidence and trust. Everyone believed that only a doctor could identify a disease and cure it. Others, who did not know the tricks of the trade, were considered doctors with no knowledge or even dangerous doctors, who could give the wrong medicine. There were other saints trying to convince the public that theirs was the right prayer technique, but since those saints could not correctly diagnose problems, no one was impressed.

Mr. Harry became close to God-Bawa, and came to understand most of his spiritual games and started treating him as a good friend only. Harry Kingson lost his respect for him and did not believe in his miracles because by then he knew that Bawa was a cheat just like any fraudulent businessman. The only difference was in the products they marketed i.e.; Bawa sold spiritual solace at a high price whereas other businessmen sold differents products. However, for Mr. Harry, God-Bawa was a very useful medium to achieve his own goals. On the other hand for God-Bawa, Mr. Harry was an equally useful medium. In a short time they became faithful friends and knew the secrets of each other's underworld businesses.

Many people believed that by just seeing the God-Bawa all their problems would disappear, therefore they went to see him, but only two types of people could talk to him directly; the first group comprised of wealthy people who could pay large amounts as donations to his establishment, and the second group consisted of social workers who were good for favorable word-of-mouth publicity and could persuade others to become his followers.

There was a new excitement in people; here was a new God with new ideas that matched the notions of most people. A new God who did not ask them to have good relations with their fellow humans. A new God who agreed that they were right and that their fellow human beings were wrong; that they were good and other human beings were bad and, that they were fit for heaven because they had joined his cult. There was a new hope for the people who believed in magical powers, a new hope for the people who believed in this incarnation of God, a new hope for those who believed that without a spiritual master one could never see God. There was a new hope for those who wanted to have a God of their own fantasy, a new God who would be satisfied with their actions. A new God who could be satisfied by money.

****

Step Three...

FAITH IN MAN-MADE MYSTERIES

Bawa's style of convincing his people was unique. A business psychologist - he praised them by saying, how pure they were. He praised their courage, their faith in God, their inner truthfulness, their wish to help the helpless, their determination, confidence, inner beauty, hard work, and ability to face adversity with gentleness. He also praised their love for God. Then he would tell them about the Supernatural Power's message through a dream or a direct message regarding the person's situation, and how it would help him or her. On top of that he had some well-known highly placed political leaders in his team who would convince rich clients about Bawa's honesty and the power of his prayers. Once a client was convinced only then would his politicians talk about a business deal.

There were many victims who bore the consequences of their foolishness. One such victim was Mr. Chaudhary. Eventually, one day after going through many struggles, Mr. Chaudhary got to meet Mr. Harry and said, "Mr. Harry, I am very unhappy. This God-Bawa has destroyed my family. This man has made my life miserable. I have never had such disappointment in my life."

Of course Harry knew the entire story, yet he pretended surprise, "Why! What happened?"

"I have lost everything. Now I have only tears," he cried hysterically.

"What happened? What happened? Tell me," asked Mr. Harry pretending, as if he knew nothing at all.

"That God-Bawa I met in your prayer room ... he promised to change my luck in weeks ... you and your friend said that the prayer was being performed to bless you with a child and you got a child. I thought that a holy man, who was being invited by highly regarded people like you, must be in possession of some godly powers. You told everyone that he has many powers and that his spiritual master could fly from one mountain to another, in seconds, who was 225 years old yet youthful looking. He could enter another's mind, and discover what was going on inside. Once, he changed his form, became a butterfly and went into someone's home and later told him everything about his extremely private life story. That man was amazed. Anything was possible for him. He could change a person from a beggar to a king or from a king to a beggar. God-Bawa could do anything; so believing your statements I went to him. He asked me to write down my problems on a piece of paper and, then in-front of my eyes, without reading it he destroyed the paper. After destroying the paper, he told me all the things that I had in my mind.... Except me nobody else knew about those problems. I kneeled down before him and, assuming he was God, I started to speak. He interrupted me saying, he knew everything. That, the day before he had had a dream about my business problems with Johnny and Kabeer and about my mother who was suffering from cancer; in a critical condition and on her death-bed. The Supernatural Power had already told him about all my other problems and had instructed him to help me.

Vice-President Lord Andrew was also sitting there while Mr. Chaudhary was talking. He too spoke of his friend who was in coma for two months. One day the doctors declared him dead, and his funeral was arranged. Everyone in his family was informed to attend the last rites. Lord Andrew was already in touch with God-Bawa and God-Bawa brought the dead man back to life. There was a photo album on his table and while I was turning the pages of that album, with many pictures of God-Bawa with famous political leaders and business people, he told me all about the big miracles he had performed for them. After that conversation, I had every confidence in him.

He explained the eleven night prayer program and told me, "The prayer will start daily at twelve midnight and continue for three hours. One night, in between, the Spirit of Death will appear. You will see him. He will ask, 'What do you want? ... What do you want? ... At that time we will break a decorated coconut. Breaking that coconut will be like offering a man's life to the Spirit of Death and that's how your mother's health will be restored. The coconut's death will replace her life." Then he explained to me some of the ancient systems of 'human sacrifice', such as: why the ancient Japanese made human pillars to protect buildings, why in Britain people put bodies into the new emerging motorways, why the Ashanti king offered the blood of 200 young women to the land upon which he built his palace, why during the third century a child's life used to be offered to bring someone else's life back, but now he could do it by only using a special coconut.

Hearing all those astonishing stories of miraculous sacrifice I made a deal with God-Bawa. I had some cash in hand and I borrowed from a bank against my inherited property. All the jewellery I had I gave to a pawnbroker for a little money, the rest I borrowed from my good friends and relatives. I gave all the money to God-Bawa's secretary and Mr. Andrew in the hope that it would be doubled in a few months.

We did everything that he asked us to do. After couple of night's prayers my wife assured me that God-Bawa was a righteous and powerful living God. She assured me that with God-Bawa's blessings everything would be all right, and that it was providence that had brought him into our life. God knows what he did to her psychologically for he changed her thoughts, and she started speaking highly of him. She said to me *"If you want to win the contest you must enter the contest, while God is favoring us"*. Apart from the personal faith in the prayers I was highly impressed with his contacts with the top leaders such as you. I remember your words, *"Opportunities come to us all, but if we are not prepared to capture them, they will pass us by."* God-Bawa had strictly forbidden my wife from disclosing the secrets of the sacred prayer to anyone or the powerful prayers would destroy everything and everyone.

Mr. Harry, my wife and I did whatever God-Bawa asked us to do, believing that God's man was honest. My mother didn't survive. We got nothing in the first month except the worry on my daughter's face. Earlier I used to be welcomed warmly into his room with a friendly smile, jokes, and laughter, but after handing over the money, God-Bawa did not even like to speak to us.

I went to his monastery several times to ask about my money. His gatekeeper always told me that God-Bawa was addressing a VIP congregation ... or God-Bawa was in the middle of a prayer ... God-Bawa was in the meeting with the president... God-Bawa was not in ... and so on. Whenever I called him, his secretary always told me that he is saying his prayers ... he has gone to Tokyo ... he is in New York ... he is in Sydney ... he is in San Francisco etc. call next week. One of my friends told me that Bawa had cheated a businessman in London for half a million pounds, and that the money was divided among a cabinet level politician, a businessman, and a king of bandits. The politician, businessman and bandit were partners in his business gang.

I am also very frightened because many people say that Henry's murder was arranged by God-Bawa. Henry was in a similar situation, and he was about to proceed to the court. His wife knew many secrets about God-Bawa; like how he abused ladies and influenced them psychologically into making their fathers or husbands to enter into business deals with Bawa's politicians, but before anything could be done legally, they were shot-down by some unknown gunmen. There were many other murders of people after their involvement with God-Bawa. Now, Mr. Harry, I am afraid. I don't know what to do and because of my daughter's career I cannot tell anyone. Please tell me what to do because you are close to God-Bawa and only you can help me. I am frightened and confused, please help me," said Mr. Chaudhary as he finished his story.

"Listen my friend; you are committing a terrible mistake. A holy man is a holy man. His life is to do good things for others. Never repeat again what you have just told me, about him, to anyone. Do not let the word 'murder' pass your lips again. If God-Bawa does not want to see you, it's all between you and him. Don't put me in the middle and don't ask me again," Harry Kingson stated.

"....Who on earth will the unhappy turn to for solace? Everyone believes that at an unhappy stage of life one should visit a holy man to seek consolation, and if one were to get cheated by that holy man, then where on earth is a safe place where a restless man could take a break?" questioned Mr. Chaudhary.

"Not everyone can stand before the fire. Only good people can reap the fruit sown by God-Bawa. We have been with him for a long time and we see his miracles every day of the year. A man who has so many doubts in his mind cannot see his miraculous powers," answered Mr. Harry boldly.

Mr. Chaudhary said, "I can't understand how a God-man can be dishonest? You being a religious person, recommend him to everyone, saying that you are in the service of ... ..." again he started crying.

"Well Mr. Chaudhary, who in the service of the public, is innocent in this world? The Railway Minister pocketed a quarter of a million, the Finance Minister has defrauded half a million, the Home Minister squandered half a million, the Chief Minister embezzled one million, and the Foreign Minister has polished off over one million and the Prime Minister made over five millions. Everyone is milking the public cow according to his or her acumen. Everyone's eyes are on the finance department. Show me one honest minister, in the country, who is living within his earnings and tell me which one of them is not religious? Then how can you think that a person wearing religious robes should not make money?

There have been thousands of religious crooks, before, in this world and there will always be. This system is very old and it will remain so. You can do nothing about this powerful system. Read this book; then you will know that this mighty system is perhaps mightier than God," Mr. Chaudhary started reading the first page which said;

Jeep Scandal 2000-jeeps for Rs 30 Crores, The Jaguar Deal - Rs 12 Crores, The BOFORs 155 mm Gun Deal - Rs 64 Crores, Hawala -Rs 65 Crores, Securities - Rs 9130.75 Crores, Fodder - Rs 750 Crores, Urea - Rs 133 Crores, Letter of Credit - Rs 112 Crores, Telecom - Rs 34.68 Crores, Ayurveda - Rs 26 Crores, Petrol Pumps - Rs 100 Crores, Housing - Rs 154000.00, Wheat/Rice - Rs 2000 Crores, Krasnopal Shells - Rs 150 Crores out of which a minimum kickback of Rs 22.5 Crores, T-90 tanks - Rs 3000 Crores, Su-30 aircrafts - Rs 36000 Crores, Sirajuddin

Scandal 1956 - Rs 60 Lakhs, Maruti 1975 - Rs 100 Crores, Indian Oil 1980 - Rs 9 Crores, Hospitals Scandal - Rs 5000 Crores, Coal Scandal Rs - 50 Crores, Locomotive Scandal - Rs 19 Crores, Sugar Scandal - Rs 5500 Crores, Purchase of Votes for getting Majority in the Parliament - Rs 5 Crores, Indian Bank Scam - Rs 100 Crores, Housing Scandal -Rs 100 Crores. (1 crore = 10 million) *'Courtesy: Tehelka.com'*

Mr. Harry continued, "That is just one page of one country, and if you read this whole file you will know that this world belongs to us and not to God. All those people are or were religious and had blind faith in some unseen power but they became billionaires by using our game plan. All those billionaires were admired by the public and in the future anyone who follows in their footsteps will surely be admired because the masses blindly follow the richest person considering him God or believing that God acts through him. This is how the system of money power and the power brokers work. This world belongs to the money-power brokers. Do you understand Mister? So don't even think of fighting the mighty tigers.

Each of these mighty tigers climbed the political ladder by using religious faith and God's name and then appeared in the news headlines as kind-hearted, benevolent and truthful people completely dedicated to the public. Don't you know that many of our Government's powerful chairs are occupied by murderers, criminals, crooks, blood suckers, cheaters and bandits? All of them claim to be; religious, truthful, innocent, and God-fearing public-servants.

For us money is like the river on which we build a dam. That dam makes us winners in the next election and while we remain in power we use that dam's power for our high utility bills, our security expenses, home entertainment, children's education, relative's expenses, girl friend's expenses, foreign travel expenses, beach house expenses, Swiss Bank accounts and high standard of living. We enjoy life. Who cares? We spend millions on parties. Let the experts say that Harry Kingson's greed is causing the death of one hundred twenty four people per day. Let them talk. The poor don't know that. Let them die. Everyone has to die. Who cares? Power is where the money is. Money speaks. People follow the lessons of a billionaire. People are inspired by billionaires, even if he or she is immoral. We have money. We can do what we want. The critic's mouth will be shut. Their tongues' will become silent unless they are determined to praise us. Money is everything Mister! You too tried to become a multi-millionaire like us, but you failed because of your own foolishness. Do you understand Mister?

A religious person is worshipped only if he has lots of property. You people consider him God only because he has two billion dollars worth of property or a palace-like monastery. You people respect him only if he has a big monument. That is why all religious heads are vying with each other in making more and more money. The more they have the more they are accepted by you, the people. Money and wealth endows higher purity upon a holy man, his devotion, reality, sincerity, and his connection with God. You wouldn't have gone to God-Bawa had he been a penniless beggar saint.

Therefore, learn to live with the reality, and not in a dream world. Be practical. If God-Bawa could make you millionaire then why shouldn't he do that favor to himself? Why does he have to depend on others' funds and offerings? God-Bawa is doing a business, in his own style, by conning greedy people like you. You wouldn't give half-a-million dollars to a truthful saint. Like every big man Bawa too must become powerful to deal with people like you. Yeah, this is the truth. Every high man is clever and also religious. A big man cheats many people and a small man cheats a few. A big man cheats big people and a small man cheats small people.

Now listen to me carefully Mr. Businessman; a turn in the road is not the end of the road unless you fail to make the turn. Here, whoever has failed is dead. Everyone looks to the one who is ahead in the race. Every racer competes with the one who is ahead. You were destroyed before reaching the goal. To race on the highway is easy and fast, but you didn't know how to make the turn at the curb, therefore; you couldn't survive. Don't blame others for this. Now you should go home and take some rest. Tell your wife that accidents happen. An accident is a lesson. Learn from these lessons; if you cannot swim, don't jump into the pool. Assess your strength then take the big step; you cannot cross a chasm in two small jumps. Don't regret if you don't succeed. Bad luck comes your way to make you strong. Learn from it. Grow wise from it. Later you will understand that your bad luck is the luckiest thing that ever happened to you.

God-Bawa was right; is right, and he will always be right. Wrong is the one who does not know how to deal with him. You reap the consequences of your ignorance. You claimed to be wise, now you need to be wiser, you need to learn more than you knew before. Don't you ever dare to say these words again 'How can a holy man ...?' A holy man has more responsibilities than a common man. He has to build bigger buildings, feed more followers, provide free accommodation to the increasing numbers of his followers, and stay ahead of the competition. How can God-Bawa afford so many things? From honest actions? What's wrong with your brain?

Now, let me tell you the facts, because now you are finished and can therefore do nothing. Listen to me carefully, because in your depression you may forget. You were one of my rising competitors in this city, which I could not tolerate anymore. We have wiped out almost all the competitors. All the powerful political leaders do what I want, because I finance them. Nobody knows that major turbulences are taking place in the country with my directions. Whoever tried to grow bigger than me did not see the next morning's sun. I figured out that your business ideas were going to affect my business in the future, and my intention is to remain on the top, which is possible only with God-Bawa's miracles. You should know that the laws of this world and God-Bawa's law are in my hands. You will be destroyed if you speak-out and say anything bad about God-Bawa. You will be made a paraplegic invalid, and you may even suffer a stroke if you do anything wrong. All your family members may go through unbearable pain. Do you understand, Mr. Chaudhary, what I am telling you?

What the hell do you want from him? I am telling you that money has gone into the Railway Minister, Foreign Minister and others' pockets. He is a holy man; he doesn't keep anything with him. He has nothing. Why do you want to trouble him? Why do you have to waste my time and his? I have explained everything to you in detail as much as I possibly could? Never bother us again. Do you know the Member of Parliament for this area? The President and the DIG of the Police department? Do you know them? They all are his disciples. And remember one more thing, one enemy is more powerful than a hundred friends," said Harry angrily and walked upstairs into his palace.

Mr. Chaudhary held his forehead and started thinking about his dead father; all his money gone, high debt, the destruction of his daughter's future, the misunderstandings with his wife, misunderstandings with his friends and, now this man was telling him to keep his mouth shut, "Oh, God, it's not easy to live in your world." He prayed a lot but he could not handle his problems.

He became depressed and his blood pressure shot up. He gave up praying. He wanted to initiate legal action against God-Bawa, but he had no money and no strength. He thought of going to the courts on his own and standing in front of the judge and telling him the truth. But he knew that Bawa's expert lawyers could convince the judge by proving that wrong was right and right was wrong, because there would be many hired witnesses available outside the court. Proceedings against God-Bawa! That would sound a bit funny to the public. He knew that no one would believe him. No one would have any sympathy for him. There is no justice without money. He needed money for lawyers. On his own he could not fight the case. For the poor, there is no hearing. Even the corrupt judge would favor God-Bawa.

Mr. Chaudhary had a million things to tell to people about this God-man, but he was speechless. There were so much going on in his mind, but there was no one who could understand his state of mind. He felt really lonely in this universe.

If Mr. Chaudhary had become a successful man, he would have perceived God in the enemy's face, he would have made a large advertisement for God-Bawa saying that, 'God-Bawa's miracles really do work. God-Bawa is the true God.' He would have advertised on national television, newspapers, and he would have covered the city with banners, flyers, and leaflets. He would have donated a huge building to the monastery that would have attracted more crowds. Like other successful businessmen, he too would have misled many more people telling them to, "Go to God-Bawa and see the real miracles of God with your own eyes, as I saw it. He can do everything that you want. He made me successful. He made my friend successful. He can do this, he can do that … …He is the real God, and so forth," But thanks to this God, he had became penniless, and therefore speechless. Even if he wanted to express his true feelings about God-Bawa, no one would believe him. Everyone would think that Chaudhary had gone crazy and he was talking rubbish because of his madness. They would say that he was slinging mud on the most holy God-man, which was proof enough of his madness. He must be beaten up or sent to a mental hospital.

For eighteen months he wandered around in the hope that some day he might get back something but after eighteen months he gave up. He realized that there was no use in wasting time. He was depressed and ill. He knew some gangsters who, for forty percent, could pull out his money from Mr. Harry and God-Bawa's pockets. Unfortunately, due to his mental illness, he forgot to approach the gang. He forgot many useful things. Eventually he disappeared. He just disappeared; nobody knew where he went including his two daughters and wife. He disappeared for good. Some people had last seen him in God-Bawa's guest-house dormitory, but he just disappeared leaving no trace on earth. God only knows where he went…

****

Step Four...

LOVE AND FAITH

Learn the Wisdom of compromise, for it is better to bend a little than
to break
... Jane Wells

Two well-wishers must keep walking the journey of life together with
perfect understanding, all the while, keeping in mind that the destructive
flame exists within everyone. It is sparked by discontent and like a fire in
the jungle it keeps growing until it becomes uncontrollable even for fire
fighters. A wise person can also become helpless, and separation the only
option left to live a better life. However, that is not the way to end up in
the struggle of life. Life can be a cinch by inch and hard by yard.

Tom and Maya knew that divorce and death are quite similar, because in
both cases one has to travel alone. The only difference is in divorce one
has to travel 'the journey of life' alone and in death one has to travel 'the
journey of the soul' alone. Both can affect the other's journey
powerfully.

Their plan was to achieve real happiness but arguments, financial
problems, unexpected accidents and other unwanted things started
befalling them that they were unable to reconcile their differences and
understanding could not help. They were not prepared for such a struggle
in their lives.

They knew that divorce was a big failure in life. They forgot all the
promises which they pronounced to the Almighty at the time of their

marriage; i.e. 1. We shall walk together in the journey of life. 2. We shall always love each other in sickness and good health, ups and downs, richness and poverty, and we shall support our marriage through its trials and triumphs, 3. We shall fly with our dreams and overcome life's obstacles, speak and listen to one another openly and honor one another, 4. We shall fulfill our social obligations and strive for perfection, respect spiritual values.

At that time they knew that the meaning of the marriage ceremony was 'commitment' or the union of two minds so that they shall walk the journey of life together on the rough road of endless unexpected trials. They knew nature's laws; 'last rites' and 'marriage ceremony' takes place only once in a life time. They listened carefully to everything that the priest explained to them, but when they were dominated by their egos, that stood between 'them and their vows', they forgot everything. They did everything wrong while controlled by anger and alcohol, as a drunk driver makes mistakes. At the actual decision-taking moments their wisdom disappeared and their faiths pushed them far apart from each other. The simple facts of life became too difficult for them to deal with. Their lives became miserable because of trivial issues.

Maya was a completely confused victim of God-Bawa's philosophy. She never had a conversation with him nor had she seen him at close quarters. All she had heard about him was from her parents and friends. Her beauty was admired by all the followers, and she was a staunch devotee of God-Bawa.

At the beginning of their love affair there was no religion between Tom and Maya. As young people often choose a mate based only on physical attraction; a smiling face was always welcomed. They thought that love would conquer all and religion was not important at that time. The only thing important was to love each other till the last breath of life and they were sure that their love would last for good. They loved each other immensely. They were willing to do anything for their love.

Many mixed marriages are very successful when they are blessed with great understanding, as usually the couple is broad-minded and capable of understanding things on a wider scale. Many couples have faced bigger problems while they belonged to the same culture, religion and similar family back grounds but in their struggle the core of faith became a powerful issue for Tom and Maya. Hate is blind to any thing good in a partner's religion and in a partner's loved ones. Problems become uncontrollable when they start condemning each other's religious heritage or parents and that is like digging out the roots of a well established foundation.

Maya was God-Bawa's follower, and Tom was a Christian. They both had a strong faith in God. Only their beliefs did not match. In his perception Tom could never accept God-Bawa as his God, and Maya could never see Jesus as her God. Tom never liked the idea of a man as a God and having his picture in the house instead of an icon of Jesus Christ. He couldn't comprehend God's presence through God-Bawa's picture just as Maya couldn't see God in the picture of Jesus. But if they had to live together compromise was necessary, so in their place of worship, they had two pictures; one of God-Bawa and the other of Jesus Christ. For a long time, they remained in agreement that God is one; though the paths are many, all paths lead to the same destination, therefore it makes no difference when one's heart is clean etc. etc. But in his heart Tom never liked God-Bawa's photo on the coffee table. It was a cause of constant irritation to him. He believed that his life partner's mentality was deteriorating because of her philosophy and Maya believed that because of his religion Tom was deaf and blind not to understand the right things.

They had hoped that one day either one would accept the other's philosophy, and start believing in his or her God instead. Whenever they tried to persuade each other, they knew the intention was to convert the other to his or her creed. Agreeing is one thing but adopting a philosophy that is poorer than one's own is quite another thing. They used to think, 'if your religion cannot teach you how to be a good human being then what is the use of following that useless concept? What was the use of admiring a tree which produces bitter fruit?'

Usually children's love unites the parents, but poverty, insecurity, faith or blind faith shook their confidence in their ability to carry the load on their shoulders. When, after the birth of their children, Tom lost his job they had big a financial problem and their misunderstandings kept increasing day by day. They could not curb their emotions and feelings anymore. They could not tolerate the insults of each other's parents and parent's religion anymore. They started fighting like cats and dogs and with no limits to using foul language. In their disturbed mental condition they kept making more and more mistakes. Eventually they brought up the subject of their respective faiths. In total exasperation Maya asked Tom, "Well, I am not asking you to throw away Jesus' picture so why do you want to remove my God-Bawa's?"

"Because God-Bawa is not God," Tom replied firmly.

"Have I ever said that Jesus is not God? If I have not, then why do you say that my God-Bawa is not God?" asked Maya with tension.

"Because he is simply not," Tom replied with surprise on his face.

"Please don't be so unfair and unreasonable. Let us live a happy life together. Do not make me say anything bad," Maya said, trying to be reasonable. So many things kept going through their minds.

Tom's thinking was: "Those who do not believe in the words of the Holy Bible are unlucky. They cannot reach heaven. The Bible states that there is only one God, and that is Jesus. There has not been any Savior before and ….,"

Maya's thinking was: "The same thing is written in God-Bawa's book as well: God-Bawa's book says that Bawa is the one and only Savior of people living at the present time. There has always been a Savior whenever needed by devotees. This time God-Bawa is the Savior. There shall always be one whenever people need him."

Tom: "Whoever wants to be saved must believe in the Bible. The Bible is old, and God-Bawa's scripture is only twenty years old."

Maya: "God-Bawa is the oldest one in the universe. It is explained clearly in chapter nine, verses 8 to 17 of the scripture on how the creator himself came in the form of God-Bawa. This is the truth. One shouldn't believe in unseen stories. The Bible is not a living witness. I can show you a million people who will tell you that there is only one savior, and he is God-Bawa.

The most intellectual of people like doctors, engineers, professors, teachers, and industrialists, members of parliament, foreigners and many Ph.D. degree holders will tell you that God-Bawa is God. The only proof you have provided for your God is the 'Bible', which was written in ancient Hebrew - a dead language. A dead language's proofs are as good as dead. I have a million living proofs. They can speak in a living language about a living God. Do you think that all of them are idiots? The whole world is worshipping Bawa's photo and admiring his spiritual powers, which have wrought miracles in their lives, their homes, their business' and their children's lives. Do you think that they all are fools? Are you the only intelligent person left in this world?"

Tom's logic was: "There is no traditional authorized Priest who can prove that God-Bawa is God."

Maya's point was: "At the time of Jesus, there was also no traditional Priest who could prove that he was God. In fact, many people did not like him saying that he was a Savior."

"We are living now and I am talking about this time," Tom said with wrinkles on his forehead.

"That's what I am saying. Talk about the present time about the living God of this time. Jesus may be a God of that time for those who lived during that period. We are living now and our God also is alive now. However, if you want it to be proven by a priest then come with me. There are many priests living in God-Bawa's monastery. Some of them hold the highest degree in scriptures and they can even chant the scriptures by-heart. They can tell you who the real God is, for the people of this time. It is simple - if your people can prove that a dead man was God, then why can't a living one be a God? If you can believe in a dead God then you must believe in a living one too. From a dead person you cannot ask for advice, but from the living one, you can..." said Maya.

"Maya, stop it! Please, I have had enough. Don't you dare say anything more against the Savior. Enough is enough, now stop it. I have had unusual events and crises before in my life, every-time I was saved by Jesus, and now I can see that you are in danger as you have started uttering malicious words about the ultimate Savior." Tom warned her with firmness.

"You also don't dare to say anything against my God; otherwise you will face miseries and calamities. If I could keep my mouth shut about your ignorant actions like kneeling down in front of a dead man's wooden statue then you should also keep your mouth shut, when I worship my living God's photo. I also have had many experiences with my God. Whenever my father and other family members called him for help, he came and helped, and no one in my family has said anything against God-Bawa. You are my husband and therefore I forgive you, otherwise my father would destroy you. Whoever speaks a bad word about our God, he or she, deserves the death penalty. No one can be forgiven for such a crime. This is the biggest crime. It is written in the holy book that: whoever speaks bad words about the God of this time should be punished with the most frightening death. His tongue should be ripped out. He should be burned alive or stoned to death so that no one in the world dare speak badly about God," with wide opened eyes Maya warned him.

"The same thing is written in my scriptures as well, but I did not frighten you to death. Now the matter has become serious. I have to tell you that if your God-Bawa is Christ then no one, in this world, would be higher than him, and he deserves the highest respect, worship, honor and all the kingly treatment, he is getting now. But if he is not God, if he is not Christ, then he is a fraud. A cheat using God's name! In that case, he deserves to be stripped naked and physically punished with one-hundred thousand needles. His eyes must be gouged out. His tongue must be tied with a rope and pulled out. His hands and legs must be pulled apart for deceiving millions of people. If you think I am talking illogically then we must wait till the reality is exposed. He must get the severest of punishments in the universe, if he is not what he is claiming to be. No crime can be bigger than the crime of deception, the biggest crime in the universe," while taking deep breath, Tom spoke out finally.

"You are not intelligent or wise enough to decide punishment. That is God's job. And God is God-Bawa. Let him decide who should be punished and who should be rewarded. You are not wise. You are wrong to suspect and doubt the real God. It is even written in the books that, 'anyone who has any kind of doubts about our living Savior must know that his or her time of doom is near'. You have doubts and that means you will be finished soon. And there will be no one to save you. You will be finished," said Maya squeezing her lips together.

"That's what exactly mentioned in our Bible which means your end is near, and no one will be there to save you as you are against the Savior," said Tom with steadfastness.

"My doomsday is not near for two reasons; First, I have a real living Savior, God-Bawa, and second, I do not believe in a fake one... For two reasons my doomsday may be near; first, because I have shared my life with a man who does not believe in God and second, because I have kept a man who believes in a fake God," replied Maya with anger in her eyes.

The children watched every incident in their parent's life. They wanted to tell them the truth from their youthful point of view and understanding. They needed to reassure their parents of their own security. They were already worried that any moment anything could happen if their parents didn't stop their destructive behavior. They were handling more then they could, but Maya and Tom kept up their destructive activity while ignoring the kids.

Tom went out of the room and closed the door. Then in front of Jesus' photo he cried inconsolably. He said, "God please help me, I know you are testing me but I am too weak for this difficult test. I cannot take it anymore my Lord. How many wrong things do I have to put up with and for what? Please God help me!"

That evening Maya also prayed in front of Bawa's photo saying, "Please Bawa help me at this defining moment in my life when my faith and belief in you and all that I hold precious in life, is in jeopardy. If I agree with him it's a sin and if I don't it's a sin. Bawa I know you are testing me but I don't know what to do to make him understand. Please Bawa, help your helpless child I am completely broken and don't know what to do except bow down before you." In this manner each kept praying for their God's help.

Finally, one day, Tom said, "Maya I just wanted to help you so that you could walk on the right track. I feel sorry for you; everything could have been wonderful, if you had accepted the real God. Your mistaken beliefs are bringing failure into my life. Now it is time for you to help yourself, our beautiful kids, and me. So far we have only stayed together because of the kids, but now I am sorry, I cannot take it anymore. Tomorrow I am going to the lawyer. I do not want you to be my life partner anymore. You do not deserve me. You deserve something else, which you will get when the time comes."

"What do you mean? What do I deserve?" asked Maya with a shock.

"Divorce," replied Tom calmness.

Maya started shaking with fear. "I have not asked my Lord to punish anyone but if you really make me unhappy and give up your responsibility to raise these kids, then you shall suffer the tortures of hell for thousands of years," said Maya agitatedly in a shaky voice.

"I have not harmed anyone so why should I be punished? Jesus is my Savior, and he will save me," answered Tom calmly.

"Now let us see who saves you. Ask your Savior to be ready as your doomsday is closer than you think. I also cannot accept a man who is against God and still shares my life. On top of that I am not committing the unforgivable sin of giving up the responsibility towards my children," said Maya in a shaking voice.

The next day, two police officers came with handcuffs and arrested Tom.

"But I have not done anything wrong," Tom said to the cops.

"You have to justify that to the Judge. We are here to do our duty," replied the cops.

They handcuffed him and put him in a cell. There was no one to get him released. 'Wife Abuse' was the case filed against him. Maya was determined to destroy him and to teach him a lesson because he had really hurt her devotional sensitivities towards God-Bawa, which traumatized her. Now, he must learn a lesson for this offense. She believed that Tom had destroyed her life and left her in the middle of the ocean with no succor or shore in sight.

Tom was in prison. He was depressed and was hoping that sooner or later Jesus would produce a miracle to help him; because his fight was for truth. He knew, from the bottom of his heart, that, 'Truth Prevails'.

After a week, Tom was released from prison. A hearing date was set. However, before the hearing date, they went to the court and filed divorce papers. After a long married life, Tom and Maya ended up with a divorce. This cleared each other's path to their so called 'monumental spiritual progress.'

Divorce became unbelievably expensive for them and devastated their wealth, their health and ruined their lives. Tom suffered from depression, physical and mental illness and could not handle the pain. Alcohol relieved his pain and eventually he became an alcoholic. Maya became jobless and took care of her three kids with the little money she got from the government welfare fund.

> *Yaha Alaga Baata Hai Ki Mai Pahichaana Na Sakee.*
> *Merii Jarurat Me Tuu Kahaa Nahee Milaa.*
> (It's beside the point that I couldn't recognize you but my God,
> where didn't you meet me in my desperate need. You have always
> been with me.)

Tom completely changed. He was no more, as he once was, smart and well dressed. He became weak and thin and had a long beard. He did not bathe for many days. He slept on the road. He was always sad. He would mutter every ten minutes, "Jeeeeeejus … … My Lord, Jeeeeeejus … … My Lord…" One night he saw the Lord laughing in his dream. He asked "Lord why are you laughing?" The Lord answered, "Because, my child, you are worried after surrendering to the Protector."

His faith was strengthened but his love for Maya remained. One evening he was sitting near a lake. He was alone and started crying. He wiped his tears with his fingers, and looking at the lake water he said, "Maya my beloved, I truly love you, but I don't really understand what went wrong. But I want to tell you my beloved, I cannot live without you. I am so confused. Again, I want to tell you I love you. Your love had nurtured me, my mind and my soul. I did everything for you. I fought with my parents... I cannot live without you. Will I ever see you and my beloved kids again?

What great love that really was. What went wrong with their relationship was a mystery. Before their marriage their life of love was like being in paradise. Their conversations were amazing. Everything they saw as a miracle of God. They believed that their lives were united by God for some great purpose. There was a time when Love had made their life heaven, perhaps heaven itself had come to earth or earth had become heaven for them. Every bird sang in a lovable voice for them. The wind whispered melodious music into their ears. The rivers sang for them in a Godly voice. The mountains smiled and the trees welcomed them with beautiful flowers and fruits. They sang God's glory and thanked God. They sang many love songs. They were filled with happiness and happiness was within and everywhere around them. *God thou art wonderful...*

> There is no more lovely, friendly, and charming relationship, communion, or company than a good marriage.
>   ... Martin Luther

What a great love that was. Those days Tom understood that 'it is a woman who makes a man'. His happiness became her happiness and her happiness became his happiness. She had a giving nature. She never lost her temper. She was kind and completely dedicated to him. Even, if he sometimes, did something wrong she did not keep that in her mind. She knew that it is the woman who makes the man. Her aim in life was to always please her husband. She treated him as her God.

On the other hand in return she got more than she gave. He always cared about her and told everyone that he had a wonderful wife. She had so many good qualities in her that he always tried to please her. He said to her that all he wanted in life was for her to always have a smile on her face. He worked hard to earn money to buy many things for her. She was interested in helping the poor. So she told her husband to help the poor and helpless. She said that she had everything and needed nothing more, and if unprivileged people could also enjoy same comfort in their lives it would make her happy. Once she saw an old man shivering in the cold and gave her coat to him in the hope that in a difficult time God would provide a coat for her husband. She explained to her husband, "He has no mother, or wife who could understand his pain. Only a mother or wife can understand the pain of a man. If I die before you, you will be alone. If you shiver in the cold, that will be my pain. Thinking of such a time I protected him so that God will help you."

Two persons became one in mind. Once he underwent a painful surgery. She stood by his side and showered him with love. He did not even know when his surgery was over. After the surgery, in the hospital ward, she started crying. He asked her why she was crying. She told him the dialogue between the burning wick and wax. A candle was burning in a shrine. As the wick was burning, the wax was melting. The wick asked the wax, "I am the one who is burning but why are you melting?"

The wax answered, "I cannot bear the burning of the one whom I have kept in my heart."

Yes, that is true. One stays alive just for the loved one. Even after death they want their loved one safe. Love is God's gift. A spiritual minded person can survive, in any condition, if he or she is not alone. Loneliness is the most painful experience. Their concern developed for each other. They always had a deep consideration for each other. The flow of their thoughts was always in the same direction. Their two hearts were one. Their two minds were one and their souls became one after the union in the ceremony of love. They always consulted each other and agreed with each other. They had no ego problems. Education, beauty and money did not count in their dedication to one another. She used to believe that if he ever got upset, then it was her fault and he believed that if she got upset then there must be something definitely wrong with him.

Their lives were a dream world. They felt each other's pain, yet pain was not a pain because their love was great enough to triumph over any pain in the world. Their love was their strength at the time of pain. They knew God had made them husband and wife so that, together, they could enjoy this world even while facing great difficulties in life. God had made them to share each other's happiness and difficulties, joys and sorrows. God had made them to help each other in the spiritual journey. They knew "true love never fails".

At that time it was impossible for them to understand how people could have bitterness in their married lives. What religion or what philosophy did those people follow that instead of loving each other, they hated? Why could they not understand that this short life is meant for love, not for hate? Why could they not understand that love unites, hate separates? That a husband and wife are joined together to collect loving memories and that the most important thing in life is to become a successful parent. It was totally incomprehensible for them that a husband and wife could hate each other.

One day Tom had even said to Maya that, he loved her so much that he couldn't even imagine living without her. He knew that when two people love each other there is always an unhappy ending. One dies first leaving behind the other. No one could understand what a person feels like when he looses half his body (wife) in old age. No one could even have the slightest clue of that tough test when a man cannot die and cannot live. A lonely life becomes more painful than death.

At the time Maya had said to Tom, "It is like the two feet of a man; one becomes immobile after the death of its travelling companion. Both rarely die together. One dies first and the other dies later. The one that is left alone must always think about the Great Soul and nothing else. Loneliness is a gift to think about God. Immortal love doesn't die. Love is a sort of invisible energy; an invisible form of God that keeps us alive; that nurtures our soul. Love is the destiny of the soul and one is restless without its rightful place to sit. That was one of the reasons, in olden times, a wife used to immolate herself at her husband's pyre."

Love is patient, love is kind. It does not envy, it does not boast, it is not proud. It is not rude, it is not self seeking, it is not easily angered, and it keeps no records of wrongs. Love does not delight in evil, but rejoices in the truth. It always protects, always trusts, always hopes, and always perseveres. Love never fails

Bible

That time, with his hands folded, Tom had started praying and thinking, "O God! What an amazing thing this love is? Love and death are both your inexplicable wonders. Will there ever be a human brain to understand and reveal the secret of these two things? My Lord only you can reveal it. Amazing!!

Then in a loving way Tom had said to Maya, "Yes, God may have thought about how people could survive without love. On this earth both far and near, without love there is only fear. People may wander alone looking here and there, not finding the Creator or any one to whom they could tell the story of their hearts, therefore, God may have created this wonderful miracle between man and woman, so that His children may not feel lonely in this fearful world. Their loneliness will lead to depression and end with nothing. They will go around searching for God and find confusion. That's why God may have created this love."

Maya had changed the topic slightly and told him about alcoholics, she said, "Many people cannot bear loneliness. Though, practically, one is always alone, but this loneliness gets further accentuated after the loss of one's beloved. One then takes recourse to drinks and narcotics, but here also the law of the Great One holds our swing. Whatever one goes through in such a situation is mainly because of a disregard for God's decision. If they do not care about themselves then how can they care about anyone else?" They both went on and on narrating the miracles of love, and eventually Tom had said, "But Maya shall I tell you one more thing?"

"Yes, do tell me"

"I love you so much. It's not possible to stay alive without love…"

"I know that. You don't have to tell me that"

But what happened when within a few years the bright days turned into dark nights? Everything turned topsy-turvy, reversed and they ended up in divorce. Even after their separation, for a long time they remained in love, they couldn't forget each other, but slowly with time changes took place.

As Maya was only thirty-two years old, and beautiful, she had many visitors coming to her home. Some of them even admired her and asked if they could help her in any way. The fact was that she loved her husband. She tried her best to fight chaos, but didn't know how to deal with the challenges.

The reason behind their separation was not only because of their different religious concepts but another, and main, reason that was a mystery, which they themselves could not understand. Everything was going smooth and well and suddenly their minds became gripped by some unknown force and they did not know how to deal with that. That stopped nourishing love. They did not know that they did not know. They did not know that they were wrong. An outsider had come between them in an unperceivable form. Fear of loosing of their dream-world and the 'I' between them had made them egoistic and stubborn and created hate and supported anger.

She wanted him to quit some bad habits and he wanted her to change her style. Tom forgot what she wanted from him and she forgot what he wanted from her. They were no more concerned about what they were not giving to each other; on the contrary, they remained concerned only about what they were not getting from each other so they became afraid of loosing each other. Through religion they tried to remove the 'I' problem.

Moreover, since it was a fight between husband and wife. No one could jump in between because only they knew the seeds of the problem. Therefore, only they could solve it. If they couldn't resolve their problem then how could others? Even God couldn't help them.

Eventually a great love of the world ended up in a sad and devastating separation. All their well meaning friends decided not to interfere in such a fight because after all it was a husband-wife fight and no wise person should think of coming between in such mysterious matters. No one came to share their sad moments. The Lord Jesus didn't come to help him nor did God-Bawa help her. Their great love died after few years and before their deaths.

****

Divorce was like death because walking the journey of life alone was not easy. Tom became a voiceless man. When he told others the reason for the break up of his family, they didn't believe him. Some of the God-Bawa's followers even said that Tom became mentally sick because he didn't believe in God-Bawa.

Tom was gripped by poverty that made him voiceless. No one was going to give him a microphone to amplify his voice as according to society's law, he did not deserve a microphone. He was not worth listening to. As a result of his alcoholic condition and poverty, he was not seen as a good man by society. People looked at him with different eyes. No more was he invited to any social gathering. He was struggling to find even a small job just to survive but there was no job for him.

Once Tom was starving and couldn't find anything to eat. He pocketed an apple from a hawker. A policeman beat him mercilessly and arrested him. Due to the endless problems in his life he was in no position to speak. Finally, when he was taken to the police inspector, he asked, "Sir could I say something?"

The Inspector said, "Go ahead my thieving friend, what do you want to say?"

Tom said, "Every child of this planet has a right to eat. Your law is wrong. Do you know how many people die of over eating in this world, and how many poor die of starvation every year? Rich thieves like corrupt politicians and high flying businessmen get rewarded and appreciated for swindling millions. When rich corrupt politicians like Mr. Andrew or wealthy businessmen like Harry Kingson steal the food of a million starving people nothing ever happens to them... On the contrary they get awards and appreciation from many organizations and great respect, but we, the helpless, get prison for just trying to put something in our stomachs, to avoid death from starvation.

Instead of telling you my life story, all I want to say to you is that you should be serving humanity not the power hungry politicians. A few ill-mannered, corrupt police and greedy politicians have traumatized the world. Evil, in a police uniform, exists in all the countries of the world. The police are not above the Supreme Judge - God. All judges, including you, shall be judged by Him. Therefore you must learn His law. Corruption in the house of justice has polluted the world and forced many God-fearing human beings to fight for justice. What is the use of constitutions and laws when all around the earth God's children are dying of hunger? Now you may lock me in the cell. I know the consequences of speaking against a police officer."

The police inspector got very angry at Tom's boldness and in a quivering voice he said, "Small mouth big talk! Who has given you permission to tell us what we ought to do? Who has given you the right to speak about the law and against our politicians and Mr. Harry Kingson? Yes, they give us money and they give 'under-the-table' donations. They deserve awards and you poor deserve prison. We arrest middle class people to seize their money and the poor to increase the number of prisoners in our files to reach a higher rank, get a higher salary, and for these reasons, I am going to lock you in prison. We are in power. We can do what we want. We need more rubbish like you to fill up our prisons. What else do you want to know? Little man, big mouth! …" Many charges were filed against Tom. Then the inspector said to the cop, "Constable! Go and lock him in the cell."

Tom said, "Oh God! Misfortunes always come alone. I thought the truth eventually wins, instead I end up in jail."

In jail Tom noticed that many prisoners were facing the consequences of standing up for the truth in their fight against inhumanity. He was lonely. Though loneliness was a painful and restless time for him, but it was also displaying signs of dignity, maturity, sensitivity, awareness, beauty and love. It was opening the window of gentleness to his soul. However, he was unable to handle all this and became depressed. He prayed to Jesus because he believed that it was Jesus' will that he should experience the bitterness of this life in order to purify himself. Sometimes he prayed, "My God people told me that divorce and death are the same for in both cases one has to travel alone. My God I am not lonely. I know you are with me now, and even after death you will be with me. Thank you for blessing me with your companionship. I am not lonely." In jail he sang the Lord's glory, from the bottom of his heart. He would never been able too sing in the same way in golden palaces. No ordinary person could sing such a hymn to God. He was extremely grateful to the Lord.

When he had nothing left except love for God, he then realized that the love for God is enough. One day, in the prison, he cried saying, "God is there no day after twelve hours of night? I can see that the distance between life and death is shortening and there is no hope of seeing the morning sun's rays. I might die in this prison... It is all right my Lord, as long as you are in my mind, it's all right. I would have not had this conversation with you and thought of you had you not put me in such a situation. I am grateful as long as you are in my thoughts and I can speak with you. Maybe you did it because it was the only way I could be with you. Maybe it was the only way to communicate with you. Thank you my God, thank you for blessing me with your company." The next morning he read a framed strip of wood that contained some lovely words titled "Footprints". It told of a little incident that reinforced his faith in the Lord. He read what it said;

FOOT PRINTS

Once, a man had a dream. He dreamed he was walking along the beach with the Lord. Across the sky flashed scenes from his life. In each scene, he noticed two sets of footprints in the sand, one belonged to him and other to the Lord.

When the last scene of his life flashed before him he looked back at the footprints in the sand. He noticed that many times along the path of his life, there was only one set of footprints. He also noticed that had happened at the very lowest and saddest times in his life.

This really bothered him and he questioned the Lord about it, "Lord, you said that once I decided to follow you, you would walk with me all the way. But I noticed that during the most troublesome times in my life, there was only one set of footprints. I don't understand why, when I needed you most, you would leave me."

The Lord replied, "My precious, precious child I love you and would never leave you during your time of trial and suffering. When you see only one set of footprints, it was then that I carried you."

Tom read it again and again. His eyes were filled with tears.

****

Step Five...

MAYA'S CONFUSED CHILDREN

Divorce was not the end of the struggle. Loneliness and the children's problems were added to their personal burdens. For the children it was very hard to choose from amongst the religions followed by their father, mother, grand parents and other relatives. No God and no religion was also an option. They could resolve the problem by becoming agnostics or atheists or both. Some people say that all religions are simply different paths to God. If that were so, then their questions were; what about the people who followed Charles Manson as their God? What about the people who followed Jim Jones and more than 900 Americans committed suicide in an isolated cult compound in Guyana called 'Jonestown', believing that they were right? What about the people who followed David Koresh – believing himself to be the final Christ and swore by the Bible - eventually 53 adults and 21 children died in the fire? Or, what about the people of Heaven's Gate- known as the UFO cult and 39 members died through a mass suicide, believing that they were right? Children knew about dozens of richest cults and their inside stories full of rape and murders.

There have been astonishing incidents in the history of blind faith. Servants, children, dependents and wives used to join their masters in the grave, so that he (the master) would enjoy the same comforts after death. Why people have to do stunning things in the name of faith? What about the 500 warriors who had their throats cut and buried with their king believing that he would need them in the hereafter too? Why people have to behave like a beast in the name of faith? What about the twenty thousand bodies that were offered to the Khan? Why people cannot become good instead of being religious and fighting like cats and rats? The obsessive struggle between one set of religious people and another is filled with confusion. This never ending battle of madness did not provide answers to the children. They could not draw any good lessons of wisdom from the history of so called Faith or stubbornness.

Maya's children knew that there were thousands of individuals who died, in the name of faith, believing that they were right. If all paths lead to God then why did they have to face destruction? Why do people board a train when they don't know its destination? Why are people convinced that their train is going to God when we have seen that they are heading into dark unknown tunnels? Though some train tickets were expensive and some were basement bargain priced they all were taking believers into unknown and opposite directions. So then why do people have to buy tickets, or sell themselves to train operators? It was too difficult for innocent kids to understand this complicated subject. Maya's husband problem was replaced by another husband problem. However, let us first have a look at the problem of her confused kids.

Neither daddy nor mummy could answer their questions such as; what was their origin, who they were, what was their destiny, what happens after death, why and how were they to judge a right religion from a wrong one, or how could they judge right from wrong?

Separation from the children was traumatic for the father. He didn't get custody to visit his children and Maya kept nurturing and teaching them the path to righteousness because believing was much better then not believing. After the divorce the children realized that, since the day their father had left home, their mother was unhappy and was facing an extremely hard time. Everyday she bowed down in front of God-Bawa's photo praying, *'please God-Bawa help me and show me the path'*. She was depressed and, in her most depressed moments, she lighted candles and incense in front of the photo and murmured in a mysterious language which children could not understand. They knew that when she was crying she didn't want them to know about her tears. However, the children knew everything except why their parents had to face such hard times even though they were so religious and God-fearing.

Everyone has his or her own way of praying, which may mean a lot to them but nothing to others. It's like music which pleases one but gives others a headache. The children were blind to the good things in her prayers. They could not understand the reason for the struggle and her way of worshipping. One day Maya kneeled down before God-Bawa's photo, and said, *"Bawa you know my tribulations, you know my problems and you know the answers. I have more than eleven kinds of pains and whichever becomes the most severe instinctively I concentrate on that forgetting all other pains. In such circumstances I forget you, but please you don't forget me, because I exist as long as you don't forget me. Please accept my offerings and help me."* Obviously, the children had never seen that photo talking, drinking or eating. They thought it was strange. How could a photo talk to her? They knew the problems that the photo had caused in their parent's lives. One of her children could not curb his curiosity and asked his mother,

"Mummy, are you all right? What are you doing? Talking to the photo? Is this the reason you had arguments with dad, and why he had to leave home? Because of the power of this photo?"

"My son it is my faith, love, and respect for God. *(the child thought 'faith for God or for Magician-Bawa?').* A man without faith is not a man. A person without faith is less than an animal. Faith is life and without faith a person is like a moving dead body. My son, at that time I was being tested. When your devotion is strong, God tests you and keeps an eye on you to see how strong your faith is? He will test you through one of your own family members or someone who is close to you. That person will make you go through hell, by doing one wrong thing after another. Then God sees how you deal with the situation. God-Bawa is a living God. Only a completely devoted person can appreciate that. I have experienced many miracles in my life, since I surrendered my life to him, and he has shown me unimaginable miracles. This is the outcome of my good deeds and God-Bawa once told my father that because I was a holy saint in a previous life, I would have the chance to recognize him in this life. My son, only a lucky person can be this close to him.

Once I did not have money and needed some desperately. I closed my eyes and meditated on him, and the moment I opened my eyes, a man approached me and offered a ten dollar bill and then disappeared. I was stunned, thrilled and my eyes filled with tears. God-Bawa had come in the form of an old man to help me. Another time I was hungry and I started praying to him and a tall man left a basket of fruits in front of me and disappeared. From time to time he came to me in the form of a driver, a tailor and a salesman." These and other experiences and stories the mother narrated.

"Mummy, I agree that God can help you through someone, but how do you know that person was inspired by God-Bawa, not by God? And if God could come to you in the form of a helper then could he not come in the form of an enemy if you worship the wrong photo? Daddy also had a photo and said the same thing about his God. That *his* devotion was being tested. He used to say that the picture was of the Savior. He used to tell us of the miracles worked by that picture and taught us to kneel down before it. Tell me mummy, who is right, you or daddy? Whose photo has the power to save and stop this destruction, his or yours?" questioned the son seriously.

"Well, don't ask such questions!" Maya became more serious, and continued, "These are intellectual and spiritual things and you are not mature enough to understand the high philosophy related to spiritualism. One should never question these things. Never, never! Do you understand, my son? I was being tested and I did my best during the period of a 'tough trial'. He was the one who filed for divorce and I took the right decision. I was right at that time I am right now and I will always be right, because God-Bawa's real followers cannot go wrong, but you should never question the ways of God." Maya insisted.

The child agreed, though his curiosity was not satisfied. The next day he asked again, "Mummy I respect you, that is why I could not say anything about God-Bawa, fearing it might hurt your feelings. I want to ask you one thing, but first, promise me that you will not mind."

"No I will not mind as long as you don't say anything against God-Bawa. I will not tolerate anything on that topic. My faith means everything to me. My faith is my life. I did not even forgive your father for that mistake. I kicked him out of my life when he started saying bad things about my God. I am also ready to leave you or anyone who tries to prejudice my mind against God-Bawa because, apart from God-Bawa, there is nothing greater in this world. I am here on this earth to devote my life to my God-Bawa," Maya said nicely,

"Well, mummy my question is very simple. Why do his followers fight with their own people and ask the photo for forgiveness? If that photo can forgive sinners, then will there be no judgment for forgiven sinners on the Day of Judgment? Why does God-Bawa's secretary, Ms. Soni, keep millions of dollars in her possession yet ignore all the homeless and helpless people?" asked the son curiously.

"My son, that money is donated by the public, not for distribution among the homeless but to build Bawa's monastery. However one day if, by God-Bawa's blessings, I am in Ms. Soni's place then I will definitely help all the homeless and helpless people. But now I am helpless and struggling to feed you children. It is through God-Bawa's miracles that I am carrying on; otherwise we would have been finished long ago. So never doubt my faith. I must tell you that only God can save and protect you in times of difficulties, so never ever have a single doubt in prayers to God. Do not repeat this mistake again," said Maya as a teacher.

"I can understand that you cannot help the poor when you don't have money, but instead of shouting you should speak nicely to daddy, which will cost you nothing. You could have good words..." Maya closed his mouth with her palm. "But mummy..."

"No, you will not speak another word. Do you understand?"

"All right mummy"

The children had numerous questions in their minds regarding many religious activities. They got tired of arguing with their mother and eventually gave up, reconciling to the fact that in this world there was no explanation for blind faith. Mummy likes mysteries, and does what she wants. No wonder, daddy couldn't agree with her mysterious ideas. Daddy was also religious and believed in mysteries, but what did they achieve except fighting, divorce, and hardship? The children needed answers, but from where could they get them?

Maya wanted her children to become religious but their concern was to find the truth of it all. They knew the reason for their parent's separation was their faith in different religions. The parent's separation had caused trauma in their lives as well. They couldn't understand why mummy and daddy had accepted a painful life because of perplexing things. Why couldn't they understand the simple fact that living a loving life was more important? Why did they remain fastened to a myth? The children were more concerned about their mummy, daddy and elders who claimed to be religious yet, behaved irreligiously.

Maya continued to worship God-Bawa's photograph. She wanted approval for her actions, by a well-reputed priest, who would tell her children that worshipping God-Bawa's photo was like worshipping God, and then she would be happy. Fortunately or unfortunately God-Bawa had become so popular that his photo was worshipped in many houses. The rich and the poor alike believed that he could change their fate for the better; consequently, no priest had the courage to tell others that God-Bawa was not God.

Any priest who spoke against God-Bawa lost his standing among people and would therefore not receive money for his own livelihood. No priest likes to be left high and dry. After all, discretion was the better part of valor. Left without a choice the priests had to keep people happy even if it entailed maintaining the mumbo-jumbo and hocus-pocus. How would they get the wherewithal to make ends meet if they were to start, hurting people's feelings by, telling the truth? As it was the people were engaged in trying to uncover out a priest's weaknesses, or what sins he had committed.

People forget the hundred good things a priest has done. They will only publicize the one bad thing he might have done. Many people take advantage of a priest's humility. If he opens his mouth and asks for donations then they are ready to malign him. At that time, no reputed priest would say that Maya was wrong in worshipping God-Bawa's photo, but on the other hand, no reputed priest would say that she was right. If she were to offer heavy donations, like Mr. Harry did, then it would be easy for her to get the approval of a reputed priest.

Unfortunately, she didn't have the power to buy the voice of a well known priest.

The children's minds were like a half recorded cassette tape. Whatever they had gone through, during their early years with their parents, were recorded in their minds. Most of their lives were shaped, during those days, while they watched the destructive fights, annoyances, irritations, conflict, anger, arguments, and foolishness. Though they wanted to say; *"stop this nonsense, o' six foot tall guys, do something good instead.,"* They couldn't say anything because, after all, they were kids, who quarrel one minute and make up the next. They were already handling much more than they could. They knew that with parent's lives, their lives were becoming insecure. It was age to establish the foundation of their future. Their shocked and disturbed minds were tossed in different directions.

Like two twins with same genes and same parents but different ways of understanding the things, the elder son learned a lot from the foolishness of his parents. He did not touch alcohol as he had seen the disastrous consequence of his father's drinking. While watching his father's difficult condition he noticed that whenever he drank he spoke rubbish. Though he sometimes spoke about essential things, but one bad sentence was like a flame powerful enough to burn down the whole house. He uttered those trouble causing words only when he was drunk. An alcoholic person cannot drive properly, cannot work properly, and does not realize what he is doing. An alcoholic person is uncontrollable, goes beyond the limit and still believes that he is absolutely right. An alcoholic is a total disaster as alcohol creates many problems in life. An alcoholic person should not be allowed to drive on the roads and should not be allowed to speak at home. The good child learned to live a good life; without a teacher, without a guide, and without any books. He learned a lot about the consequences of anger, the consequences of blind faith and the consequences of disregarding humanity. He made up his mind never to touch alcohol, cigarettes or any other narcotics, and never do those things that his father did.

But, the younger son turned bad. He developed anger, anxiety and a foul tongue. He imitated his father, started drinking and associating with drug addicts. Two brothers with opposite views; one hated alcohol and the other inherited it. His mother's love was blind to his bad company, and too weak to bring him back onto the right track. Her love was too deep and blind to see the unhealthy future in her child's activities. Though a mother's love was essential to raise beautiful children, but a good father's presence was also needed to instill discipline in them; to set the foundation for their entire future. In the absence of either of the two, the child got his foundation, early in his life, from the internet and cheap television shows, which eventually cost him immensely. He had gone through thousands of unhealthy messages on the internet and movies. Much of the GIGO (garbage in garbage out) remained GIGI.

The bad child's world was not inspired by the example of humanity (Lord Ram), but rather by money-minded enormously rich, wicked and immoral film stars. All his friends watched millions of alcohol related, drug related and smoking related advertisements in their early years. They listened to brain damaging hard rock music, listened to mind disturbing stories and watched violent movies, which caused fear, nervousness, hopelessness, anger and anxiety in them. In their early youth they had watched thousands and thousands of murders on the television and in the movies. They started their early lives with toy guns and toy swords. Those slow poison-like television shows were seeded into their subconscious minds forever.

The kind of books they read, the kind of movies they watched, the kind of music they listened to, all played a part in their upbringing. Their animal-like attitude became shocking. Bad language and anger became their ornaments. Conditioned by the media they became conditioned like robots and possessed ugly thoughts, actions, habits and characters. They had no manners, no respect for elders, no respect for teachers and no respect for parents. With no discipline in life they learned that in the world, *"money is the only aim of life."* Their philosophy was, *"if it feels good, do it."* In the company of those bad kids, Maya's child lost the true aim of his life. There was no father and mother couldn't play the role of father as well. Because of the divorce, the financial struggle and the children's darkening future Maya became depressed. Faith and God-Bawa's Photo was the only hope left for her. Otherwise she would have probably ended her life.

The mind of one of her children was seething with doubts and questions, which neither his mother nor the priest could explain. He couldn't understand why grown up people such as, holy men, religious men, doctors, engineers and so forth, have to lie? Was it really a tough job for them to confess, and say 'No, sorry we do not know anything about God?'

The child shook his head in confusion. "Why do people make simple things so difficult to comprehend? Why, in this whole cycle of 'endless imitation,' do we have to acquire the 'frosty weight' of man made confusion? Why does the 'Sea of Faith' have to be at the ebb all the time? Is the human being really on a 'darkening plain', swept by confusing alarms of struggle and fight, where ignorant armies clash by night? Why this ignorance and all pervasive confusion? One God; but so many religions, so many philosophies, and so many ways... Why can't human beings be just human? After following the so called 'path of virtue' why does he or she have to behave like an animal?" The child's pure and unencumbered mind was free of any prejudice. The pure-minded child was the 'Best Philosopher', 'The Mighty Prophet!' ... ... A wonderful field to sow beautiful seeds, but he needed the right food for the mind, the right education, the right parents, the right guidance, and the right seeds at the right time. Every child born into the world was a new thought of God, an ever fresh, radiant philosophy, and radiant possibility. Beautiful children...

****

Part Two

SAINT DIWAREE

Step Six...

PENNILESS SAINT DIWAREE

Saints are like jewels on this earth. They are light-bearers. They are born only to do good things, they live just to do good things, and die leaving behind inspiring examples for seekers. An orange tree is born to give oranges and will always give oranges, even if people throw stones at it. Likewise saints are born only to serve humanity. They are born to spread a new aroma and to clean up the polluted atmosphere. They don't go looking for fame, that's why many saints are unknown to this world. Those unknown saints didn't even know they were saints and after giving a gift to this world they passed away. Saints are far from greed, anger, and ego therefore they can advise confused people what to do at times of triumph and trial in life. Their priceless words are nectar to aspirants. They produce the food for the seeker's mind. Whatever beauty we see in this world, is only because of the saints who have lived here from time to time. There have always been good people in this world and there shall always be, so we have one more reason to thank God that he did not leave us alone in this world.

Saints love God. Their forsaking attachment to the world and their love for God cannot be compared with that of the ordinary human being. Unfortunately, there are many wicked people in the garb of saints and many saints are in the uniform of common people, and a few saints are in the uniform of saints. However, one should not try to judge others because we human beings are only authorized to judge ourselves. Maya knew that the rich and busy God-Bawa wouldn't come to her home, so a poor and free saint was the only option for her.

The following week Maya brought a Saint into her home. His name was Diwaree. Diwaree had strictly forbidden the use of all honorific titles along with his name. He believed that praise from people would only feed his ego, which he wanted to keep suppressed. He had instructed everyone to simply call him Diwaree and not "Saint Diwaree", "His Holiness Diwaree", "Esteemed Diwaree", "Reverend Diwaree", "Diwaree Maharaj" etc. For this reason he was known by the simple name of 'Diwaree'. The reason for the name Diwaree ('Diwaar'- a Hindi word meaning a wall) was because of the fact that he used to sleep on the stump of a wall of a broken monument.

Diwaree had been living on a diet of only fruit and milk for seventeen years. He was very strict about what he consumed and spoke. During those seventeen years he became popular and immediately realized that being popular is dangerous for the soul, so he quickly changed his identity and disappeared from that place. He stayed away from anything that did not make him feel good including popularity. He had just one long cloth around his body. He loved the simple life and preferred intensive continence and penance in order to please God. He was past middle age, had thinned out gray hair and a long flowing gray beard. He had acquired the impressive personality of an experienced holy man. His practical and simple life-style attracted a lot of people.

Some people believed that Diwaree was born in the 18th century, yet he looked like a sixty-five year old man. This was mainly on account of divine acts, divine living and divine thoughts. If any one offered money to please him, Diwaree would spurn the offerings saying, "Take away your money, my ignorant child. Do you think your money will please me? Go and give this money to those greedy conventionally clad sharks that go by the name of 'His Holiness Greatest Saint', who really crave the money and wish to have the largest monastery on an Island or on a mountain. If you want to give something, give Him (God) your truthfulness. Pick up all your money and get out of here."

Several times he disappeared from one place and reappeared somewhere else and started living under a new identity. He lived on a wall for a long time. His spirituality, total indifference and disdainful attitude towards money, appealed to people's hearts and attracted a lot of them. They thought that he was a truly holy man. A holy man who didn't accept money from people was really a person who could bless them with true wealth. His life style was as strictly prescribed in the ancient scriptures. His life had been entirely devoted to God, and to the selfless service of people. His popularity grew by leaps and bounds. For many people to be touched by him was the same as being blessed by God.

Many rich people offered him money but he never accepted it. One day a rich man humbly offered him a huge palatial building. Diwaree didn't accept his offering. This added to his fame manifold. For Diwaree, his purity was his wealth, because he knew many people had tried to make a name in the world by erecting huge buildings, but that method of impressing others did not impress him. He was doing something unique that would satisfy his inner soul. He would only be satisfied if he did something really worthwhile in this God-given life.

Diwaree did not make any disciples. Even if someone was truly willing to dedicate his whole life still he would not accept him as a disciple. Though a few people lived around him and cooked for him, sat around him, listened to him, ate simple food and lived a simple life, yet he didn't accept anyone as his disciple. There was a reason he did not to accept anyone as a disciple and that piece of information was one of the most interesting things to know.

Maya was very happy that a great saint had sanctified her home. Diwaree said to Maya, "Problems in life come automatically therefore one doesn't need to invite them. You don't need to make life more painful. God did not make your life tough. It was you who intended to make it thus. Therefore, you got what your soul wanted and what you deserved. God merely fulfills the wishes of the soul. Your wish was to live like this and your husband's hidden need was to be alone - on his own. Your stubbornness awakened the evil anger in each other which was sleeping like a harmless snake. This spiritually destructive and evil anger is sleeping within everyone. Maya, one second's anger can change an entire life, it's direction and its destiny as well. Anger is not the proper time to make any decision.

Every human being is free to make his or her choice but after choosing, the choice may control them. You chose to go through this suffering so that your soul could move closer to the Truth. In life suffering is the only way to learn. Your soul knew it. Though you could have learned all this without going through the agony, but unfortunately there is no better teacher than suffering. You cannot believe that fire burns until you burn your finger, but when you burn your finger then you know it. Then you can become a perfect teacher and teach others that fire can really burn. You have shaped your life like this to discover the truth of it. The word 'divorce' doesn't exist in the dictionary of righteous people. For the sake of your children you could have discovered pleasure in pain and pain in pleasure. You could have compromised at a certain point, as buyers and sellers have to meet somewhere, to make a deal successful. However, I will pray to God for your well-being and that of your lovely kids. Always feel God's presence within you. As long as you feel His presence within you, you are not alone, and you are living with a loving and caring God. In divorce and death one must always walk with God and think only of God," that was all Diwaree said to her.

With their mother's permission the children put some questions to Diwaree. Diwaree said to them, "You are children and you will not understand it now, but must have faith. You still have long way to go on the path of life, which will keep teaching you. Live with righteous intention."

Her children were impressed by Diwaree's life, though he did not teach them anything nor tell them what to do and what not to. He did not even answer any of their questions; yet there was a little improvement in their lives. Just by living with him their minds were changed. They thought that if a man could accept such a tough life, for God, and never complain, so must we also learn something from that. They also learned that a religious man is one, who never harms others and helps helpless people with pure and selfless living. Imagine the changes if the children had lived with Diwaree for at least just one week.... !

****

Step Seven...

TWO WEAKNESSES IN THE
HOLY SAINT?

Diwaree believed that the human body is perishable therefore one should do one's best to please God with all one's might. One should eat only vegetables throughout one's whole life, love animals, love human beings, remain celibate, speak the truth, have only clean thoughts, and even accept death through starvation for the sake of the truth. This perishable body is God's greatest gift to the soul, which should be used to produce a gift for God. This body is just a tool to achieve the aim of the soul; therefore, one must live a life such, that after leaving this body, God should be happy with its performance.

Diwaree's amazing life was a living example of Vairaagya (true stoical dejection). He had unlimited good qualities but those good qualities were not counted by God because God had created human beings only to do good things. He had only two weaknesses in him.

The first weakness was: he did not want people to know that he could change his mind - if that change were necessary - for self-perfection. He was too orthodox. He could only act in conformity with the traditional image, which was already in his follower's minds; so he would not wear stitched clothes. He knew that wearing normal stitched clothes was the same as wearing his unstitched sacking. For him western style clothes or eastern traditional clothes made no difference when leading a holy life, but if he were to appear in public wearing sewn clothes, people would be shocked. They would not respect him anymore. They would hate him and think that instead of strengthening their beliefs, he had ruined their faith. People did not want him to appear in stitched clothes. People wanted him to remain as he was.

The second weakness in Diwaree was; though he said all religions are the same but somehow he did not praise prophesizm because they slaughtered innocent beings. His question was; 'How can a believer slaughter innocent human beings?' He couldn't swallow their philosophy of *"convert or kill non-believers"*. Being a saint he knew that he should respect all religions, therefore; he did not say anything about them, but his subconscious mind couldn't accept such things.

Apart from that, a man once started spreading the idea that Diwaree was 192 years old. Diwaree did not either confirm or deny this story. His lack of clarity kept people in suspense.

Now the question was, 'were these Diwaree's weaknesses, or that of his believers'? It was very hard to answer. He preferred to live according to the conceptions of his believers, as he didn't like to offend their sentiments or spiritual feelings. He did not have the courage to bring the truth to his lips. He was helpless to change unless he changed into a new being and started teaching a new philosophy which taught that a man's thoughts and karma would be more important than his dress. In this life, he could not teach that.

'Karma - is the sum of a person's actions in the previous life that decides his or her fate in his rebirth. This truth reflects the system that this life is one of a chain of successive lives by transmigration of one's soul. Each renewed life's course in this material world is conditioned by its 'Karma' in the preceding one, until through perfection it reaches its destiny - The God.

Diwaree was not really concerned about consequences in the next life. Diwaree didn't want to say anything about his past, and why he had become what he was. He knew that a closed fist could possibly contain diamonds worth a millions, but an open fist immediately reveals its emptiness. Therefore, he didn't open his fist or reveal his cards, so to say. He used to think, *'Let people guess what is in my fist. Let them find out what I bear in my folded palm.'* He had many reasons for not telling anyone about his personal life. He knew it is not easy to survive in this world and he had no 'true friend' in this world that he could tell all the hidden facts of his heart. The fact was that a secret part of his brain kept trying to heal the wounds of his childhood. The emotional loss of his parents and their good natures was enormous. No one could even imagine how good those parents were. Their goal in life was to be the kind of parents God wanted them to be.

Deep in his heart he had especially loving memories of his mother and he believed that there was no one quite like his mother in this universe. His mother's beautiful soul had illuminated his life. Her soul remained connected with him after the cutting of the umbilical cord and even after her death. He missed his mother and only he knew how much, and only he could understand how good and how truthful she was. This inexplicable union of mother and son or father and son could be explained only by God. If the mother is good then there is no power on this earth which can stop a child from dedicating his life to God.

Dozens of beautiful memories remained hidden in his heart. No wealth, no fame and no achievement could fill the wound of losing such a loving and truthful mother. He knew that a mother is nature's best creation, for Divine God himself appears in the form of a mother to nourish an infant physically and mentally.

When he looked at a bird feeding its little ones, from his wall, he would get really astounding thoughts; *'My God! What an amazing miracle of yours!! Are you feeding this closed-eyed or is its mother feeding it?*

One of his prayers was; *'my beautiful Mother, giver of birth - your love has nourished my body and my soul, your love has enriched my mind and, whatever I am today is because of your love. Everyday I just want to present a beautiful flower unto your beautiful hands, and your beautiful fingers; the flowers of love, flowers of respect, truthfulness, kindness, compassion, virtuous living and many other flowers I must keep trying to present everyday unto your unbelievable - now invisible - hands.'*

He knew that God's greatest gift to a soul is a "Good Mother". He knew that his mother was a truthful lady who had taught him the values of 'Paap' (sin), 'Punya' (selfless action for the benefit of others)' and 'Karma.' Indelibly ingrained in his subconscious and conscious mind was not to do paap for money, and not get captured by greed, lust, and anger. He was always grateful to God for granting him such amazing gift – a truthful mother. He sometimes prayed *"God in the next life, please grant me such a truthful mother"*. His mother was not just an example of a good mother but her amazing truthfulness had touched the core of his heart. She was not concerned about the rules of Mother-Dharma (duty of a good mother) but those good qualities were natural to her. She strongly believed that God would 'feed' him if he lived a pure life. The whole world must be grateful for a good mother who produces a good gift for this needy world.

Diwaree believed; 'People act for money. Money is powerful. It can make one act like a saint, like a priest, like a soldier. If you feed a dolphin it will dance for you. Everyone dances for money; for the poor it is food, but for the rich its fun. This world acts on the instructions of rich people's money. Money power can take a soul to heaven or hell. If 'Paap', 'Punya' and Karma are not kept in mind then need turns into greed. The greater the greed, the greater is the destruction. He knew that there are good saints and bad saints, good priests and bad priests, good doctors and bad doctors, good lawyers and bad lawyers, good politicians and bad politicians, good businessmen and bad as well. In every profession there are good as well as greedy people. His mother had taught him not to go after money and that God would definitely take care of him. He respected her and believed in her teaching that God would take care of him. His favorite song was:

Tere Pujan Ko Bhagawaan Banaa Man Mandir Aalishaan.
(My God please beautify this mind-temple, just to worship you with it beautifully. Please make my mind beautiful so that I can worship you with it.)

Tuu Hee Jal Me Tuu Hee Thal Me Tuu Har Daal Ke Har Paatan Me.
Teraa Ruup anuup Jahaan Banaa Man Mandir Aalishaan.
(Your presence is in the water, on the earth, in every leaf of every tree. Your beautiful form is beyond the comprehension of all the minds of this world. Please beautify my mind so that I can worship you everywhere through it.)

Kisane Jaanee Teree Maaya, Kisane Bhed Tumhaara Paaya.
Haare Rishi Muni Kari Kari Dhyaan, Banaa Man Mandir Aalishaan.
(My God, who could understand the secrets of your divine Leela. Great
sages and saints eventually gave up, after thinking and thinking and
meditating over and over again. Please beautify my mind-temple so that I
can worship you in it)

****

Diwaree was old then. In fact, he needed medication because there was
much pain in his body, but he believed if he deserved better health, then
God would make him consume some suitable medicine through food or
the environment. He knew the healing process needed man's effort and
God's help. In other words God can quickly heal a wound if the man
applies a bandage to it. This law applies to spiritual improvement as
well; man must try for excellence and God helps. For physical recovery,
he did whatever he could on his own, but if further, expensive medicines
were recommended, he didn't want to go to rich people for help. The
amount of money he would consume through medicine, to stay alive for
one year, would be enough to feed a hard working laborer's children for
six years. What was the use of staying in an old, high maintenance
house? If his Karma was good God may give him a brand new house. He
knew that as long as God kept him alive, he would survive.

Through his mother's inspiring life, he believed that pain was a gift from
God. The more pain he got the more he concentrated on God, which was
a constant Sadhana (struggle to achieve). For him a painful body was like
a baking oven where his mind became focused on the principles of a true
life. He knew that God has made this wonderful thing called pain which
taught him infinite things and made life meaningful. More pain taught
him to pray more and more pain made him a better person. Pain, the
great creation of the Creator, nurtured his soul amazingly. There was no
other way for the soul to evolve. Though nobody likes to be in pain he
happily accepted it as a gift from God. Through the pain, again and
again, his mother's teachings kept stirring in his mind, *"My beloved son,
do not go after money. Money can buy you medicine and many other
things but live an honest life instead. God will take care of you."* These
words of his mother kept ringing in his ears whenever he felt like talking
to her during the days of his sickness. But he never asked anyone for

help except God. Those days Diwaree often used to murmur the
following hymns;

Yaa Dehee kaa Garab Na Keejai. Udi Gayaa Hans Tambure Kaa.
(O man, never be too proud of this body, because the bird may fly away
from the nest, anytime.)

Aayaa Thaa Kis Kaam Ko soyaa Chaadar Taan.
Surat Sambhaal Ye Gaaphilaa, Apanaa aaap Pahichaan.
(O man, for what purpose have you come into this world, but kept
sleeping under the comfortable blanket. O man, take care of yourself;
recognize the self.)

Jaa marane Se Jag Dare, mere Man aanand,
Kab Marihon.Kab Paayihao, Puuran Paramaanand.
(The whole world is afraid of death but to me it is the most pleasant thing
because it takes me to God - full of bliss and realization of reality of
self.)

Swaas Swaas Pai Naam Le Brithaa Swaas Mat Khoya,
Naa Jaane Usa Swaas Kaa Aavan Hoy Ki Na Hoy.
(O man, keep repeating God's name with each and every breath. You
never know whether the next breath will be exhaled or not.)

Diwaar Jo Din Aaj Hai So din Naahi Haal.
Cheti Sake To Cheti Le, Maut Paree Hai Khyaal.
(O man, the opportunity you have today is not going to come back
tomorrow. Try to understand if you can, because death is moving around
your head all the time.)

Diwaar Sotaa Kyaa Kare, Jaago Japo Muraar,
Ek din Hai sovanaa, Laabe Pair Pasaar.
(O man, for what purpose are you sleeping for so long, wake up and
pray, because eventually one day you will have to sleep with outstretched
legs.)

Durlabh Maanush Janm Hai Hoy Na Duujee Baar,
Pakka Phal Jo Gira Pada, Lage Na Duujee Baar.

(O man, it's impossible to get this human body, you won't be able to get it back once it is dead. As ripened fruit cannot be put back on the tree once it is plucked away. Over the span of your entire life you have a certain number of breaths, once they are gone, they are gone.)

Sansaara Swapn Tulyo Hi Raag Dveshadi Sankulah,
Swakaale Satyavadbhaati, Prabodho Satyavadbhavet.
(The world is filled with the dreams of love and hate, everything is just a dream. This dream appears to be real as long as you remain unenlightened (sleeping), but becomes unreal when you are awake.)

Das Dwaare Kaa Peejaraa, Taame Panchee Paun.
Rahe Achambha Hote hai, Gaye Achambha kaun.
(This soul-bird is dwelling in the ten opened-doors cage. Surprise is; it can stay in it for years. It's not a surprise if it flies away.)

Kyaa Bharosa Isa Deh Kaa, Vinas Jaat Chhan Maahi.
Saas Saas Sumiran Karo, Aurou Jatan Kachu Naahi.
(O man, life has no certainty; it can end at any minute. Keep thinking of the Lord with each and every breath, as there is no other way.)

Na Maanusham Binaanyatra Tatwagyaanam Na Labhyate.
(Except this human life there is no other species on earth through which soul can obtain the Truth.)

Binaa Dehen Kasyaapi Purushaartho Na Vidhyate.
(Without the body no soul can achieve it's aim.)

Din Te Pahar Pahar Te Ghadiyaan Aayu Ghate Tana Chheejai.
(With each and every minute and each and every day life is getting closer to its end.)

Aath Pahar Bahataa Rahe Prem Kahaavai Soya.
(Constant flow of loving thought is called Love.)

Bholee Tiriyaa Rovan Laagee, Bichur Gayee meree Jodee.
Kahata Kabeer Suno Bhai Saadho Jina Jodi Tina Todi.
(Innocent wife started crying saying my companion is gone. Diwaree says, O innocent lady, listen to me; the one who connected it – he has disconnected.)

Bade Bhaag Maanusha Tan Paawaa, Sur durlabh sab Granthahi Gawaa.
Nar Tanu Paaya vishaya Man Dehi, Palati Sudhaa Te Bish Lehee.
(The human body is obtained with great blessings, which Gods and
scriptures sing about. After getting this human body, one who destroys it
in pleasures, he is collecting the poison and neglecting the nectar.)

M. L. Singh, a philosophy professor, was impressed by a conversation he
had had with Diwaree. As a result of that conversation he decided to
become Diwaree's disciple, or if Diwaree would not accept him as his
disciple, then he would live near him. Though M. L. Singh knew that
Diwaree did not take any disciples he still went to live with him for a
week.

The impressive conversation had left an indelible imprint on his mind, at
a time when he was totally depressed. The main cause of depression was
gossip by the school management about him. People who gossiped with
him also gossiped about him in his absence. They would make the gossip
spicy so that everyone listened with rabbit-like ears. To make the gossip
interesting they lied a lot. The gossip broke his heart, ruined his life and
resulted in many tragedies and upheavals in his life.

He cried with the heartache, had blood-pressure and sleepless nights.
Eventually he learned that this life is too short to be spent in fault-
finding, holding grudges or keeping memories of wrongs done to him.
He had then decided to bring down the curtain on all ungodly schemes
and to seek shelter with a holy man. He went to stay with Diwaree.
Diwaree had told him that he would have to live as he (Diwaree) lived.
He promised Diwaree saying, "Yes I will live the way you live, my
Master."

"Don't use high flying words for me like; Master, Your Highness,
Reverend, Your Holiness, Sir, Lord, Esteemed or whatever. ... I am none
of that. I am a simple man. My name is Diwaree, and just call me
Diwaree." insisted Diwaree.

"Okay Diwaree. I will call you Diwaree," promised M. L. Singh.
The next morning, Diwaree woke up 3.30 a.m. for his daily routine of
early morning prayers. Singh also woke up at the same time. Singh had

heard that 3.30 a.m. is the best time for prayers. On the fourth morning Singh said to Diwaree, "Diwaree, I feel sorry for those unlucky people who sin by sleeping at the best time for prayers. These ignorant people are condemned not to have the great blessing of praying early in the morning. They are wasting the actual time of prayer, sleeping in sloth and ignorance. These bad people are really ignorant and unlucky."

"What's wrong with you Mr. Singh? What prayers are you doing? What prayer… It would have been much better if you hadn't been up, and remained sleeping like everyone else. It would have been better if you had remained in bed instead," said an upset Diwaree.

"But why? Diwaree, why?" Singh asked him.

"Then you would not criticize others," answered Diwaree. After a pause Diwaree again said, "Sleeping men don't do those things that you are doing. You have come here to become good. I didn't ask you to wake-up early in the morning; to criticize others, to display how good you are, how bad they are, how wise you are, and how ignorant they are. I didn't ask you to become a judge to judge all others. I didn't ask you to find the wrong others are doing. That's the mistake every human being on earth has done. The moment they start doing something in God's name they start considering themselves superior and hate others. When they start following a religion or a saint they get bloated with ego and start hating others. I shall never keep such an egoistic man with me. I shall never keep a loose-tongued person near me, which invites sin and miseries for the soul. It's better to live alone than to be with a gossiping person. If you criticize others, then you better leave this place, don't pollute the atmosphere here and my mind. You better take your blanket and get out from here, right now…" said disturbed Diwaree to M. L. Singh.

M. L. Singh was very upset and shaking with fear for he had disturbed the Holy Saint. An imperfect person should not live with a holy man for long, and if he does he must be careful, but Singh didn't realize his own imperfectness. Though he was a professor of philosophy, and had taught students that carrying tales is a big sin. He had heard many times from holy preachers and read in many books that gossiping is a sin, but he never realized that he was a part of it. He thought he was perfect. He apologized in a shaking voice, "Please Diwaree, forgive me. Forgive me please I promise that I shall never ever again criticize anyone. I realize now that I was terribly wrong, but nobody had told me before, that gossiping is bad. I didn't know what was right and what was wrong. Please don't throw me out. I want to live with you. I am really miserable out there."

Diwaree taught Mr. Singh to strive for self perfection and not to hate others. He said, "M. L. Singh the greatest imperfection is; to see imperfections in others. Gossip is the outcome of seeing imperfections in others. If you judge people you cannot love them. It makes you to hate them. Gossip creates hate. How can you help them if you hate them and how can you be holy if you hate God's creatures? God dwells in everyone, so, never hate, never gossip, criticize or speak harshly. Not even by mistake. God is listening to each and every word you speak and grasping each and every thought in your mind."

These words of Diwaree touched the inner core of his heart, and were indelibly imprinted there. That was the moment M. L. Singh made up his mind to live with Diwaree permanently and cleanse his polluted mind. He wanted to be initiated by Diwaree because becoming his disciple would be his greatest achievement, one which no one else had ever achieved. His bad reputation would be dissolved automatically. People who previously disrespected him would now know that he had become a pure saint. Before accepting his request Diwaree asked him to do several things. Diwaree asked him, "Is there anyone in your life whom you do not like or with whom you do not speak, for some reason?"

"Yes, there are a few. One of them is my relative and another is my colleague at work, and I also have some disagreements with my brother," was Singh's answer.

"First of all, if you want to live a holy life, go back to them and beg for their forgiveness. You must forgive them, as a relative must forgive another relative otherwise he is not a true relative. The wife must forgive her husband otherwise she is not a good wife, and the husband must forgive his wife otherwise he is not a good husband. You have to forgive your neighbor if he or she had committed any mistake. You have to forgive them and beg for their forgiveness as well. God may question them on your personality, on things, which you may have not realized yourself, but they know. You have to pass the test in the home where you lived. Mr. Singh, no human being, on earth, is created to produce enemies. The more enemies you have the harder it will be for you to become holy. Unless you are holy in your thoughts and actions, you cannot please God. No man can become holy by having enmity with even a single person. So, go and ask for their forgiveness," insisted Diwaree.

"Diwaree, I understand the significance of this valuable lesson from a saint but that is the most difficult thing for me to do. They are the reason I am here to renounce everything. I am disgusted, discontented, dissatisfied, unhappy, restless, and frustrated because of them. These are the people who had broken my heart and disturbed my peace. Their actions had forced me to do bad things, and they had ruined my road to virtue and righteousness. They made me to do undesirable things when my anger had risen to its peak. They all are bad people. I don't want see them anymore or plead for their forgiveness."

"They are the reason you are here. You must be grateful to them because of their efforts you are now with a saint", said Diwaree. "You must thank them. After quarrelling with them bow down your head, in the house of worship, and pray for forgiveness to the deity, which should be easy for you. You must bow down your arrogant head to the person with whom you fight - because the same God's interconnected invisible energy is pumping in his heart as well as yours. The Living God is in the heart, which you have hurt hence you need his forgiveness in order to please God. Therefore you must ask for forgiveness of those who want you to leave your stubbornness, doggedness and arrogant attitude. What kind of philosophy have you been teaching in college? I did not ask you to count their weaknesses, but discover your own. I did not ask you to change their attitudes but your own. I did not ask you to improve their lives, but your own. If you cannot improve your own life then how can you dream of improving theirs? Why are you dreaming of living a holy life? If you cannot realize your own weaknesses then why should they realize their own? If you cannot discard your pig-headedness how can you become holy? As long as you hate even one God-made-Temple you hate God, who is dwelling in that Temple and as long as you hate God, you cannot live with me, so fold up your blanket and get out of here."

"Diwaree, I cannot make them understand. Please forgive me. They are evil animals and need to be controlled and chained by government law. They are like scorpions," reasoned M. L. Singh.

"A scorpion bites because that is in his nature, but a human being is created to protect him. God has given you the intellect to find the cure for a scorpion's bite, but a scorpion is not blessed with that intellect, he only acts on the instinct for survival. So if you want live with me do what I ask you to. If you want to become a saint you cannot remain poisonous. Anger and hate are not the signs of a good person. In other words you cannot hate anyone. Hate is a stumbling block, an unbreakable wall between you and your God. Only an all-loving person, who knows life is too short to hold grudges, can become holy. The wise cannot hate night. Days and nights, are two aspects of creation. Darkness is necessary to bring out the value of light. Ignorance has to exist to realize the value of wisdom. Bad has to be there to perceive the value of good. Happiness and unhappiness, joy and sorrow, gain and loss, laughter and tears, ups and downs are two faces of life. A saint has to love all kinds of people and everyone; not as father or brother, but as a saint. He must forgive everyone and must be forgiven by everyone. Even the animals in the jungle must say about him, "the saint has not harmed any creature," thus taught Diwaree to M. L. Singh.

Mr. Singh grew wiser. Slowly he made up his mind to appreciate the value of life and did so. When everybody forgave him, he reimbursed all the money he owed, and gave up all the bad habits that Diwaree wanted him to give up. He then begged his wife and children for their permission. After a long conversation and efforts they agreed to let him to live with the Saint. After accomplishing everything he requested Diwaree to accept him as a disciple. Diwaree refused and explained his reasons,

"M. L. Singh, I cannot make anyone a disciple because, I myself don't know where God will send me. If I don't know what he is going to make out of me and what will happen to me after death, then how can I take responsibility for you? How can I put myself between God and you? I know many, so called, saints who had done exactly that and they were worshipped by millions and millions of followers. It is easy, for whoever has confidence to claim to be a knower of God's secrets and God's special agent sent to this world, to be worshipped by millions of people and for generations. People from all the corners of the world will flock to him, and in a few hundred years, he will be known as the founder of a religion. But the question is why should I lie? That's the biggest mistake a saint can make after renouncing everything. I cannot lie in the name of God and make you a disciple," clearly explained Diwaree. Mr. Singh understood the saint's truthfulness, and he was happy just by living near a wonderful saint for that was a great blessing.

After couple of days M. L. Singh witnessed an unusual argument between a very famous champion and a feeble man. The feeble man shouted at the champion saying that he was a crooked, wicked, ill-disciplined champion. The champion became very angry and went to beat him up. Diwaree asked the champion, "Man, you have beaten up all the champions of the world, can't you digest a few words of this feeble man?" the champion paused for a minute and then understood the message. Diwaree then said, "Stronger is the one who is strong in mind. Brave is the one who can forgive wrongdoers. One who knows non-violence, means gentleness, kindness, forgiveness, humanity, compassion and love, he is a true champion. If you don't accept his evil words it will never harm you. No one has ever harmed his stomach by swallowing evil words or by not accepting them. If somebody came to give you something, and you refuse to take it, he will have to keep it with him. Become strong enough to inhale bad wind, if you have inhaled, then you will be a true champion." After understanding and practicing the message of Diwaree the champion had peace of mind and lived a blissful life. Everyday Mr. Singh was gaining new perceptions while living with the Saint. Some of the incidents he observed are related below:

One day Diwaree, in a conversation, said to M. L. Singh, "M. L. Singh, why do I live without shelter? Do you think it doesn't bother me when it rains? Off course it does. But then I see people who are poorer than me, living in this world without shelter; for they also are God's children. Why should they suffer like that? I have two blankets and next to me is a poor man, who doesn't have even one. I eat bread with many varieties of vegetables and he eats it with salt and water. I am a human being, I cannot see such things. If they don't have shelter then I too should live without. If they don't have bread to eat then I too must not have any. I compare myself with those broken Temples of God. I accept sufferings willingly, because righteousness is a gift for me, to nourish my soul. I must live my life for my soul. Let my body suffer."

"What difference does it make, if you live without a house and some people live in a house with twenty rooms and seventeen of them are empty? All rooms are filled with toys, furniture, and show cases. Shouldn't we rather be teaching them, that they should share their assets with the unprivileged?" questioned M. L. Singh in a friendly, humble tone.

"God has produced one dwelling unit for everybody. I have given that to someone else. Now about teaching the whole world, first of all I will reap the fruit of my Karma and they will reap the fruits of theirs. I cannot change the world but I can change myself. For me; to believe in my own thought - to believe what is true for me in my private heart - shall be true for all people. To change everything I simply change my attitude. If I change myself it will definitely make a difference in this world. That will be my gift to God. Many people don't understand teaching. They listen for hours and hours and finally they do what they want to. If I were to start teaching, then after my death, people might start a religious business in my name, which I am against. Becoming better is far better than teaching or following someone (dead or alive). However, it is true that I should teach the world, but they don't come to me for learning, they go to other spiritual leaders who advertise their wares on the television and guarantee safety in this life and promise heaven after death.

If they would have come to me I would have opened their minds by saying, 'Hey man, what is this con game you are playing? You are grabbing the money of a million people; enough for six generations of your descendants, and dreaming of going to heaven? You cheat! Do you and your leader, think that you can fool God? Why are you keeping these photos and other religious things in your prayer room? Do you think you have become intelligent enough to fool your Maker? Hungry for fame

and never satiated with the material life! Bad kids of an innocent mother!
You want more and more! Greedy fellows! Dreaming of heaven? And
above all preaching to Diwaree? Taking advantage of his poverty and
humility? You want to fool Diwaree? You want to make him your
spiritual guide to hide your dirty heads under his clean umbrella? Go and
throw away all your money and property. Distribute it among the needy
people. Give to those whose need is greater than yours. Purge yourself of
your sins. Make friends with all your family members, neighbors and
other people with whom you do not talk or whom you hate. Then, after
cleaning up your mind come to me; only then will I decide whether you
should be accepted as my student or not.'

Again I would tell them, 'I am Diwaree. I am not a goody-goody fun
loving man. I do not laugh and joke in God's name. It is not God's path.
I do not make a business out of spirituality. I am not a dirty politician
who would use God's name and religion to gather votes, gain power to
make money. If you are looking for someone who can amuse you in the
name of religion then go to others. There are many imposters eagerly
waiting to embrace people like you. They are ready to knock at your
doors to tie an unbreakable master-follower relationship with you. They
are waiting to remove your sins, unhappiness, sufferings, and guarantee
you success in this life - and heaven after your death. Go to them and
offer your meaningless lives to them. Lustful, greedy, dirty and selfish
people find like-minded masters to guide them. This is a market where
you will find anything you want. However if you want God you will
have to lead a truthful life. Lies and truth cannot go together, as dark and
light cannot co-exist. If you are looking for God you will find God.' Mr.
Singh sighed as he learned these amazing things.

****

One day a man came to Diwaree and said, "Hey Diwaree, you know you
are a damn fool. Everything you do, you do for fame. You are the most
ignorant man in the world...." and many other bad things - he kept on
and on and Diwaree listened silently.
Diwaree thought to himself, *"My God, you are testing my strength; I
must do that which will make you feel proud of me."* Again he explained
to Mr. Singh, "If you don't accept somebody's gift, then it will remain

with them yet be kind to him. Anyone can be good to a good person but you have to be good to the one who is not good to you. You must continue worshipping your inner . God with compassion." At any disturbing situation he used to repeat the meaningful magical mantra; 'God...God...God...'

****

Once the country's most powerful politician, who had the power to change the fate of the country, came to Diwaree and wanted to make him his spiritual master. Diwaree said to him, "Mr. Politician, there are many people who come to me and ask for my blessings especially at the time of elections. I know why you want my blessings; because you are a politician and not a saint or a religious man. I know you can change the fate of the country and you want to change your fate by using Diwaree's name. Unfortunately, I am not an agent of God. Do not force me to tell lies. You want me to predict, whether you will win the election or not. So my answer is I don't know. That is the plain truth. I am telling you the plain truth because I have no intention of extracting anything from your pocket, nor do I want your admiration, and since I don't want anything from you, I am telling you the plain truth. If you are filled with the truth, God will make you a winner. That's all I know. Now Mr. Politician, as to whether you will have victory or not. The answer is to ask yourself, if you have done everything truthfully then you will have victory, otherwise not. God will make you a winner or loser; whatever you deserve. I am not God nor do I have a vision of His plan.

Now the answer to your next question, about how many people, who are deceitful without blinking an eyelid, are successful in politics. My answer is; they are not successful. Their victory is the sign of their downfall. They have charted a course of deceit and lies. After their victory or success their greed is fuelled even more. Their Karma will catch up to them either in this life or the next, and then there will be no escape from Karmic retribution. Therefore a liar's victory is the start of his downfall." This plain truth Diwaree told him.

Once a visitor offered him food and said something quietly. In reply Diwaree told him, "You can feed me, but in return if you want me to promise you heaven or success, then I prefer to stay hungry. Success or failure, hell or heaven, that is between you and your God. Yet as a human being you must love a hungry person if you can. Give love to a neglected person. You must show love to a child of God whom you hate, avoid dirty language and speak the truth. A saint's duty is to give healthy food to people's brain, and your duty is to give food to a hungry saint. Thus, we both must keep doing our duty, and leave the rest up to God."

****

One day Diwaree spoke to M. L. Singh on the worship of God and how a saint must worship God. "Mr. Singh only a person who is fulfilled with truth can understand God. One who does not have truth, integrity and honesty is not a man, and no matter how big a 'nest' he has, his nest is nothing but a tomb for the ego. He is bound to go through problems. Merciful God blesses a liar with ignorance. For a liar being blessed with ignorance is a gift. That ignorance brings suffering into his life. The more an ignorant person suffers the more he learns. The more he learns the more he understands, the more he understands the more he perfects himself. The more he perfects himself the more he understands God, the more he understands God the more good deeds he performs and then God is pleased with him. Suffering is a blessing to an ignorant person, indeed, a perfect boon. There are people who suffer but do not learn which then makes their own life more difficult and more painful. However, a father cannot be happy when one of his children puts himself in a painful situation. The father is happy when a child learns without going through suffering.

If you deserve problems on account of your lies then you will receive them no matter where you live. No one can run away from problems. The more you try to run away from problems the more they stick to you. Even if you commit suicide you will have to face the same problems after death. The moment you leave this body the same problems will be waiting to welcome you at the next door. Problems will follow you like your shadow, but you must stick with righteousness. Charity must start from home, charity must start from this place, and right from this moment. Whether you are a train driver or a taxi driver you must take all passengers safely to their destination. Don not drink and drive.

1. For a saint this earth is his home. The more he purifies himself the
    more the people of this home will prosper with wisdom. All these
    beings are individual 'home shrines' and the saint must clean up their
    inner rooms and thus beautify this God-created beautiful earth, so
    that people may enjoy living here.
2. A house is the shrine for a house holder. If he follows the moral
    principles of life; blessed will his kids be. Anyone can buy a big
    house but one who creates love, virtue and a peaceful atmosphere
    within the house... It is his duty to worship all the deities living in
    the house by becoming good a parent or house-holder, which is
    possible only with his own sacrifice. Through his own sacrifice
    changes the life of everyone in the family.
3. A village is the shrine for the head of a village. God has appointed
    him to worship every deity (living beings) in his village.
4. The community is the shrine for a priest. With his truthful
    performance his people will be blessed with a Godly life. It is the
    priest's duty to guide the community righteously through his living.
5. The country is the shrine for a King (Ruler). King is a beggar like
    clean purified great soul that after winning God's trust he is blessed
    to have an opportunity to serve a nation. Though anyone can become
    hypocrite and betray God but a country will prosper only if a ruler
    can set an example by sacrificing his wealth for others. He must
    sacrifice his wealth for the most unprivileged people. He must make
    sure that his country's richest people's money is distributed among
    the poorest people and let everyone share Earth's gift equally. His
    duty is to worship every member of his country.

This world is my home, wherein I live, and all these creatures are God's
deities in my home. I have to improve the standard of my home because
there is no another earth to where we can shift. Someone may still live on
this earth, after our deaths, and we must remove all the garbage for them.
That is why saints are born.

According to me, this earth is destroyed by the activities of rascals and
the inactivity of good people. The rascals are also willing to change their
ways but first they want greedy people to become responsible. The
responsible people must sacrifice their lives to clean up the dirt from the
shrine-home. This is what I follow in my life. You were a father of three

children, that's why after completing your duty and responsibility as a father, you needed their permission to live with me. Now you have to become holy because this is like your new birth. Now you have to worship every deity within this world-shrine. Love them, not as a man, not as a woman, not as a father, but as a saint. Now this world is your home-shrine. You are a worshipper in this universal shrine. For you every individual is God's shrine." M. L. Singh was really astonished to learn about the responsibilities of a saint..

****

Once a rich man told him, "I purchased land, because its price was rising very fast."

"What a fool you are…" the man interrupted and asked, "But why?"

"The price is increasing fast but life is decreasing faster. By the time the price gets really high, you'll be dead. What will you take with you, except hypocrisy?"

Diwaree then gave him a needle saying, "After our deaths we will meet again, bring it there and then return it to me. Till then keep it in your possession as my property," When Diwaree had left the rich man thought, "How can I take a needle with me after my death?" Then he realized, "If I cannot take one needle with me, then what can I take?" Finally he understood the Saint's message; "*You shall not be able to take anything with you except good or bad Karma*". Diwaree's ways of saying things were very different but practical. Prof. Singh had to take a deep breath every time.

****

The next day's conversation was even more remarkable; He called M. L. Singh and asked him, "Listen to me my son; will you do me a favor after my death?"

"Yes, I will do anything you say Diwaree."

"Then listen to me carefully. You know I am old now and I may die anytime. When you bury my body make sure that there is no monument on the top of the grave. The land over my grave should be cultivated and seeds must be sown there or people should use the land as a farm to grow fruits and vegetables. That will provide peace to my soul. If you don't do this then people may start organizing prayers at my burial site. If they make a tomb on top of my grave, then I will be punished by nature. This land does not belong to the dead. This land belongs to those who are alive; they need it to build their houses. Those who are alive need to plant seeds and cultivate it to feed their children," thus explained Diwaree in detail.

Then he added, "Make sure that people do not perform Jalasamadhi (consigning the dead body to the waters) for me. This is not only a sin but also unhygienic. One should not pollute the water because whoever drinks or uses that water may suffer with some kind of disease. So if you consign my body to the waters, my soul will be punished indirectly. Therefore, I insist that you do not consign my body to the waters after my death. And if you do, the responsibility shall be yours and you may have to face the consequences. Also make sure people don't put it in the Tower of Silence because that may also pollute the atmosphere.

At the time of the burial pray to mother earth reciting the following verses, "Return to your Mother Earth, may she be kind to you and you lie lightly on her lap, may she not oppress you, may she hug you, cuddle you and assimilate you like an unborn infant," and then pray to Mother Earth with the following verse, "Open thy arms, O Mother Earth; receive your child with gentle pressure and with loving welcome. Enshroud him tenderly as a mother folds her soft vestment round the child she loves." (Rigved X.18.11)

Then put the soil on the face of my dead body while reciting the word *Tattwamasi*. Then bow down to Mother Earth and again pray. Once you have covered my face then ask all others to put some soil on my body while reciting the same word *Tattwamasi, Tattwamasi*.

I have told you the method of disposal of my body after my death, I have done my duty and you have agreed to do what I have requested you to do. Will you do all these things?" he asked again to make sure.

"Yes, Diwaree, I shall comply with your wishes", assured Singh.

At that time, Tom's divorced wife Maya was there. She was listening to the whole conversation and was amazed. She murmured; "...wow! The living example of a great soul – Diwaree - wants his body to be disposed off in the soil with a clean and sinless reputation. He is not one of those materialistic saints who want fame even after death. What a great saint - concerned about all human beings of the earth..." Looking at the kind-hearted wise saint Diwaree's simple life and meaningful thoughts, Maya was highly impressed. Her eyes filled with tears.

While listening to this conversation, Maya learned that Diwaree did not talk openly about the huge houses and huge churches, mosques and temples on acres and acres of land all over the world, but she understood what was wrong with the human mentality. She understood why there is suffering in our world. Diwaree did not like the foolish idea of putting an expensive diamond in a dead person's mouth, offering money, offering jewellery, or placing many expensive things next to a dead body believing that the dead will receive them, instead he preferred that those expensive things be given to a needy person. He knew that there are people who have buried their dead with much gold and diamonds because they forgot their humanity and that poor people face hardship on account of their ignorance. The system is unequal because of greedy and fame hungry rich people and their protector saints. Diwaree was full of truth. His truthfulness touched the depths of Maya's heart.

Like Maya, many media people were impressed by Diwaree's truly renounced life. Many people like God-Bawa were disturbed, because some enormously rich people had started believing in Diwaree's way of life. He seemed spiritually rich yet very simple. He did not need money. For the rich miserly people it was easier to follow Diwaree's philosophy. By following his philosophy, they could be considered followers of a holy man without having to spend a single penny. If the rich and the miserly had gone to God-Bawa, God-Bawa would have definitely extracted some money from them for the construction of some building, shrine etc. But they didn't have to give anything to Diwaree, not even a single penny. Diwaree was neither interested in people's money nor accepting anyone as a disciple. Even if a powerful person with a high reputation came to him he still wouldn't bless him.

When more and more products and services enter into the market, it is natural for the consumers to start comparing a new product with the one they have been using for a long time. Eventually, they would opt for the better and cost effective product. When Diwaree's name and fame appeared on the horizon, it was natural for God-Bawa to take a note of it. Till then God-Bawa had a sort of spiritual monopoly. God-Bawa's close disciples had done their best to convince everyone that God-Bawa was the best saint in the world. There had never been anyone like him nor would there be in the future. Those who moved away from God-Bawa would face desolation and total annihilation. Their bodies and even their entire families would be consigned to the tombs. Those who had left him faced endless tragedies, disasters, endless sickness, their children died, their parents died, houses collapsed, businesses collapsed and so on.... God-Bawa's disciples cited numerous examples of such cases to keep God-Bawa's flock intact. Yet God-Bawa perceived a challenge to his hegemony in Diwaree's blemish-free reputation and selfless commitment. God-Bawa was afraid and saw a menacing threat in Diwaree's clean and simple image.

****

Step Eight ...

GOD-BAWA AND SAINT DIWAREE

Many others, who were in the same vocation as God-Bawa, were concerned about Diwaree's rising reputation. Just like politicians, all these so-called saints and preachers, were competing with each other. They preached in public that criticizing or gossiping is a sin, but after finishing their sermons, criticized everyone else to prove that all the other preachers were ignorant. Each one said the others were charlatans, imposters, pretenders, frauds and cheats who only misled the public to make money.

For God-Bawa, there remained only a few competitors. Diwaree was one of his main obstacles and rivals. Since the day, Diwaree had refused to take a big donation from a rich man, he attracted everyone's attention and God-Bawa's followers started admiring him. When God-Bawa heard about Diwaree's disdainful rejection of money or earthly riches, he was deeply perturbed.

One of Bawa's close disciples was Maya's class-mate. He was rich but he did not have a 'wealth of personality'. For that reason he could not be with her but she had always stayed in his mind and after her divorce he got more concerned about her whereabouts. When he heard that instead of God-Bawa she might start following Saint Diwaree, his mind became restless. He started whispering the words into the air, 'Diwaree is a problem', Diwaree is a problem....' Already perturbed, God-Bawa's curious ears could not ignore those words.

God-Bawa's business was being adversely affected by Diwaree's life of simple living. God-Bawa wanted to make him realize, as a friend, that he was harming him publicly for nothing, but Diwaree wouldn't pay any attention. God-Bawa started thinking of ways to remove this obstacle;

Diwaree was making a dent in his reputation. Though Bawa had several ideas to solve this problem, such as; allegations of moral turpitude, to be made through his hired ladies, putting slow poison in his food, getting him arrested by the police on trumped up charges, sending him to jail for a lifetime, using special political tricks, and so on. He knew that destructive weapons can be useful during a war. For God-Bawa this world was a battle-field where any tool was be used as a weapon.. Diwaree could be used as a weapon to win over all the saints of this world. As big companies buy small companies when they come into competition, Bawa thought of merging Diwaree's name with his mission.

One day the clever God-Bawa sent a follower to Diwaree to fetch him to his monastery. The follower sought out Diwaree and said humbly, "God-Bawa has invited you to his monastery office."

"Why can he not come to me? What does he think of himself? Does he think that he is a big man? Does he think that he is greater than me? Does he think that he is a great personality? ... If so, then go and tell him that Diwaree refuses to come to such an egotistic man. For what? Is it because that on account of his wealth he considers himself superior to others? Well, he is superior to only materialistic-minded ignoramuses, who get impressed by his property, those greedy ones who want something from him and of which he is not capable. I have renounced the material world. I do not need anything from him. He is the king of his palace and I am a king of my 'wall'. Ask him to come to me instead, if he wants to meet me," Diwaree answered in a bold way.

The follower told God-Bawa everything. God-Bawa thought for a long time on how to solve this problem. Finally, one night at around eleven o' clock, with Mr. Harry Kingson, he went to visit Diwaree.

When they arrived in the area where Diwaree lived, they couldn't find him. They did not see anybody of whom they could ask directions. Eventually they saw a beggar sitting by the side of the road. He was an old, bald, and simple poor beggar with a long beard. Harry Kingson hit the beggar's bald head with his bent finger and asked him, "Hey man! Do you know where Diwaree lives?"

"He must be somewhere here or over there," the beggar humbly answered with folded hands and bowed head.

They looked around and came back again to the old beggar and, throwing a dollar bill on his head, with an arrogant voice Harry Kingson asked, "Do you know who we are, and what we asked you for? Take this dollar bill and come with us, show us where exactly he lives."

That old beggar said, with folded hands and bowed head, "I am Diwaree."

"Oh! You are Diwaree! Then why did you not tell us before? We heard you sleep on a wall but how come you are here? We thought you are just a beggar having a nap. Anyway, we have come to see you," said Harry Kingson and then he picked up his dollar bill.

"Actually that's true I sleep on a wall, this is my praying place. When I pray, I always sit on the ground, to bow my head on the ground. I love this Mother Earth and therefore love to bow my arrogant and egotistic head down upon her skin. Anyway, I have the whole night left for praying. Guests get first priority. You are my guests. Guests seldom come. They might come in the form of God. For this reason you have precedence. Let's go to the wall. It's only a five minutes walk from here," Diwaree said.

Diwaree walked slowly. God-Bawa and Mr. Harry followed him. In less than five minutes they reached 'Diwaree's wall'. Diwaree climbed on the wall, sat there for few seconds to pray before turning to his guests, and then the conversation started. Mr. Harry made the introductions.

"This is His Holiness His Highness God-Miracle-Bawa and I am Harry Kingson," introduced Mr. Harry.

"Oh! God-Bawa God-God! hak... hak... hak ... ... God-Bawa? God-Bawa hak hak ... ... oh I cannot believe it! You are here. I can't believe it. You are the great God-Bawa and I am but a poor man. I am surprised that you have come to this poor man's place. But you are welcome ... ... I have heard a lot about you. Thank you for coming to me. Please have a seat. Take this wooden plank. hak... hak... That's all I have to welcome guests. Sorry about it," said the astonished Diwaree giving them the wooden plank.

Harry Kingson took the wooden plank from Diwaree's hands and passed it to God-Bawa.

God-Bawa sat on the plank. Harry Kingson sat on a rock and Diwaree sat on his perch on the wall.

"Sorry Diwaree, I hit your head with my bent finger. It was just a misunderstanding," apologized Harry Kingson.

"What difference does that make?" said Diwaree.

"I disturbed you while you were praying. I didn't know that you were praying as there was no incense or any candle burning, nor any symbol of God. ... Sorry," said Harry Kingson behaving like a reasonable person.

"Prayers, that's all right. I can do that later. You have come all the way from your palace to my humble abode. There must be something urgent for you to have taken so much trouble to come here, at this time?" the curious Diwaree asked.

"That is true Diwaree, as you know, I don't go to anyone. I have come here to speak with you about something very secret. I have a problem. I would have solved this problem easily but I thought it was better to solve it with a better understanding. This is a confidential conversation we don't want anyone else to hear it," God-Bawa said.

"That's all right, no one is here. I live alone. There is only my son M. L. Singh but he is far from here. It's middle of the night and he is sleeping anyway," assured Diwaree.

God-Bawa started to explain, "Diwaree, whatever you do, you are doing it for nothing. You are getting nothing and my mission is being affected a great deal because of your useless actions. Why do we not form a coalition and make this world aware of our purpose and powers? Together, we can do a lot. You come and live with me. I will give you a nice house with all the facilities including television, a telephone, refrigerator, two servants and good food. You will get lots of respect. What else do you need?"

"God-Bawa, I am old. At any moment I may get God's summons. I have this body for only a short time. I've never had any intention of doing anything except live a pure life. That's the only aim of my life. I want to live a pure life and never do anything wrong for money. I may have to live with sufferings, but I have to lead an immaculate life. God will take care of me, as he has always done," said Diwaree humbly..

God-Bawa was a little emotional with his touching response, then he explained to Diwaree, "Diwaree, you are a talented and an impressive speaker. If you come out of your self-imposed oblivion do you know what you can do? You can make millions of followers in just one year. I am telling you that you have accumulated a treasure, now use it. In one year, you will see that you have shaken not only this country but also the whole world. I will tell you how to go about it. All you need to do is issue the following statement in public saying;

'I am Diwaree. I am impressed by God-Bawa's powers, and I have not seen anyone greater than him, therefore, I have surrendered myself before His Highness and joined his great mission. I am no more Diwaree but God-Bawa's disciple'. All you have to do is just say these words. That's it!

And listen to me Diwaree, in two years you will have the tallest building in the world. You will have more property than any businessman in the world. You know all the needy, and the greedy people are under my control whether he or she is a businessman, magician, priest, preacher or a politician. It is our brains that are motivating even the biggest politicians and business people. People like the President will come to meet you. You will become the advisor to the bigwigs of different political and non-political groups. When ever a VIP comes to me I will send him to you, telling him, *'my disciple Diwaree will advise you correctly as I have doubled his soul powers'.* Diwaree, I will teach you every single thing. Listen Diwaree, this is the time for you to reap the fruit of your austerity. Now be prepared to achieve great things in life. Diwaree, live while you are alive, don't die before you are dead. Live an enjoyable life.

You have led a very good and impressive life with sincerity, that's all I was looking for. You know that all political leaders, including the President, are beholden to me for my advice. With your help, I can shake the whole world. That's all I need. Come with me and you will see the wonders of my monastery. Diwaree, every ascetic and every holy man has reaped the fruits of his austerity. Do something in life. Don't die without doing something. So far you have done nothing. Now, you have a chance to prove that you have strength and powers. You will get everything that you never had," said God-Bawa as he explained the plan.

"God-Bawa, I am a God-fearing man. I have never made one single disciple with the fear that if God were to question me as to where I would finally take that disciple, I would have no answer. I know a little lie can impress the whole world, but I don't want to do that God-Bawa. According to my understanding the biggest sin is brainwashing. I know that by brainwashing one can build the largest church in the heart of the city. If we brainwash a billionaire, it's possible to do many things. Brainwashing is the most profitable business in the world. But, God-Bawa how will I answer God's question. I know what it is, God knows it, a brainwashed follower may not know it but the brainwasher knows it, and we know it." Diwaree explained his fear of God and his point of view.

God-Bawa argued and questioned impatiently;

Q: "Who has seen God,? Have you, Diwaree?" demanded God-Bawa.
A: "Well, God-Bawa, tell me who has not seen God, haven't you?" said Diwaree.
Q: "Is there any single thing which can prove God?" again questioned God-Bawa.
A: "Is there any single thing which doesn't prove God?" questioned Diwaree.

Q: "Is there anyone who can prove God's existence, can you?" questioned God-Bawa.

A: "Is there anyone who can prove God's non-existence, can you?" questioned Diwaree.

Q: "Who has seen God's Judgment?"

A: "Who has not seen God's Judgment?"

Q: "Why do you have to believe in so called judgment?" said God-Bawa.

A: "Haven't you seen a beggar, then why don't you believe in His Judgment?" questioned Diwaree.

Q: "Why do you have to believe in illusions?" questioned God-Bawa.

A: "Why don't you believe in his laws when the sun rises on time and the trees are giving fruits?" said Diwaree.

Question followed question, the argument went on for a while. After few minutes the atmosphere became quite charged. They stopped the argument. Then after a minute Diwaree continued,

"If you cannot prove his non-existence then why don't you believe in his judgment? I know you have promised millions of followers to save them after death. According to your philosophy there is neither a judge nor a judgment for those forgiven disciples, or you have some special collaboration with the Judge. But God-Bawa, to me, there is nothing in this world which refutes the law of the Supreme Judge and His existence. I can find nothing which denies God's existence, not one single thing. Each and every single thing is a proof of God. Every single thing I see in this universe speaks to me loudly, of the Creator's powers and inconceivable wonders. When he shows me; I see. When he makes me happy; I am happy. When he feeds me; I am fed. He operates my body; including my brain. Without him I would not have speech, hearing, vision and couldn't even move my body. When he moves me I move. When he makes me sleep I sleep. But, when I hear your negative statements I am astonished that God should have some purpose in creating such a person as you. There has to be a definite reason. It really surprises me when a creature does not accept his creator. It's really surprising, when a man sees the sun and does not believe in it after using its life sustaining warmth and light, or does not believe in food after having it consumed it. In this world of God, what could be a bigger surprise than this?

God-Bawa, to make it simpler, you have a wrist-watch, which means there is someone who has made it. This universe is speaking through everything, from everywhere such as; trees, birds, animals, human beings etc., which is proof of God. Look at the leaves and look at the flowers. Are they not speaking of the miracle of God? God-Bawa, come closer; feel your heartbeat or your pulse beat. It is the living witness to prove God's existence. One who looks for proof will find that every single thing is a proof of God's existence. God is an astonishing Artist, whose invisible hands have designed the wonders of this universe. God-Bawa I cannot find even one single thing, which does not bear the proof. Every human being, every creature including this whole planetary system is functioning at his behest. What about the billions of stars, in the galaxy not deviating, from their assigned orbits, by even a fraction of a millimeter? Are those things not speaking clearly of God? You want more proofs?

He lives in the hearts of every human being, which are his self-created residences. The human being's mind is the Creator's sanctified sanctorum. I do not want to destroy his sanctified sanctorum. These are the reasons; I say that the biggest sins in the world are brainwashing and deception. God-Bawa, once you mislead a person towards an unknown destiny, he is lost for as long as he remains deceived. His mind cannot evolve further. He cannot walk with nature. He cannot accept the simple truth of God. This is happening to all of your followers. Mr. God-Bawa! Misleading is a sin. Do not cheat them for your pleasure and fun. Let them find their own creator. Let them communicate with Him directly. Do not hold and use them. Let them achieve the aim of their lives. This is what I believe," explained Diwaree.

After listening calmly God-Bawa became grumpy inside and still trying to convince Diwaree he said,

"Diwaree, God does not live in human beings. There are a million proofs I can furnish that only the evil Satan lives in human beings. I cannot see any human being, in this world, who does not function without the power of Satan. Forget about where he lives and where he doesn't, my point is, there is no God's justice and only Satan rules the world. They are all confused and blind human beings, filled with distress and misery. Now I will tell you about misleading; it's not we who mislead them, they themselves want to be misled. I am merely fulfilling their wishes. They feel satisfied. In this way I am doing a good job by providing peace to their restless minds. I am making them feel relaxed, by saying that they can look at me if they cannot see God. Together with you, we will do the same and our mission will spread all over the world," explained God-Bawa.

"There is only one God, so there has to be only one path. We already have so many religions, so many paths and so many Gods. Each continent has its own religion and its own God. We already have enough God-leaders, and enough religions to make people hate each other. Why should I help in adding one more to it?" Diwaree asked him.

"Diwaree, the children of God are all coming to the center from the East, West, North and South. The one who is coming from the South is walking towards the North, and one who is coming from the North is walking towards the South. You cannot question them; *'Hey! Seekers, why are you walking in opposite directions?'* reasoned God-Bawa.

"Clever words cannot change the truth Mr. God-Bawa. Fools will agree with those ideas, but don't try to fool me. I am not looking for pleasure. I don't like people who fool others with tricky words and complicated language. Misleading with clever words is not good. Many times M. L. Singh requested me to accept him as a disciple, but my conscience did not allow me to do so. I didn't like to give more drugs to drug addicts to keep them high. Off course, the drug addict would be thankful for more drugs, but I know that his brain cells will get destroyed, and he will be unable to recognize God's miracles. That's a sin. Mr. God-Bawa, I told you I am a God-fearing man. What they want that is none of my business. I am concerned about my Karma. Again I will say, 'misleading or brainwashing is the same as murdering God's children'. It is the same as destroying God's shrine's; his sanctified sanctorum. Now, I don't want to talk any more," concluded Diwaree and remained silent after that. In his silence perhaps he started praying.

"Well Diwaree it is now up to you. .... I have tried. I have done my duty," and concluding with this final statement God-Bawa walked away with Harry Kingson giving him a funny look.

In the morning, before four a.m., Diwaree just disappeared. He used to wake up early in the morning for his prayers but M. L. Singh didn't hear anything, nor did he notice anything in the night. What happened to Diwaree? God knows where he went... he just disappeared without leaving any trace. M. L. Singh searched all over but couldn't find him.

Nobody knew where Diwaree had gone! ... His followers were left in the middle of a mist of confusion. Where Diwaree had gone was a mystery ...

Mr. Singh cried very much, when he could not find his beloved Master. Though, he was not a philosopher like Diwaree, but he used to be a professor of philosophy and by living with Diwaree he was constantly thinking about God, the Mind, Consciousness, Sub-consciousness, Conscience, Buddhi, Gumption, Wisdom, Death, Karma, Rebirth and all that was written in the scriptures and what Diwaree was practicing. In only a few months he was completely changed by living near him. His diary of quotations: "Thus Revealed the Sages of Sanatan Dharma" was an interesting collection of ancient scriptures.

The Bhagwad Gita was his favorite scripture. He had understood the essence of all the scriptures while living with his beloved master. He knew the secret of the; Yoga of Dejection, Yoga of Wisdom, Yoga of Action, Yoga of Disciplines, Yoga of Renunciation, Yoga of Meditation, Knowledge, Realization, Absolute God, real Science and the Royal secret, Divine manifestations, vision of cosmic body, Devotion, Body and its Knower, Three Qualities of nature, Supreme self, Discrimination between the godly and demoniac properties, Division of three kinds of faith, and Yoga of freedom through renunciation. He knew why people face towards the east (sun) or north (pole star) while praying, why people move clockwise at certain ceremonies, why people bow down their heads to the ground, why people pray to the sun, moon and other planets. He knew why people worship the air, fire, rivers, mountains, trees, and other creatures including human beings. He had a vast knowledge of all the religions. He knew many things about the soul, the mind, and death of a body. He knew the facts about the real and unreal worlds, and how to control the mind in adverse situations.

But, when the time came he could not stop crying. He couldn't handle the loss of his beloved Master. He kept crying like a baby, saying, "Master, master, my beloved master, where have you gone without telling me... why did you leave me alone...why... my beloved master where have you gone...?

****

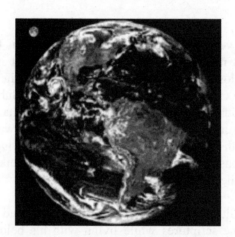

This earth is alive. From His cave in the center of the Earth God watches over His creations. When the soul of one of His creations has outgrown its body, God puts that soul into a more evolved body.

****

Step Nine...

WORLD FAMOUS GOD-BAWA

After Saint Diwaree's disappearance God-Miracle-Bawa became world famous. He had a big monastery with many admirers, followers, and disciples. He had dozens of buildings with many rooms, and a well organized guest house with five star hotel facilities for all VIPs. It was difficult to count the air-conditioners, personal telephones, mobile phones, servants, cars, trucks, drivers, kitchens, and food facilities, cooking utensils, free cooks, waiters, cleaners, gate-keepers, cattle, farms and buildings. For his own use he had a Rolls Royce, like the one Mr. Harry Kingson had. He had his private airplane and two pilots, a helicopter and helipad inside the monastery.

Millions of people were mesmerized after seeing his enormous property. Each year thousands and thousands of people became his followers. He appeared on the national and international televisions and sometimes on the front pages of newspapers.

He used to wear a long gown with long sleeves. Nobody knew that he hid things under his sleeves, and with a thin hair-like thread (fine colorless thin fishing line, almost invisible) he could pull out the tucked up object, and bring it into his palm, in front of hundreds of people. He could perform stunning magic. He would ask them, *"what do you want to see?"* and if a person would say *"I want to see roses"*, he would say, *"So be it"* and in a split second a rose would appear. Nobody could catch him because nobody could understand his interesting methods. Therefore, they believed that God-Bawa was God because he could create so many things with his powers. It was proof that his miracles could change one's luck.

However, God-Bawa did not need to produce miracles anymore, as the enormous crowds and his immense riches automatically attracted thousands and thousands of money-minded innocent people who became his followers. God-Bawa also guaranteed them heaven. If a follower's forefathers were returning from the grave, God-Bawa could fix that problem. If a follower's forefathers were not able to enter heaven, God-Bawa could arrange that too. He guaranteed salvation to those who were initiated and offered an initiation fee. The amount of offering for initiation was not fixed, it varied from the rich to the poor. However, heaven was guaranteed to everyone. Some people offered two hundred dollars and other people, like Harry Kingson, offered two hundred thousand, but heaven was guaranteed to every useful person.

To accommodate his admirers for free, God-Bawa had a guest house. There were three categories in his guest house. The first type was for only those rich people who could offer heavy donations. The second type was for middle-class people who came there to enjoy, and paid the nominal charges. The third type of living accommodation was dormitories with no beds. The poor, who couldn't afford it or who didn't want to pay the nominal cost and still wanted to enjoy safety, could stay in the dormitories. Some of them were afraid to stay in city hotels because they had had terrible experiences with the local people and commission agents who functioned incognito.

God-Bawa had a free food distribution center for poor people, where sometimes the rich people also went to enjoy the religious simplicity. He kept a few orphans in his orphan's home and opened a small free medical clinic for the poor. The free clinic and orphan's home were weapons to shut the mouths of his critics, and allow his admirers to shout from their roof-tops that God-Bawa's organization was providing free services to the poor. So then how could he be considered inhumane by foolish people? Anyway, they had dozens of news clippings, to prove that he had done an unlimited number of good things.

Almost everyone worked for free. Unpaid volunteers worked in the clinic, cottage industries, guest houses and kitchens. He had a few specially paid volunteers who maintained his secret tax accounts and legal papers.

God-Bawa had millions of followers all around the world. Whoever wanted to win an election went to God-Bawa for his blessings. God-Bawa had a special arrangement with the candidate to the effect that if he won he would remit an agreed amount to his registered charitable establishment from the government budget in addition to doing some favors in his pending legal cases. The candidate would also grant a business deal to Harry Kingson. After these agreements God-Bawa's photo would appear in the newspapers, with the candidate. When they saw the photo all his gullible followers understood that they were to cast their vote for that candidate, as he believed in God-Bawa, and Bawa had approved him. The politician's victory was almost certain. Therefore, many candidates wanted to prove that they had been God-Bawa's followers and would remain so for good. A candidate's victory was as good as a victory for God-Bawa and Mr. Harry. The victory further boosted the reputation of God-Bawa as well as that of the winning candidate.

God-Bawa was a precious jewel, for any party's representative. God-Bawa would only support the politician who could offer the most money and most political favors. If a politician happened to be more famous than God-Bawa, then he was accepted without a deal. God-Bawa's doors were always unconditionally open to welcome the world's most powerful leaders. A famous politician's popularity automatically attracted the public. The people believed that the reason behind a politician's success was God-Bawa's spiritual blessings.

If a candidate happened to be reasonably powerful but not willing to contribute generously to God-Bawa's 'Charitable Trust', then he could go to any popular religious shrine, and invoke the blessings of that shrine's God in his endeavors. God-Bawa did not object to this, yet in his subtle and crafty way he would plant an idea that the blessings of a 'living saint' were really more effective. Whatever God-Bawa said was accepted as the 'gospel truth' and coming from the mouth of a world-renowned spiritual person, was like coming from God. Yet, if a poor yet learned person said the same or even better, people paid scant attention to that poor person. A poor person, no matter how educated he may be was a non-entity in the eyes of the people. It was better if that poor man could prepare attractive speeches for God-Bawa.

God-Bawl was not alone in this multi-million dollar spirituality business. A whole lot of corrupt politicians, mafia, and gang leaders were intimately involved. Many people's survival, livelihood, respect, business and even their family members' livelihood were connected with this so-called holy cause of spiritual enlightenment.

****

God-Bawa's disciples had a standard procedure to convince a new seeker to make him or her surrender before Bawa, and to get initiated. Some of the salient points of the technique were very innovative. The eight main arguments to convincing a potential disciple were:

1.   Like you I too was having many bewildering experiences; I had more than my share of family and other problems. Finally, I found God-Bawa and the day he blessed me I got peace, satisfaction, harmony, tranquility and other good things. My life changed.

2.   Don't wait for your ship to come in, swim out to it. Life is short. It ends without any notice. Human life is a door to heaven and only God-Bawa is the key bearer of the door to heaven.

3.   The aim of human life is to find God, and God-Bawa is the only one who has the gift to guide lesser mortals like us. He has achieved these special spiritual powers after a life of long hardship and special prayers. He knows everything that we don't, his eyes are open and ours are closed, he can enter our minds but we cannot enter his. He can read our minds but we cannot read his.

4.   A bad person will not be able to recognize God-Bawa. They presume him to be a common man. Many people were destroyed when they doubted or opposed God-Bawa. There are thousands of examples of how the foolish were destroyed.

5.   Everyone comes into this world with nothing. With death everyone leaves everything behind. Your family members will

dispose off your body but now they are just using you for their own benefit. Use this life for God.

6. The enormously increasing population, great destruction, natural calamities and wars around the world are all precursors of God's arrival on earth. God-Bawa is God's chosen representative to solve all the problems of humankind. He is our only Savior.

7. Oh! You are lucky that you have come all the way here. Only a lucky soul can become his follower. His followers are safe in this life, and when God-Bawa takes all their responsibilities; their business booms, success comes their way; all their wishes are fulfilled including their children's marriages, their health problems, business problems, and other problems are solved. Those who put their lives in his hands are safe in this life and the next.

8. Only God-Bawa has constant communication with the Creator; he is the only one with a direct link and is in constant communion with the Almighty. At the moment of death, God-Bawa comes to receive his follower, takes him or her into his loving arms, and then to heaven.

'Complete destruction' and 'absolute success' were the two words used over and over again to make anyone who hesitated take the desired plunge in God-Bawa's cesspool of spirituality. 'Death' was the main word - the trump card - to break the resistance of any doubting Thomas.

****

Step Ten...

MESSIAH MET GOD–BAWA

God-Bawa enjoyed all kinds of luxuries. To all his followers, he said that he prayed after midnight, but those who lived with him knew that he never prayed. His followers believed that he was an incarnation of truth, but his closest disciples knew that his reputation was built on a foundation of tricks, and every brick in his establishment was made out of a solid lie. For him there was no God, therefore there was no fear of God.

An interesting fact was that most of his followers believed in God's constructive and destructive powers, but he did not. He himself was an atheist, so even if the true God were to appear in front of him, he wouldn't have believed. He never believed in the philosophy of his followers. He believed only in two things - 'money' and 'safe fun'.

He did not often say that he was God but when his prosperous devotees were sitting in the congregation, only then would he utter; *'I am God'*. However, he was aware that all his followers called him God. He had also seen that in many photos, books, stories, advertisements, movies, cassettes, newspapers, pamphlets and flyers, that he was referred to as Christ, Prophet, Avatar or God. Of course, he was aware that his photos were being worshipped by millions of believers, and in fact he was the one who had advised his media department to distribute more and more of his photos among the followers. People used to light candles, incense and kneel down in front of those photos. He knew all about these practices...

He made others feel that they were never alone, as they were always in his thoughts, but an interesting fact was that he himself was a very lonely man, as was there was no one to listen to him. No one thought that he could be a lonely man. He knew that no one was his true well-wisher. Everyone came to him to get something. Everyone told him their problems and asked for help. He kept thinking that there was no one whom he could consult about his own inner problems and to share his deep thoughts. No one was going to share the consequences of his terrible deeds; which sometimes made him restless. He could not sleep during the nights, thinking of what would become of him after his death. He was afraid, but no one could know his fear, consequently no one knew the reason for his fear. He didn't know how to interpret Devi's warning.

Devi's warning was the most stunning thing in his life, which came about this way. One day Devi Messiah came to him. She looked into his eyes and said to him, "You are not what you are claiming to be, so stop it now."

God-Bawa looked into her eyes, and tried to read the depths of the ocean. With great surprise, he started to think, 'Who is this? So far in my lifetime, no one has made such a statement to me in such a way. What shall I answer now?'

"Who are you?" asked the confused God-Bawa.
"If I tell you, you will not believe me," replied Devi.

"Why will I not believe?" asked God-Bawa.
"Because you do not understand," answered Devi.

"Can you make me understand?" asked God-Bawa.
"Yes I can, but you will loose everything you have," replied Devi.

"Then what is the use of knowing you?" asked God-Bawa.
"Don't be afraid of losing everything, as you will gain everything you need," reassured Devi.

"What do you mean? Don't I have all the good things available in this world, including; my five Rolls Royce cars, helicopter, airplane, and this property? What else do I need now?" asked God-Bawa.

"If you have everything but not the truth, it means, you have nothing. If you have nothing but the truth, it means you have everything. Now you have nothing except dirt and dust. But if I tell you who I am then you will have truth and you will lose all the things you have now. You will lose the curtain of dirt and dust. I will place you in daylight and you will see who I am. Now you are in terrible darkness and that's the reason every moment you are committing a new sin, and you are aware of those sins," said Devi.

"Darkness? Committing a sin every moment? Curtain of dirt and dust? What's all this?" uttered God-Bawa.

"You don't know what you are standing on, what are her powers, where you came from, what is the soul, the mind, consciousness, death and God. You don't know why you have come into this world, and where you will go after death?" said Devi.

"Nobody knows these things, then how can you? Even, if you know, what is the use of knowing them and why do you want to teach me all these things?" questioned God-Bawa.

"I am a helper. I am here to help you. If you let me teach you then you should listen quietly, with no preconceptions in your mind. In only few hours you will know who I am. If you let me teach you for three days you will know the difference between good Karma and bad Karma.

I have come to give you a feeling of reality and to help you. Helping is my nature. I do not take anything from people. That is why, I have no material things. Someone has given me a room to live in for one month and I have only two blankets and some necessary things in a bag.

I don't make any advertisements nor do many people know me. I have changed my name many times. When I was in Asia my name was different. When I was in America my name was different and when I was in Europe and Africa my names were different. A flower will remain a flower, no matter by which name you call it. The sun will remain the sun, you can call him by any name. You may never have heard my name.

Last night you cried in loneliness as if you were afraid of death. Your conscience is telling you that enough is enough. Stop it now before God's summon. You are worried that the consequences of your misdeeds would cost you when you die, because you know what you have done, and I know too. Only you and I know. I must give you a chance, so that there will be no excuse that this earth was without a teacher of truth, and you will have no excuse to say that no one told you about the existence of the path of virtue.

When I open your eyes you will know where you are, and where you will go after your death. With your new learning, all your followers will have a chance to hear the good news about the real God. However, at the same time they will find out what you have been. Remember, your followers will hate you for your past misdeeds, but in return they will get everything. But now, you are the wall between them and me. I am the light. If you want them to see the light you have to stand aside, or demolish yourself. They don't belong to you. You did not create them. They are not your children. They are the children of this Earth. I have to tell them the relationship between their mother Earth and themselves. I am telling you again, you will lose everything but you will redeem your soul," added Devi.

Frightened and angry, God-Bawa rang the bell and two caretakers came in and said with folded hands, "Yes our Lord".

"Take her away and put her out beyond the boundaries of my monastery," ordered God-Bawa.

Devi Messiah said while slowly walking out, "I will walk myself; I don't stay where people don't want me."

Since the day Devi Messiah walked out from God-Bawa's monastery, he became very restless. He could not sleep during the nights. He felt very lonely even in the middle of a crowd. No one could understand his fear and loneliness. The following week he had a dream. In his dream the Earth said to God-Bawa,

"I am watching all your actions. I know what you are doing. You blind fellow! You thought that there is no one, in this world, to watch over your actions. I know you started preaching to people while you yourself remained a pretender, a cheat and a liar with a hunger for fame. You told them to go to God with offerings and ask Him for nothing except wisdom, devotion, and his blessings.

You started preaching to people; not to be greedy, not to gather more than what was actually required, not to crave for fame and not to try to become someone special. You told them that a religious garb does not make anyone holy, and they should not hanker after palace-like houses when small houses could meet their needs. You told them to renounce the material world, and donate as much as they could in order to receive compensation after death. But, you on the other hand used your clever tricks and grabbed their money.

You kept increasing; your property, your buildings, your palaces, expensive Rolls Royce, helicopter, airplanes and business enterprises. You appeared in newspapers, distributed your photographs, made advertisements and used publicity agents. You set out to enrich your own "Empire." You fooled everyone. You ignorant little man, you thought that in this manner you could fool the whole world. I have been keeping my eyes on you. I know the kind of tricks that you have been playing to gather more and more money. I know the tricks you use to fool credulous people, and your so called 'magic cures'. You thought no one will understand your clever tricks, like

- creating fire without any match stick or a lighter, while hiding a little phosphorus underneath the camphor and cotton, which burned with the contact of the water sprinkled over it;
- hiding a carbon paper in the first page of your prayer book, which you used to give to visitors to write down their problems and then destroying the top paper and pretending that you had read their minds;
- hiding things inside your sleeve, then pulling them out with an invisible thread to bring them into your palm;
- creating ash with mercuric chloride and aluminum;

- reading a newspaper with eyes wrapped with a cloth while actually reading from the gap that is formed where the cloth goes over the nose;
- burning a dollar-bill and later bringing out the same number dollar bill, while the number on the burnt bill was already written;
- hiding an idol in the soil with wet peas hidden beneath. Later when the peas used to swell while germinating the idol used to get pushed up, and many other tricks … …

You have violated my law - the law of the universe by fooling the public with your deceitful magic. You brainwashed them and made them blind to the real miracles of nature. You numbed their brains, and prevented them from understanding the real super natural miracles that were taking place every day in the lives of each one of them. You have violated the law by telling the public that you were God. You thought there was no one to watch over your dirty actions, what you think, what you plan and what you do. You thought no one knew your terrible deeds, which you did alone and in collaboration with your partner Mr. Harry.

For decades you have been fooling my innocent children. I know everything you have done while you were alone or with your clients in your room. I know how many people you have murdered. I know what you have done to Chaudhary's wife and other innocent ladies. I know how you used their wives and daughters to grab all their property and demolished them because they could have become Harry's future competitors.

Yes God-Bawa, you forgot that, I am the one who gave you birth. I am the one who created you. I am the one who gave you this mind. I am the one who provided the energy to keep your brain cells alive. Now you know that someone exists who knows your secrets," concluded Devi Messiah Earth. With those words the dream was over.

****

Step Eleven...

WARNING TO HARRY IN HIS DREAM

After warning God-Bawa, Devi Messiah also warned Harry Kingson in his dreams. She was showing her palms and saying to Harry Kingson, "My puppet! Dance as much as you want! I have given you a short life. Do not forget that you are being watched. I grow people like you on these palms, and then crush them with my fingers. You have no understanding of the powers of these palms. I have grown many like you on these palms. They have danced, the way they wanted.

Those ignorant people could feel the power of my invisible hands, yet they ignored it. They said there was no need to worry about those powers for when it comes to the crunch; they would know how to deal with the situation.   They said they had many years to go before the final rendezvous with the Maker. There is no immediate cause to worry, therefore, they should eat, drink and have fun, whilst they could have it. They said, 'Dead is yesterday, unborn is tomorrow, why worry if today is sweet'. They said, 'the past is history, the future is a mystery, the present is for enjoyment, eat drink, have fun, and do that what feels good'. Your hunger for money, fame, fun, luxury, enjoyments and pleasure kept increasing day by day. I gave you money for a good cause but with that money you created Andrew and this God-Bawa." Then she said to everyone in the public gathering in God-Bawa's monastery,

"You people think that you are functioning on your own, not knowing the fact that it is me, the Earth, who is working for you twenty four hours a day, seven days a week and three hundred and sixty five days a year. I am working very hard to raise you. I made your body out of the chemicals from my own body therefore, all the parts of your body belong to me. Do you have any idea how hard I work for you? You ignorant children!" Then she pointed to God-Bawa in public and said, "Do you think that this cheat is really being kind to you? Don't you know that this man has been fooling you for many decades? You understand other things very well, then how is it you don't understand the difference between God and a cheat?

I am the Earth. I am your Mother. I love you, but you don't want to understand your Mother and Her love. I grow you on my palm. Whenever you are on a sinful path, I shake my palm. My palm-shaking is like an earthquake in your life. I do that to remind you that I am here beneath your feet. Bend down and look at me and understand that I do exist! Here, right here.

I do exist, I am your God. From where did you get the idea that God is up in the sky? Use your brains. If I am up in the sky, then two persons pointing up in the sky at the same time, one in Tokyo and the other in Washington DC, would be pointing in opposite directions. If I were to be up there, then who would be right? The man in Tokyo or the one in Washington DC? Why do you have to follow the wrong concepts? Why have you become so stubborn? Why can't you understand simple facts?

It's me, the Earth, underneath your feet and I am alive, therefore you are. I carry you on my back. I am the provider and the savior. My natural powers are beyond your imaginations. You cannot understand them because you do not believe in me. You do not believe in the truth. You believe in liars and cheats like this ignorant Bawa. This fool is a fraud and I am the truth. You can understand daylight only if you are living in daylight. You cannot understand my powers because your egos have kicked you into the darkness of this Bawa's cesspool. You have sold your life to this ignorant cheat, and you love his mysteries. You do not pay attention to the great mysteries of my body, like the whirlpools, tornadoes and conch-shells, the spirals on your fingers, and the spiraled DNA of your body. You don't believe the miracles of your heart beat, your pulse, vision, hearing, winter, fall, summer, months, years, day, and nights, otherwise I would teach you their secrets and you would understand the Father and the Mother.

Whenever I tried to tell you about the great mysteries of my body you started wailing. You enjoyed this cheat's confusing sermons. Why do you have to follow this cheat, Bawa's destructive path? Do you really know who this man is? Have I not given you understanding so that you can follow the right path? Am I not producing enough miracles to make you understand my powers? Do you really have to follow this dishonest man who leads you away from God? Why can't you realize that this cheat Bawa is a crawling sin on my back? Why do you have to support this cancer?

No one can bring you closer to me except you. Whenever I teach you, through sufferings, you make promises to me saying, *'God next time when you give me more than my basic needs then I will distribute it among your suffering children. I will follow your wishes. I will not hate anyone and I will have love for everyone.'* I trust you, and when I give you enormous powers to help the unprivileged and helpless, you become hypocrite and forgetting your promises start multiplying your fame and having endless fun. You started following the philosophy of this hypocrite ignorant man and started believing that the giver is God-Bawa. You blind babies! Let me open your sealed eyelids. It's not painful. Now you are grown-up enough to bear this little pain. You can make computers, airplanes and satellites. You have the capability to understand the movement of other planets, and much more. Nothing is wrong with your understanding capability. It's just a matter of pulling apart your eyelids. You will love to live in the world of reality."

Pointing towards one of God-Bawa's followers Mother Earth said, "Once I tried to open this ignorant man's eyes. He said, 'Don't open my eyes. Do not hurt me. It is painful. Let me remain as I am. All my friends have the same way of living. I am wiser than you, and I know what to do, and I know what I am doing. Don't spoil my fun, otherwise ... ...'

Pointing to another follower of God-Bawa Mother Earth said to everyone, "Once a courageous man said to this fool *"God is the giver, not the God-Bawa"*. This foolish follower started preaching to that man, "God says this... God thinks this... God likes this... God does... God's rule is this... God's way of giving is this..." and so on. This senseless man kept going on and on until he got tired.

That brave man replied to this fool, 'I did not ask you to preach to me. I am just saying that God-Bawa is not the giver. The giver is God. That's it.'
This fool answered, 'God-Bawa is no less than God. In fact there is only one God and that is God-Bawa."

The Earth said, "Now I ask this fool; did God authorize you to speak out on his behalf? How did you know; what God says, what God thinks, what God likes, and what God's rule is? Why did you not tell me about yourself instead? Such as; what you think, what is on your disturbed dirty mind, what is your ulterior game-plan, what you like, what you don't like and so on. ... What made you to speak about God, about whom you know nothing, and hide everything about yourself?

You puppets, dance in an abnormal way. The moment I start crushing you in my palm, it becomes too painful for you and then you beg for mercy crying, *"Mother! Help! Help! ... Father, help! Help! ... Please help. What sin have I committed that you do not listen to my wails?" With folded hands I bow down to you saying, 'What should I do now? Please tell me what I can do for you, to be forgiven by you. Please tell me how I can please you."*

Again Mother Earth said, "Ask the photos you worship, ask the religious monuments, search the scriptures and ask any preacher. You shall never find the answers. You believe in Bawa's magic only. You believe those who do not even know where exactly they are in the solar system and where they are heading to in the future. Who do not know; where they are in this universe, what this Earth is, and which is Devalok (abode of Gods and deities), what their mother and father have done for them and what is going to happen in the future. They think that their mother is meant to only provide them fun and amusement.

Go to God-Bawa, have more fun in God's name. Go to any other charlatan, and there are many of them around, promising to save you after death. Give them another five thousand green bucks for their organization and get a certified rain check from them, to enter heaven. Work for them for free; spend your life and energy in promoting their organizations. Find quotations in the scriptures to prop up God-Bawa as a Savior, or the only living Savior. Hear it again and again from the mouth of hired preachers and blind followers. Gather more and more proofs that you are right, and only you are right. Don't even think of questioning where heaven is, and where God-Bawa is going to take you. Instead of questioning, concoct more and more proofs to prop up this 'cheat' as a God, which in other words - 'God is a cheat'. Keep fabricating more and more proofs to magnify that God is a cheat, and I, the Earth, am nothing. Try your best to prove that right is wrong, and wrong is right. You are born to oppose God, and to support the antithesis of God. The Creator has given you this life and brain to support arguments against his own existence.

I am your God. I exist is not because of you, but you owe your existence to me. My mind is the creator of all minds. My mind is not an invention of your mind, but your mind is produced by me. I am the life giver to your brain. You call me by any name you wish; Vishnu, Allah, Muhammad, Moses, Jesus, Buddha, Mahvira, Nanak, Shankara, Creator, Father or Mother Nature. It makes no difference to me. I can produce brave and great souls who speak the truth and therefore, many poets call me the 'Main Artist'. Those truth speakers sacrifice their lives, and I grant them new life. I teach many realities of life and this universe, and visit you, from time to time, whenever you need me.

It's your life and it's your choice. My puppets! Dance the way you want and dance as much as you can. I have given you a short life and don't forget that you are being watched and your actions are being recorded. I can crush you at any moment, and you won't even know who crushed you. You are blind to my existence and keep asking; 'who has seen the future?' Set up a fake God ... and do whatever you like, but remember that you are constantly under my scanner.

I am your constant companion. I can be your greatest help or your heaviest burden. I can push you to success, or drag you to failure.

I can be completely at your command. Most of the things you do, you could turn over to me, and I will do them quickly and correctly. I am the beloved of all great men. Those who are great, I have made them great.

Those who are failures, I have made them failures. Your destiny is controlled by my invisible (to you) law.

I am not a machine, though I work with precision. You may run me for your profit or for ruin - it makes no difference to me.

Take me, understand me, respect me and I will place you in heaven. Disregard me, and I will destroy you in hell. You know who I am. I am your best friend, or your worst enemy - I AM YOUR GOD!

And listen to me Ha..." suddenly Harry woke up. His dream was interrupted. He opened his eyes and looked around with surprise. He became very frightened. He started shaking with fear.

Natalee asked, "What, what, what? What happened? Tell me what happened?"

Harry said in a low voice, "I am not feeling well … pain in my body… and I feel frightened …oh."

"What? What did you say?" asked Natalee Kingson surprised. By then Harry was fully awake.

"Oh! No, I was just thinking about something. Anyway ... it's nothing," Harry mumbled.

"Please tell me, what's the matter? Are you all right? Something is wrong, you look disturbed," said disturbed Natalee.

Mr. Harry did not say anything to Natalee. Natalee once again cursed her luck and said to herself, "We live in one room, but our worlds are different. So close - but so far apart. Together - but lonely. We are husband and wife – but cannot understand each other. We share the same bed - but we don't share our thoughts and feelings. We sleep in the same room yet we are miles apart … miles and miles of distance...Oh God," she pressed her head with both hands.

****

The distance increased as the years rolled by. She couldn't understand why he had to go elsewhere while sleeping with her. Though she too went to different places while sleeping with him, but she believed that he couldn't guess what was on her mind. Though they shared the same bed - communication between them had ceased to exist.

One day, suddenly, after coming back from the doctor's office Mr. Harry showed himself to be a totally changed person. Such a complete and sudden metamorphosis was as surprising as it was unexpected. It seemed that he had resolved to be the dutiful husband. Though he had a couple of urgent business plans to think about, but leaving everything behind he made coffee. Natalee saw him bringing two cups of coffee. He then affectionately invited her to join him at the dining table. As if in a dream, Natalee sat with him and Harry started the conversation,

"Look Natalee. Enough has happened between us that were undesirable and avoidable. For my part, I want to make up for my acts of omission or commission which might have brought our relationship to this sorry pass. I want to apologize for my misdeeds," said Mr. Harry with humility.

Such a confession from Harry was totally unexpected. Natalee Kingson was surprised to hear such words. At first she thought it might be some new game of his. A man whose philosophy has been, *"if you don't lie down, no one can walk on you"*. A man who never believed God's invisible hands were far more powerful than all of man's philosophies. A man, who believed that 'no one could remain standing forever'. A man who was full of anger, quarrelling everyday on every new issue and a man full of wily games. What was his plan now?

Not knowing how to react to such an abject surrender by Harry, she just responded, "I don't know what acts of omission or commission you are talking about. Our relationship has been quite all right. There are always ups and downs in every relation, and ours has been no exception," then she waited for his response.

"There is no point in ignoring the facts. You know perfectly well, as I do, that there have been only 'downs' in our life. Now, I have to put a stop to it. I want to change my life completely. Henceforth, there will be no place for double-dealing, crime, sin or pretense in my life. Believe me Natalee! I hate wrong doings and injustice. I always hated them. Now I know life is a long lesson in 'humanity'. Please try to understand my feelings," said Harry. There was real sincerity in his voice. Natalee could feel the 'I' between them had become a much diminished thing.

"Well, it is not only you but I too would like to move away from sin and the path of folly. We all want to live a truthful life with a clean conscience. We all reap what we sow. We all know that good deeds will bring good results sooner or later. Bad deeds will inexorably lead us to disaster and tragedy, but I must confess that I am completely taken aback by the metamorphosis that has taken place in you. Let me also make a confession. My jealousy has been destructive. Your egotistic approach in moral and other matters had fueled my jealousy. I too provoked you into using physical violence against me. I also used profane and abusive language against you. We were trying to destroy each other's ego by destroying each other. Anyway, the moment we realize our follies we can always start anew," said Natalee with more positive feeling.

"Just one wrong ingredient can spoil the taste of food. Since the day Ruby came between us, my jealousy developed like a destructive fire. I used to get upset, especially, when you admired her and other ladies who look at rich men and play games with them. I knew she was more beautiful than me but I was helpless. I wanted your complete attention because I was married to you. I surrendered my life to you and in return I needed your love. I couldn't control my jealousy. I did many wrong things, which I cannot tell anyone. Now I know; no woman should try to win her husband with the power of the law. No woman should think that legal, social, and religious rules are tools to win her husband. Love is the only power that can win a husband's heart. Love needs to be nourished everyday, like a child. Unfortunately I forgot all these things," admitted Natalee admitting the powers of Love.

"I could not control my anger, madness overtook me. I could not control my ego; rather I was controlled by my ego. I thought I was right, and fighting for the truth. Today, I came to the conclusion that a man's biggest enemy is his ego, which fuels anger. I know that I alone shall pay for my sins." said Harry Kingson with wrinkles on his forehead.

"I don't know how you have come to this point where you are willing to change. Today, for the first time we are admitting our bad deeds. It is the first time I have ever seen such a thing since we got married. For me, it's like a dream coming true. I can't believe this miracle," said Natalee.

"Yes, miracles do happen in life, don't they?" Harry said with a little smile but sadness on his face.

"Today your openness and accompanying humility has me wanting to dedicate myself to you. I feel like doing more and more good things to please you. The whole purpose of my life now will be only to please you and bring a smile to your face, nothing else, nothing else," said Natalee with tears in her eyes.

"If you are happy, then I also am happy. Your happiness is my happiness," Harry placed his hand on Natalee's forearm.

"I wish we had lived to give happiness to each other from the very beginning. No woman can become happy by upsetting her husband. We kept sitting in judgment of each other's actions," said Natalee wiping off her tears.

"I wanted to hear words of appreciation from you. The day you said, "*So what! There are many like you... My in-laws and many... much better than you...*" Harry couldn't say anymore, he couldn't stop his tears.

"Those words were etched into my brain," he continued. "My ego was deeply hurt. Since that day my ego controlled me. For me there was no pleasure in life except to succeed by hook or by crook. The ego could not let any challenge stand. I was determined to show you, how much other people admire me. That was the day when I started using religion, priests and preachers towards satisfying my insatiable ego. I started visiting the shrine and kept donating a few dollars everyday. The priest started praising me in front of you. It was a pleasant breath of temporary relief. I loved the admiration and it was that, that took me to God-Bawa. I was clever. God-Bawa and the shrine were like my toys. Nobody knows just how I have used them. I did many bad things with God-Bawa, which I cannot tell anyone," said Harry – in a little confession.

"I knew you had done some bad things with that God-Bawa, but I could not say anything. After committing those crimes and shouting at me, you would humbly bow down before the shrine in front of everyone. I had seen your humility in public. I wanted to see the same humble attitude at home as well. I said many prayers, fasted for many days. I visited many psychiatrists and astrologists to improve our relationship. To improve your attitude I did everything they advised me.

I wore the Virgin Mother's pendant, Devi's bangle, Buddha's amulets, Christ's cross, Guru's medals, Silver bracelets, the Egyptian ankh, Coral stone, Hatha jodi, Elk teeth, rabbit's foot and I avoided the number thirteen, number eight, Saturdays, black cats, broken mirrors, and looking at bad signs. But, nobody told me that only real humility works. I believed in all superstitions but not in Karma. My stubborn ego kept me deaf to the miracles of humility. All my friends and family members kept energizing my ego. One of my my mistakes was that I never put any effort into looking at the situation through your eyes, and make myself humble. I know I did not do my duty properly," told Natalee.

"Natalee, any decision I took in anger was wrong, yet my ego made me believe that I was right. My ego made me fight against the tiger. I knew that the reputations of the most powerful men including Mr. Prince, Mr. President and Mr. Prime Minister could be demolished in no time. Most of my people loved to gossip about me. They were curious to find out if a rich man also could have problems in life, and they wanted to prove that after accumulating enormous amounts of sinful money God's justice could be seen in this life. Playing sinful tricks was nothing, but the foolishness of an ignorant man. I knew all rich people tend to marry once and stay married. That helps conserve wealth, and of course, staying together is the secret of success.

My enemies and those who were jealous of my achievements were waiting for the scandals to emerge. The stronger I became, the more enemies I had. The more enemies I had the more gatekeepers and security people I needed to hire. With my progress their jealousy increased. My own people were waiting for rumors and scandals to erupt and terrifying things to happen to me. Everyone was eager to discover if the most famous, successful and richest business man could face the miseries of this world. They wanted to prove that one can have everything in life yet not be happy. The man, who played so many smart games to become the richest, could have a miserable married life. They wanted to prove that one can have a palace-like house in town with depressing, turbulence and darkness hidden inside. One who could have a huge bank account yet his 'marital bliss account' could be full of stress, irritation, suspicion, distrust, anger, breakdown, frustration and depression. Their sadistic pleasure in seeing my utter ruin could happen only through Natalee Kingson. A woman is a powerful person who can make anything out of a man. She can decorate a house with love and she can damage it permanently. A woman is a flame and a flower too. If she is fire she can be ice too. If she is constructive she can be destructive too. She can be kind and also cruel. She can be sweet and also bitter. She can be a savior and a devil too. I wish I could have understood the powers of a woman and respected her. I knew it, but my ego blinded me and did not allow me to realize the strength of the tigers," said Mr. Harry admitting his wife's superior power.

"A man has all those qualities as well. He too is fire and ice. He also can be constructive and destructive. He too can be kind and cruel. He too can be a savior and also a devil. But it is true that a woman is the one who can make anything out of a man. I know a woman can produce a Hitler and she can produce a Gandhi as well. It was my duty to make things better for both of us. It was my duty to direct my efforts to good things and attain self-perfection. I needed your help but there was no such hope and I didn't know what was to be done," said Natalee admitting the potential of man's power and her faults.

"Surprising as it may seem, I too wanted your help rather than being pushed into a quagmire. When I committed all those sins with God-Bawa, I thought that my life was ruined and God would surely not forgive me. I have been a sad and an unhappy man all along," confessed Mr. Harry with a regretful mood.

"A woman's heart does not like sin. God has designed a woman's heart for love and compassion, but when it is shaken it can shake the mountains. Its compassion and passion can be the cause of world peace or world war. It is every woman's duty to save her husband from sin and to put him on the path of virtue, so that their children can grasp the essence of life. Goodness is the only real assets parents have to pass on to the next generation.

Learning about all those lies, corruption, and sins, I was too weak to handle the situation, and I had no idea how to take the first step to make a better life. My destructive anger made me to do all the wrong things, and my ego kept persuading me that I was one hundred percent right. My fuel-like ego did not allow me to suggest that you put out the 'fire'. It kept alive the destructive flame. Burning our own house we watched the fire and smoke and our egos kept encouraging and pushing us. Seeing our confusion many people took advantage of our foolishness, and many women misguided me. Now, finally we know that only we can extinguish our burning house. Only we can douse our anger before anger burns us completely. Only we can demolish our egos before our egos demolish us," said Natalee Kingson wisely.

"Oh God! What have we done in the last few years?" said Mr. Harry while squeezing his forehead with fingers.

"Would you like to have another cup of coffee?" asked Natalee.

"No, thank you, I am fine," Mr. Harry answered humbly.

"Come let's go out into the garden," proposed Natalee: took his hand.

Stepping out together both had different feelings. Thousands of stories had filled Natalee like a balloon and now she had a chance to exhale the stifling air in her heart. They had so much to talk about, so much to tell to each other. They sat on the grass holding each other's hands and kept talking.

> The lightening and thunder they come and they go but the stars and stillness is always at home. Real fried is the one who takes you for what you are.

"We made many mistakes in life just to learn a simple lesson. We did not realize our own mistakes nor did we learn from the mistakes of others.

Where we stand today is not the goal of life. Coming all the way here was an unnecessary journey and a waste of precious time. After going through a long journey, we find that we have traveled only a few yards and our destiny - to understand God's miracles - is miles and miles away. It is already too late to cover the distance. We cannot taste the fruit of life - truth. A wife's life is meaningless if she cannot make her husband satisfied, but my beloved I love you," said Natalee with wet eyes.

"You know everything about me and yet you still love me - this is love. You took me for what I am and you remained... Love is not an accident or a coincidence. It's a collection of memories in decades of companionship, and the eventual realization of the amazing things God can show us on the journey of life," "Oh God...," he sighed, "I too will love you as I should, because you deserve love," said Harry.

"I will respect you as I should because a husband deserves respect," replied Natalee.

"Natalee, from now on I will always worship and consider you the gateway to God," said Mr. Harry.

"I am so happy today. I never thought that such a day and time would come and I will take every opportunity to respect you... worship you. Thou art my God, and I was dying to get thy permission to worship thee," said Natalee again, tears rolling down her cheeks.

"But, there is one piece of bad news, my beloved Natalee," said Mr. Harry with a little sadness on his face.

"There can be no bad news now. All news will be good news. I have everything I wanted. Now no bad news can affect me. My dream has come true. Now all sorrows will be turned into happiness," said Natalee with confidence, tears and a loving smile.

Mr. Harry paused for a second, and a wave of thoughts passed through his mind. He thought; 'if I tell her now, her smiling face will turn to stone. Let her smile as long as she can. She has had blood pressure, diabetes and several other diseases due to her mental anguish, anger and jealousy. She hasn't had a good experience with her husband so far, therefore, I will not tell her the bad news of my disease, but I will also not hide it from her because, a wife is a true friend and nothing should be hidden from her.'

The next day Natalee Kingson in a singing mood said, "By the way my fragrance of rose, my flower of heaven, my twinkling star, my peaceful moon, my shining sun, my honey boney, tell me what was that bad news you were going to tell me yesterday," She smiled at Mr. Harry's back as she put her arms around his shoulders and said in a loving way, "Won't you tell me?"

Harry held her hands and said slowly, "Natalee, you know that for the last one week I have been visiting doctors. I used to say, if you don't lie down, no one can walk on you, but the new question is for how long one can remain standing? No one can remain standing forever. Natalee! Nothing is more inevitable than change. Man proposes God disposes. Though I have had couple of warnings from Devi Messiah, but this may be the final warning she is giving me through a doctor.

I was having a terrible pain in my body. The doctors could not diagnose the reason for the pain. After the fifth day's checkup the doctor told me that it is an incurable disease that has reached an advanced stage and there is little chance of my survival. This is God's final warning and it broke my heart. Half my strength is gone. I have not told anyone this bad news. I was shocked and wondering how to face the ultimate reality. Then I made up my mind to resolve all the problems and misunderstandings with you. I realized that I have done many bad things and I would not be able to forgive myself if I didn't resolve these issues. I have cancer."

"What! What!! What!!! What are you saying?" asked a puzzled Natalee.

"Yes Natalee, it's true," said Mr. Harry squeezing his lips and face.

She kept staring at him and in a few minutes her color changed and her face became pale, her eyes closed, as she hung on to him and then slowly fell to the floor. She never stood up after that.

Natalee's sudden death left Harry shocked. In a mood of utter dejection
and gloom he cried, "Oh! God..." Not knowing that nobody ever came
back after death, and believing that their mother had just fallen down, the
children said, "Wake up! Mummy, wake up. I have to speak with you
about something very urgent," but mummy did not wake up. She was
gone.

For the children it was difficult to understand that the mother who gave
them birth, fed them when they were hungry, clothed them and protected
them like a real God was now suddenly gone.. "But where? God what is
all this...?" They only knew that the one they loved so much and who
had loved them, like only a mother can, would have to be consigned to
flames. They couldn't believe that it could happen so suddenly. No one
was prepared for such an event. Who could understand the inexorable
law of God? That the soul had gone to its eternal resting abode. The last
rites and condolences were over in three days.

Many of her clothes were in good condition and Harry wanted to donate
them to a charitable organization. He hid all the expensive jewelry,
diamonds, rubies, gold necklaces, bangles, rings and watches. He put all
the other unwanted stuff in a truck. She had over seven hundred
expensive dresses, five hundred and thirty five pair of shoes many
towels, napkins, bed sheets, pillows, gowns, shawls umbrellas, duvets,
pajamas etc. Everything was loaded into trucks to be donated among the
poor. Some other unwanted items were also donated to OXFAM and
UNICEF, including a small check. The check presentation ceremony was
covered by the media. With all this publicity Harry earned the reputation
of being a 'generous and kind man'.

On the same day, after completing the last rites, he telephoned Dr.
Mathew – a well-known doctor in the Sloan-Kettering Memorial Cancer
Center in New York. He explained his situation to Dr. Mathew. Dr.
Mathew asked him to come to New York. On the following day he flew
with Ruby to New York on the Concord. Dr. Mathew was at John F.
Kennedy airport to receive him. Dr. Mathew assured him that his
hospital had the best technology and most patients were cured. Since his
was a case of early detection, the prognosis was very optimistic. "Let's

pray and hope for the best. Under your care all will be well. I am sure about it," said Harry.

While he was struggling and fighting the pain he prayed, "God, if I am cured, I will offer one thousand dollars to a church, one thousand dollars to a shrine, and one thousand dollars to a mosque. I will walk to your home barefoot. I will climb up to your church on the holy mountain. I will go to other holy places. I will eat only two times a day for five days. I will not eat meat on Fridays. I will not drink water on Sunday mornings. I will organize a five days non-stop prayer at your shrine. I will wear cotton clothes for one week. I will light one hundred candles in church. I will take a bath in the holy lake early in the morning for eight days. I will chant the scriptures daily and light four oil lamps and incense in front of your statue."

There were many human sharks who fished in the cesspool of death and disease. They claimed that they could arouse the concerned Gods and prevail upon them to change the fate of the unfortunate victims of such a disease. They guaranteed recovery. Their charges were very high, and fixed according to the wealth of a patient. With Mr. Harry's kind of wealth they expected millions. Hoping to grab millions of dollars many of these people started knocking at the doors of Harry's well-wishers and in turn they began to search. Many of these tricksters started moving around him like vultures and Harry was aware of their presence. By living with God-Bawa he had gained that wisdom. However at the most difficult time of their lives many learned people also get confused and they forget whom to deal with and whom they shouldn't. Sometimes they end up with these sharks, like Mr. Chaudhary. Bad luck is added to all the other problems. But for the experienced Harry this was not a problem.

Though a hospital is one of the main portals to exit this world, but he put it out of his mind. Most people lose health while in the process of earning more and more money, and then they lose the money when trying to regain health. But, here the case was different. If he died there was a huge death benefit from insurance. However, he was optimistic that he would not die, because of the money he had. Money-power works everywhere. His money would do every thing possible to save him. The doctors also assured him that they were trying their best. Some business-minded doctors wanted him to stay longer so that they could keep updating their daily visit report and make money. They reasoned that once he died the flow of income would come to an end. A dead man doesn't buy expensive medicine. Though there is a long line of patients in reputed hospitals - business is business. He was on his deathbed. Ruby was with him most of the time; she would bring him food and tried to cheer him up. Once he told to Ruby,

"Many saints have told me that a woman is unholy, and the root of all sin. Since my personal experiences with my wife were bad, their philosophy appealed to me, and believing in their preaching I donated a lot of my money to their organizations, so as to please God. Otherwise, I would have donated that money to the unprivileged and the needy. They said that they were celibates, therefore fit for heaven. Those who could not make themselves fit could also achieve heaven, by donating money to their organizations. They took advantage of my disturbed family life. To feed my ego they praised me in public," said Harry as he related his strange story.

In the hospital bed Mr. Harry realized the significance of the love between a husband and a wife, but it was too late for him to reap its fruits. This was the time he should have had to love Natalee. It would have been nice having his wife by his side. Now he would never taste the fruit of a great understanding.

Now he understood that all those expensive luxury items are good only as long as the body is healthy. He understood that by doing good deeds nothing could go wrong, and he could still write a check for helpless people. He was able to sign his name and the check book was just lying on the table. His condition was deteriorating day by day and, like every-one of us, with every moment he was stepping towards death. In a few days he might not be able to sign the check. With his one check, thousands of dying people could have their lives back or thousands of suffering people could get a smile on their faces, thousands of people could have love in their lives, and education as well, but the greatest disease would not release him.

He believed in God and his religious knowledge was very good, better than many a well-educated scholar. Only rich people like him could understand such high philosophy. He had prayed to God for more and more money and now he prayed for good health. He did not believe in loving a helpless person because his philosophy of life, death, the poor, the helpless and God had nothing to do with money. He knew that everyone gets impressed with an expensive house or expensive cars but donating that amount selflessly was a foolish idea. He would rather be happy to write a check for any tax exempt organization where his name would be engraved, and he would be remembered by the public after his death. His philosophy was; *'in this world everything is done by God. Nothing can take place without his will. The one who deserves to be a millionaire he makes him millionaire, and the one who deserves to be penniless he makes him penniless. Giving money to the poor is against his will. Beggars should not be encouraged to beg. Anonymous charity is a foolish concept. Those who donate to a big shrine get the fruit immediately; their names being announced in public, propagated by the media, the public becomes a witness to their generosity, people respect them, their name is engraved on a stone tablet, displayed in a prominent place and after death the name remains there.* He knew that once man dies everything is washed away. Life comes into existence mysteriously and leaves as mysteriously. Man comes into the world with God's wish and leaves with His wish. Everything goes according to His wishes. He was exactly like Lord Alberto who had a vast knowledge of the scriptures, but was zero in helping others.

Mr. Harry's condition was deteriorating. He had lost 45 pounds in a few weeks. In the beginning he was scared of the needles and drills, and even more so later when he underwent horrific chemotherapy, the doctors installed a tube in his chest and put everything through the tube. They gave him as much dosage as they could without killing him. The chemo-treatment started damaging his inner organs. Most of the time he was high on painkillers, and didn't even know about the surgery and lung biopsy carried out on him. The second wave of chemo-treatment halted the leukemia, but it came back quickly so they gave him another round of chemo. He was having spells of unconsciousness. Once, returning to consciousness, he opened his eyes and said, "Ruby I am in great pain. This is the time when money cannot help. I want you to listen to my last words. Ask the doctors to give me more morphine, and ask the holy men to pray for me. I may not survive this time. Please make sure that both my children are all right. Tell my son that he should take care of all the business and buildings on Marine Drive, and here on Park Avenue and 5th Avenue. My insurance papers are in the underground safe box in the basement. Most of the premiums have been paid on time. The total death benefit is in the millions. He is the 1st beneficiary. All the other confidential papers are in there. This is the key to that safe, give it to my son, he knows the secret code to open it. I am going through a painful death. Oh God!"

Ruby said, "Don't worry my friend. God is with you. He is blessing you. We have prayed at 15 Mosques, 5 shrines, 20 Temples, 2 Synagogues, 2 Gurdwaras and 21 Churches. Everywhere prayers are being said for you. More than twenty priests are praying daily in the morning and evening. We have paid them for one full month of prayers. Their combined prayers are definitely going to work."

Each second Mr. Harry was slipping closer to death - his final destiny. In his unbearable pain he just wanted to die. He started praying, "God, please take me away from this painful world quickly," God heard him, appeared in front of him and said, "Did you call me?"

"Who are you?"

"I am the Lord of Death whom you just asked to take you away. Are you ready?"

"No! No! No!   Of course not! I just said it, I didn't mean it, I have a couple of important things to do, I have to sign some property papers and my son is coming here to meet me. He is on his way, and I have to check the business accounts. I am sorry. I didn't mean it, please go away."

"O man. You still have all the time in the world, you are not yet dead. These breaths are priceless. These precious moments are beyond estimate. Use them, understand them and invest them, for you may not get back this gift. Once your time is over, everything will be gone. Once they put you in a box, insert you into the crematory furnace and push the button, in four hours you will be gone. What will be the meaning of your life? Understand man... You will take nothing with you, except Karma. Don't worry about anything, worry is your biggest enemy, worry raids your treasure of gifts, worry takes away the joy of living. Worry brings diseases like; diabetes, cancer and heart disease and it kills you. Stop worrying now and start thinking constructively about the important jobs."

Suddenly Harry became unconscious and fell to the ground. Ruby lifted him up and asked, "What happened?"

Ruby called the nurse and Dr. Mathew came to the spot. Again, uncontrollably, Harry fell to the floor. The doctor laid him down and gave him CPR and a cardiac massage. Harry opened his eyes and said to the doctor,
"Doctor! ...too much pain... too much ... . take me to a better hospital please." After that he could recognize visitors but couldn't speak at all. He couldn't write because his hands were attached to many tubes such as the glucose drip, blood drip etc. He opened his eyes for a second, trying to move his body, and a thought came to his mind, 'Oh! God, I used to believe that with money I could buy everything, but today I know that I cannot buy even a few more breaths of life. When I was healthy, I bought shrines, deities, preachers and a reputation, but now I cannot buy a few extra minutes of life. Now I am in the most expensive hospital in the world, but I cannot buy life. Now I know money can buy a bed but not sleep. Money can buy books but not wisdom, a house but not a home, a woman but not a wife, material things but not virtue, doctors but not life. Now I am willing to pay one million dollars for ten minutes of life, but nothing is possible ... your will ... God thou art great."

The good thing about the disease was that he had resolved his problems with his wife before her death. He watched his dying as a scene on TV screen. He had enough time to resolve any other problems if he wanted, as God had given him enough time to accomplish the important things in the 'journey of the soul'. His friends and well - wishers could also learn from it, and do what they had to do. Everybody has to die but that clear warning was a chance to do what had not been done yet.

Harry wanted to tell to his son about his assets, but by the time the son arrived his speech had gone. There had been many sunrises which turned into day and evenings and eventually became nights, but this night he had a strange feeling. He was discontented with all the unreal achievements in his life and his bad son.

He played the movie of his life from the beginning up to the current time, and was filled with regret and disappointment. He realized that he had been surrounded by selfish people throughout his life and no one had encouraged him to do the right things. He was about to make up his mind to donate a heavy portion of his property or all of it to some welfare society. His mind had completely changed. Throughout life, he never believed that God could do things but tonight he believed that only God could do anything and everything. Till yesterday he could not understand what God wanted from him, but today a disappointed Harry was about to donate all his assets. But, the problem was he couldn't speak, and couldn't move at all. Again and again he kept falling unconscious and whenever he regained consciousness, his breath was slowing down. Only God knew what was going on in his unconscious mind. He might have been waiting for someone - or his beloved's touch at the time of saying good bye to this world. Who knew what was happening to him at that moment? We wish we could ask him. A candle was still burning next to God's picture. His credit cards, check book and a few prayer books were on the table. Half of his body had gone cold. It was 2.00 a.m., in the morning his eyes and mouth were half-open. He breathed his last. At 2.30 a.m. a nurse pulled aside the curtain and came out from his room with the doctor. The doctor said to the children, "Sorry, he is no more."

Everyone watched the pyre in which the body was kept with wood all around it. The expensive casket was not visible. The son lit the fire and in minutes it spread all over the body. When this once powerful man became helpless, then God-Bawa poured clarified butter and camphor onto the pyre, which made flames rise higher. All his friends and well wishers watched the flames, which was reduced to ashes in just a few hours.

Different people were suggesting different things such as; the breaking of a coconut, breaking the skull and burning the brain with clarified butter, burial, which turns the body into millions of worms, burial at sea, an expensive casket, expensive cemetery, an expensive sandalwood coffin, an expensive silk cloth to wrap the body, and offerings of expensive diamonds. They talked of Alexander's smartness in fooling the public, Shah Jahan's philosophy of love that caused the death of a million people, etc. etc. One old man who was listening to all this talk for almost one hour started yawning and said, "O little mortal, what havoc you created in such a short life!! Man when will you become a human?"

Mostly the people were thinking; 'God, how many things can you show us just in one life... unlimited and unexpected things to see. When we replay the movie of our own lives we get really astonished to see your wonders and ours. God, no wonder you are great. The next day a condolence meeting was held in the shrine. Some well known priests, preachers and holy men addressed the gathering. In the congregation a Hindu sage said,

||*Ishaavaasyamidam Sarvam, Yadkinchid jagatyaanjagat.*
Tena Tyakten Bhunjeethaa, Maa Gridhah Kasyaswidhhanam.||
(O man, whatever you possess or whatever exists in this world, all that belongs to God, therefore take only that part which is necessary for your survival, and the rest return to God. How you eventually die is quite unimportant, but by far the more important is how you live. Your destiny will be decided according to your living.)

*

**|| *Tattwamasi*||

Body is made out of soil and shall be returned to the soil only. Time belongs to God. He has loaned it to us. Let us use every minute - every moment - in the best way we can. All the land you have occupied leaving that behind you may need just a two yard piece of land, and eventually your ashes would become an integral part of mother earth. Do you know where you will go then?

*

> Touch the earth, honor the earth; her plains, her valleys, her hills and her seas; rest your spirit in her solitary places.
> ... Henry Beston.

Then a Christian Father said while holding his holy scripture;

Mere Vajuud Ko Mere Daaman se Alag Karane Waale,
Yaad Rakh Teree Aakhirii Manjil Mai Hee Huun.

(A man was blowing away the dust from his shirt and the dust said to him, "Blowing me away from your shirt, O man, don't forget, I am your final destiny. One day you shall be assimilated with me. Dust to dust. Ashes to ashes!")

*

A Buddhist monk came onto the stage and said;
Eka Chutakee Raakh Lekara Haatha Me,
Kabhee Apane Baare Mai Bhee To Soch.

(O man! From the pyre take a speck of ash on your palm, and looking at it, think sometime about yourself too. One day you shall be turned into the ash powder. If there is no Nirvana you get re-united with your loved one. However, there is a land of the living and a land of the dead; and the linking bridge is 'honor for ancestors'. Respect them and maintain the bridge. Harry's wife died sometime ago, she was alone in heaven. Now he has gone to her and thus they are reunited. Do you know where they are?)

*

Then one of his friends read a poem, as Harry's message to everyone;

My memories of thee and yours of me are filled with love and laughter forever.
You'll see no reason to worry, or question God as to why you have lost me.
No reason to say goodbye. We were together and we will be together.
It was time for my journey home, a beautiful and peaceful trip which, like everyone, I must make alone.
Once you complete your journey you will also walk like me.
I am not allowed to tell you the secrets of this journey but you will see it soon.
So just be strong and keep a smile, know God is more powerful than anything.
We'll only be apart for a little while. Then we'll meet again.

*

Man comes into existence with His will and disappears with His will.
(Anonymous)

*

A Saint said; O man, at the end of the day, what are you?
As an infant you came into this world, Parents and relatives rejoice in
happiness. They nourish you with love. You play with toys, start school,
play games, and have fun. In your marriage procession people rejoice
singing, dancing and congratulating you.

Then you acquire wealth and become father and later grandfather.
Then you start recollecting many memories of the past bitter and sweet,
all astonishing. Captured by diseases, pain in the body and pain in the
mind, eventually you give up.

The beloved son carries you in a bier and consigns you to the cemetery
or crematorium. Everyone sighs; where have you gone? You disappear.
At the end of the day, what are you? You flew away like a bird leaving
behind the cage. Nobody knew what happened.
Everyone sighs again and says; "God you are great."

*

Finally his family priest sang a song;

"O mind, O mind, you are so weak and dirty,
You are so weak and dirty.

You cannot do that which one should do,
You do that which you should not.

You live here and in seconds, travel to London, Miami, Paris, Rajasthan
or Hong Kong and then come back quickly and no one knows where you
have been traveling. Mind o mind! …

O mind! In seconds you go to the Himalayan Mountains, a friend's
house, enemy's house but no one knows whom you have been visiting.
Mind o mind! …

Mind O mind! What an amazing thing you can do,
Mind o mind, you can cause Nagasaki, Hiroshima, Jalianwala Bagh and
the World Trade Center. You have divided the land into many countries
to fight. You have divided the Mother's body into many many parts.

Mind O mind! What an amazing thing you can do!
Mind ... you are so weak, ugly and dirty."

After listening to these desperate and helpless outpourings against the
vagaries of uncontrolled and uncontrollable minds, the Mind itself
decided to plead for itself, and replied, "Listen my friend don't accuse
me too much for every misdeed. Everyone accuses me, but do not forget;

I am not weak, but the most strong one.
I am so strong, when I want to do something, I do that.

I am not impure, but the most holy and pure I am. I did not cause any
havoc when I was with Mahatma Gandhi, when I was with Dag
Hammarskjold, Jesus Christ, Mother Teresa, Ram, Mahaveera, and when
I was with Gautama Buddha, and there were many, whom you do not
know otherwise I would tell you their names as well.

I am not dirty. It is you who have become dirty.
Change your path, I am always with you, and I can be a gift to you."

Again, remember one thing my friend whoever establishes friendship
with me I guide him, and whoever considers me dirty, I put him down. I
throw them from the mountains, when they reach the peak. When I throw
them, their back-bone breaks, then they know that there exists some
super intelligence."

Listen to me my friend! There are many good people who have made my
reputation high. And many bad people who have destroyed my
reputation. That is what you are, my friend..."

"Friend my friend..."
"Mind! O mind. ... Mind O mind ..."

These words ended the song.
Old God-Bawa's partner was dead but the story did not end here. In fact
the real story started from here; because, the real journey starts after
death.

Bhagwan - the Lord Krishna said in Gita, "That (soul) which is embodied experiences the body's childhood, youth and old age, and also the time acquires another body. Self is not killed when the body dies. There was never a time when I did not exist, nor you, nor any of these ruling princes. And neither will there ever come a time when we cease to be.

Stages of Life from the Cradle to the Grave". At left is a flourishing green tree, at right a symbolic weeping willow.

1). "A wailing infant, first she plays, Unconscious of her future days." (Infant in cradle).

2). Her girlish pastimes reveal for show The cares which woman's life must know. (Young girl with doll.)

3). Her ripened beauty all confess And wonder at her loveliness. (Late teen girl in grownup clothes.)

4). A husband's arms, in hope and pride, Enclasp her now, a lovely bride. (Bride in white dress and veil.)

5). A mother's anxious love and care With toilful(?) heart is hers to share.

6). Dressed to go outdoors, Now to the poor her hands dispense the blessings of benevolence. (Young mother holding baby.)

7). (first declining step): Absorbed in household duties now, The weight of toil(?) contracts her brow. (Middle-aged woman.)

8). (suggesting the latter stages of mourning, perhaps her husband has died): She now resigns all earthbound care,   And lifts her soul to heaven in prayer.

9). At eighty years, her well-stored mind, Imparts its blessings to her kind. (Old, wearing spectacles.)

10). The hoary head, us all should bless, Who abound in ways of righteousness. (Bent over, using cane.)

11) "The body sinks and wastes away, The spirit cannot know dismay."(?) (Sitting in chair, knitting.)

Funeral scene. There are smaller vignettes under each of the nine steps of the arch. (Vignette under arch.)

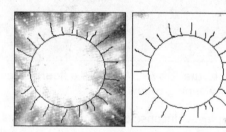 

Night Sun - Morning Sun - at Noon - Evening Sun - at Night

"You should know that the sun does not die in the evening. It sets on this side and rises somewhere else. The sun exists even during the middle of night. You exist even after the death of this body. Body expires but Karma remains with you."

Step Twelve...

DAY OF JUDGMENT

Devi Messiah said, "Welcome Harry, I told you that after death you will come to me. This is the truth. I kept reminding you again and again through numerous messages. I gave you a couple of major warnings such as; changing the color of your hair, wrinkles on your face, and diseases to tell you that each day you are moving closer to death's point - the door. At every second every human being is stepping closer to death, but I gave you special warnings, still you did not balance your way of life, and money remained the aim of your life, till the last breath. You neglected everything including the next step of the real journey which starts from right here, known as the; 'journey of the soul'. Now you know those warnings were right, that leaving everything behind, you have to face this ultimate reality alone.

First, listen to the real journey of an ignorant man who behaved exactly as you did. He was Anna Mario. The beggar you had seen many times on television, in the newspapers and many times with your own eyes while you were in your body. Once you had even ordered a temple worker to remove him from that palace-like clean area. I had told you in your dream and the same story I will narrate once again, so that you will know nothing is here without a reason.

Did you see 'Anna Mario'? How many times he had begged me saying; *"Mother, Mother, take me away from this world, I cannot bear it."*

There was a time when Anna Mario, the beggar, was dancing like you, and people hailed him the king. He loved the praise. At that time he thought he was the only one, and should remain on the top. There should be no one else above him, everyone must think about him, talk about him, and praise him. Many times I warned him that, his way of dancing was not the right way, and he should not try to amaze people with his sinful dances. When Mario was, like you, in his previous life, he was one of the 'central male characters' in the media, surrounded by many people. He had so many well-wishers, friends, relatives, doctors, priests, saints, managers, and accountants who were willing to do anything for his benefit. He bought buildings, houses, property, reputation, relationships, health, and guarantee for heaven.

Harry, exactly like you, I gave him a high social rank. He enjoyed that rank. He became more and more concerned about protecting that rank. Later, he would do anything to protect his possessions. He committed dozens of crimes, as you did. He ignored me and the Father's law. He did not keep his promise. He just wanted to multiply his money and fame. The worship of mammon became the 'be all' of his life.

Like your greed Mario's too caused 124 deaths each day. I (Mother Earth) was producing sufficient for each and every child but because of your insatiable greed, many people in the world suffered from hunger and disease. Many people could not buy sufficient food for the day. Many people could not buy clothes to cover their bodies. Many people suffered from the cold. They couldn't get an umbrella for the rain. They could not buy slippers to protect their feet. Many people could not get married. Many people could not get an education and medication.

Harry, I kept showing you the living example of Mario the beggar, and told you not to commit the same mistakes in life. You saw all those things with your own eyes and on the television as well, but you kept ignoring them. You offered obeisance in the shrines, and you listened to praise from your hired preachers. You carried on with your grandiose and pompous show, but ignored all the sufferings of Anna Mario.

Through God-Bawa's organization you started a home for orphans, opened a clinic for the poor and a school for the children of the poor just to increase your business, yet that couldn't cover one percent of your sins. Looking at these institutions, people admired your philanthropy and concern for the poor deprived, down-trodden and the unprivileged.

Everyone knew about the dozens of good things you had done but only I know how many bad things you have done. The only good thing you did in your life-time, with the proper intention, was donating that four-wheeled wooden trolley to the disabled Anna Mario. Nobody knows that but I do.

You knew common people did not realize that it was your greed that was causing 124 deaths each day, and thousands and thousands suffered a fate worse than death. Their utter poverty had played havoc with their lives and educational chances to the extent that many of them eventually became monks just for their survival."

Devi-Earth continued, saying; "I was producing enough for my all children, but you occupied a huge part of my body (land) so that you could sell it in the future and thus double your money in a short time. The rulers of a rich country do not allow a poor country's people to cultivate their fertile land, which is useless to them but is life for the poor. I made them king so that they could bring justice to my poor children. I wanted other jobless children to cultivate that land, grow food for their stomachs, live happily, lovingly and also learn of my miracles but you did not listen to me.

Harry Kingson, exactly like you, Anna Mario also was aware of his own bad deeds because I had sent him into the world with sufficient brains to understand what was right and what was wrong. He ignored what was right. He wanted a verbal certificate from a socially authorized religious person, who would say to him, 'I shall grant you Heaven.' As God-Bawa had promised you Heaven his spiritual master did the same.

Like Anna Mario you too were initiated through God-Bawa. He convinced you that his authority to save the deserving people was granted to him, by the most powerful master of the world. He convinced you that *"in this world only his master had that power. The master also got that power from his great master and great grand master. The master was the 17th successor of that power bearing a lineage that originated since the time of the creation and then disappeared. It was restored by the cult founder, who lived in the 11th century. He was a real messiah of God...,"* He needed money to extend his establishment. For that so called 'good cause' you kept giving a fixed amount out of your tax deductible income and in return heaven was guaranteed to you.

You may still remember after getting that heaven's guarantee, I (Mother Earth) appeared in your dreams and warned you, *"Harry, I have to tell you to forget about God-Bawa's promise to grant you heaven. God-Bawa is responsible for his own Karma as you are responsible for your own. You reap the fruit of your bad Karma and he too will reap the fruit of his bad Karma. I have said that if you follow the God-Bawa then I would save you. I have never said that God-Bawa has any connection with God. I have gifted you with a discerning intellect. You are smart when maintaining your hidden accounts, then how could you be so foolish in choosing a spiritual guide like God-Bawa? Or are you trying to fool God?*

In your past life you had been through worse than Anna Mario. That time you promised me to be upright, sincere, honest, and obedient and never to misuse God's gifted powers. Trusting in your prayers, I gave you enormous money, and see now what you have done. With that money you bought houses, cars, wines, cigarettes and dozens of pretty ladies were at your call. You enjoyed unprecedented luxuries, which have been inaccessible to Maharajas, Kings, and Badshahs. Anything you wanted you could do but remember I had told you that you shall never achieve happiness, because that was not the purpose you were created for, and I told you not to blame me in future if ever again you become like Anna Mario, a beggar. Don't ask me that question again 'God what have you done to me? ...and I asked you, why were you so cruel to yourself?' you still remember this warning, don't you?

You know the words I spoke in your dreams, *'Again I am telling you that you are cruel to yourself. Be kind to yourself. Otherwise you have to go through bitter lessons again and again till you pass the examination'* Everyone is their own worst enemy or their own best friend. I only produce the fruit of the seed that you have sowed. I tried to make you understand, but even after those warnings, you never paid any heed to my advice.

Anna Mario was exactly like you. He never listened to me. He became completely deaf to God's appeals. After his death, he was reborn into a poor family. His mother and father were very poor and they had a genetic disease. Because of that disease they died during his early youth. The child was raised by a relative. He inherited the same disease, as his parents. He could not work at any job and took to begging. Within a few years his body had become black because of the cold of winter and the heat of summer. His hair was matted and a foul smell emanated from his body that prevented anyone from going near him. Every two months, he started loosing a part of his body. Sometimes a finger, the next time two fingers and next time yet another two fingers, and then he lost both his feet in one month. He could not even talk properly. He could understand almost everything, but physically he became very weak. Early one morning, when he awoke, he couldn't open one of his eyes. Later, he realized that he had lost one eye and after two weeks he lost the second eye also. He had much physical pain and the agony of rejection, dejection and neglect which no one else could even imagine. Thus I (Devi Messiah) made him a kind-hearted human being. And Harry Kingson you are about to get a similar judgment as Anna Mario got. Are you aware of that?"

At the time of his final Judgment he urged God (Judge), "I made one shrine for you when I was alive."

"Whose name is written at the front door on the right hand side of that shrine, mine or yours?" the Judge questioned.

"Mine," Harry Kingson replied.

"Then, did you make that shrine for me or for yourself?" the Judge asked.

"But, I installed your idols inside?" Harry Kingson answered.

"Does that idol look like me, or is it based on your imagination?" the Judge asked.

"But, I didn't know then that your real form is like this," Harry Kingson said.

"Then why did you mislead people into thinking that I - Almighty, Omnipotent Omnipresent God look like your imaginary idol?" asked the Judge.

The Judge stood up from the chair and held Harry Kingson's hand and took him to a place filled with millions of dead people. Then the Judge said to Harry, "Now, come here Harry! I will show you how many shrines you have made for me, and how many shrines of mine you have demolished." He pointed to 1.13 million dead bodies, "These are the bodies of those, who died on account of your crass greed and dirty politics.

In just twenty-five years you demolished more then one million shrines of mine. I made them with my own hands and you demolished them like a cruel Satan. Even just one of my hand-made-shrines cannot be compared with the shrines made by you people. And listen to me Harry, anyone who hates my hand-made shrines cannot enter into my kingdom.

And now, I will tell you how many of my shrines were locked up by you, while you were involved in the "Brainwashing Program" of God-Bawa. Whoever was treated by that program, he or she, could never understand me. You locked up their brains. Brainwashing is the same as demolishing (murdering) my shrines. When God-Bawa locked their brains, with the help of your money, they got confused. They gave money to God-Bawa. You and Bawa enjoyed that money and fame. Now, look at these millions of shrines whose doors were locked to me for their lifetime. I tried to unlock their brains, but you gave the key to God-Bawa. I asked God-Bawa to unlock their brains or hand over the key to me. God-Bawa said, *"Don't disturb me, otherwise you will not see the 'next morning's sun"*. God-Bawa violated my law - the law of the Universe. He fooled the public with his deceitful magic and deceitful philosophy. He brainwashed them, and made them blind to the real miracles of the Universe. Thus he locked all the shrines and prevented them from seeing the real natural miracles taking place in the daily lives of each and every one of them.

I kept building my shrines, in the hope that when I enter within the light's reflection would immediately bring out the best news in the world; The Day of Destiny, Apocalypse, The End of Time, Doomsday, Beginning of a new world, the Earth blessed by the Savior, Judgment Day, 'Pralay in Shristichakra', the Day of Christ, or the appearance of the Avatar. However, you kept them locked up for your pleasure. You kept demolishing my hand-made shrines. You and God-Bawa were Hitlers and Aurangzebs of this age.

Do you have any idea how painful that was for me? How many Hitlers ... ...," Devi Messiah paused for a minute and then again continued. "You were capable of helping innumerable persons. You could have made thousands of shelters, schools, collages, hospitals and you could have donated clothes and other necessities to thousands of needy persons. You could have financed the marriages of thousands of unmarried couples and empowered thousands of orphans to learn some trade and live with dignity in society and you could have left opened their doors for my light. You could have brought happiness, wisdom and love into their depressing lives.

But, you could not even protect one shrine of mine, the one named Natalee. She knew everything you did. I knew she was mentally ill and you were capable enough to protect her. That weak woman I handed you in the hope that with your powers you would protect her, but your charity could not start at home; consequently that shrine tumbled down in the absence of your support. You tried to protect your son and daughter, so that they would protect your assets. You kept four orphans in God-Bawa's monastery to gather donations in the orphans' name, to shut the critic's mouths and to get tax benefits from the government and for legal reasons. You published all your good deeds, and hid all the evil deeds. Even if you think, you have protected my six shrines (four orphans and two of your children) then redeem them out of the 1.13 million demolished ones. Each and every one was a monument of worship, so called House of God was a Qutab Minar. Your shrines were built out of the bones and blood of my shrines (my living kids). Now you have seen my sin-screening system, and realize that no one can hide even a single sin from the Judge?

Yes, Harry, I live in the shrines, which I have created. The one, who hates my hand-made shrines, hates me! The one, who locks up my shrines, locks his door to heaven! The one, who demolishes my shrine, demolishes his own mind!" said the Judge.
"Like Anna Mario, the beggar, you destroyed many of my beautiful shrines. Now, you need to walk on the path Anna Mario – beggar - has already walked."

The Judge said to Harry "You belong to that place..." Pointing with his index finger he showed him the place. .... Full of diseases, miseries, pain, confusions, snakes, scorpions, cobras, swords, arrows, knives, and guns ... "Oh God," uttered Harry and fainted.

Then the Judge-God said, "The 'Forgiver' is also my name. You could have been finished for ever and ever in hell. It's not a punishment but it's a blessing for you. I have granted you one more intolerably sickening life to purify yourself. During that course you shall use your mind properly. You will learn to become a human being. Also, I need some living examples of the terrifying conditions on earth for sleeping ignorant people to learn from."

After the judgment, in a village, he became a normal man like any others but suddenly he underwent a tragedy. He saw some pimples on his right hand. He thought he would recover, but they remained there for a long time. Finally, he showed the pimples to a doctor and everyone found out that it was the beginning of a contagious disease. Everyone told him that according to religious rules and also the doctor's warning he couldn't live with his own people and within an hour his world of dreams disappeared from in front of his eyes.

That same day every one in his family forced him to leave his home. Even his wife could not face the reality. She could not let him stay fearing that she too would be chased out of the house. He (Harry) begged his good friends to help him. Everyone refused him and he had to leave. Everyone left him fearing that he might become a burden on them. Left with no choice he walked out of the house alone to face the reality of life. He had brought some food with him but that would last for only a few days. He had taken two blankets with him, one of which one was stolen on the fourth evening. He was left with nothing. No clothes to wear, no food to eat, and no money to buy any medicines. (Yes, my dear ones, this was the same Harry Kingson.)

He felt as if the whole world had rejected him. He was left alone to bear the pain of rejection, dejection, neglect and the feeling of being unwanted in this world. He knew that death was painful but committing suicide was not an option, so he had to tread the most difficult path of life to survive…. He became a beggar.

He lost everything including his fingers, feet and eyes. Nobody could recognize him except a few beggars. Those beggars came to know him by the name of Anna Mario Junior or Harry Mario because the cart he had, belonged to the late Anna Mario. Those beggars knew that a few months before a beggar named Anna Mario had lived there in similar terrible conditions. He had died and left his wooden cart behind. One day as Harry Mario was pulling his body along he found the cart lying near the river. He got on the cart and sat on it. After sliding on it for about two yards, he became very happy. Bringing his finger-less hands together in prayer he said, "Thank you my kind God! Thank you for giving me this cart. Now, I have something to move my body from here to there. Thank you my kind Lord, thank you…," then he cried.

He would be grateful to God if he could get back at least one finger, because he desperately needed a finger to scratch his body when it got too itchy. Then again he would cry out, "Thank you my kind God! Thank you for giving me back one finger."

****

Harry Mario sat on a four-wheel wooden cart. He had no hands and no feet. Nobody in the world knew him except a worshipper at the shrine, and a few beggars. He had no shelter. Having no means to buy food, he sometimes starved for days on end. He needed many things but his first need was to put something into his empty stomach. Hunger was really painful. Stretching out his hands he used to beg to every passing visitor, *"O kind gentleman, please have pity on me, give me something, in God's name. Oh! Blessed Sir, please give me a little, and God will bless you with a lot."* Most of the people looked at him and thought he was a trickster taking advantage of his illness. People didn't see at him as he was (in pain); they only saw him according to the color of their eye glasses. Therefore some people thought he was a trickster, others felt sorry for him and some kind hearted people helped him. Many people hated him. One day, a shrine member threw him out of the shrine boundary.

The next morning's sun woke him up and with that came the pangs of hunger gnashing his innards. Looking at the shrine from a far distance and bringing his fingerless hands together to his forehead, he bowed to the deities and said, "My God, it's too painful. I cannot live with this perpetual hunger with nothing to eat for days. My God help me. ...Death passes near me. Neither can I die nor can I survive the pain... God, I have no strength to take it anymore..., my God...please my God...Oh my God! ... Merciful and kind God! Help me please."

Due to his completely changed appearance none of his friends or family could recognize him any more. Also nobody knew how bright his brain was. When he got a trolley to move around he prayed to God in a murmur; *"My God! One day if you bless me with money I will do ....I will please you ... as a mark of my utter devotion ... for providing me with this cart. Thank you God! Thank you for helping me with this trolley. I desperately needed it...Thank you."*

The president of the shrine ordered a worker to move him away from the shrine because a dirty beggar didn't match the beautiful shining palace like shrine. Looking at the shrine from far away and joining his fingerless hands together he prayed, "My God! Oh my God! Please help make my moments easy. Please give me something to eat. My God it is too painful to live like this .... I cannot bear this pain anymore. I don't want to die but I cannot live. I don't want to live but I don't know how to die. My God! I am suffering ... please help me. Help me, Father help me! O God! Help me. Help me please. God what sins have I committed that you can't forgive me? Am I not your child? Won't you see my ill-health and the fire of hunger in my stomach?"

He surrendered himself to God, when he had nothing to give. ... He was that same Mr. Harry Kingson who once upon a time was known as the richest businessman and friend of powerful politicians. Then he wouldn't listen to God. Now he wanted God to listen to him and was willing to surrender, but his empty handed surrender was useless to God.

He was still like the late Anna Mario Senior, who once said, *"God if you give me half-a-million in a lottery, I will build a shrine for you and I will make you famous."* However, God was not amused with such prayers. Even after going through so much of suffering Anna Mario Senior also could not understand what God had wanted and what God didn't want. Therefore God had to teach him through a more painful lesson, so that he would realize that if he built a shrine it would be in His fame. He should realize that, one should not tag God's name on to anything, when it is actually being done for one's own fame. He should realize that God is not homeless, nor He is bothered about His own fame.

This Harry Mario had never listened to God when he was a rich man, in his previous life, and named Mr. Harry Kingson. Greed was a serious disease - a great obstacle on the path of the soul's destiny. When he was gripped by it, he couldn't hear his 'inner voice' because he had enjoyed getting more and more. That pleasure made him so deaf, that he hadn't hesitated in using religion or God's name to satisfy his greed. He had not hesitated to indulge in any forbidden 'sins'. The word 'sin' was misinterpreted by his priest. In his dictionary it was the 'Race of Greedy Competitors'. At that time, he did not surrender to God when his coffers were full of gold coins. However, God was not going to listen to his wailing until his thinking was changed. God wanted to hear from him;

"My God! I will never build monuments in your name but mean't for my fame. I shall never again use religion and people's sentiments for my political games. I will never play those games again and I will worship all the members of the home-shrine. I will never build big houses to satisfy my ego. I will never waste your money on frivolous things. O God! One day if you give me money, I will worship you in your hand-made temples, I will give food, blankets, shoes, and shelter to the poor people who suffer like me and I will fix the candle of Love and the candle of Education beside it, so that when you enter you can light them with your powerful light of Love and Wisdom. God, I now know you dwell in them. I understand that you live in the shrines which are made by you. You do not live in those man-made shrines. Man-made shrines are the tyrannical symbols of your shrine's broken bones and blood. God I will live a humble life and listen to your voice always. Now I know how to listen your voice..."

He had suffered a lot. When he perfected himself, his prayers would tell God that he was perfect. The language of his heart would be clear. Though, now Harry Mario had lost his sight, he knew the value of real vision. ... Now that he was deaf and wished to hear someone's voice he couldn't and he now knew the value of hearing. He was mute and desperately wanted to say something to someone. He tried to open his mouth to say something but it wouldn't open. He now understood the value of the gift of speech, and learned how to use this gift. He wanted to go somewhere but he couldn't walk... He thought, *"My God, there are so many things to learn..."*

One day, Harry Mario's brother got a message that Harry may die soon. He went to see him and found him after facing many difficulties. He saw Harry Mario lying on the sidewalk. He said, 'Mario I am here.' He did not respond. He touched Mario's shoulder and said, 'Mario I am your brother, look at me. I am here.' He asked again "Mario can you hear me?" Mario remained silent.

Mario's brother opened his lunch-box and took out some food and put it into his mouth with a spoon. Mario ate that food happily, and finished all the food. The brother then gave him water to drink. He drank the water. After drinking the water the brother noticed Mario's lips stretching slightly and guessed that Mario was smiling. He asked, "Mario, are you smiling, my brother? ... Can you understand I am here?"

Mario couldn't speak anything. After few minutes, his brother saw a tear rolling down Mario's cheek.

Mario's brother cried trying to imagine what was going on in his brother's mind. He might be thinking of the parents who had brought them up lovingly and could not stay with them for long because of their ill health. They've gone from this world, now they might be watching the loving son taking his last breaths. God, so many thoughts must be going through his mind.

However, as Mario could not speak he could not say 'thanks' to the food giver. He understood how it felt, when someone puts food in the mouth of a helpless person. He now understood the value of food. He would never throw food in the garbage can anymore. He would not throw away even one single grain of rice. He now knew the value of a grain of rice and value of a piece of bread. He understood the value of vision, feet, fingers and all the parts of the body.

"Oh! God ... my kind God." the brother uttered.

****

Step Thirteen…

DISPOSING OF DIWAREE'S
DEAD BODY

On the fourth day, after his murder, Diwaree's body was found in the jungle. The body was swollen and flies were buzzing all around it. It was in a frightening condition. Just looking at it gave rise to many questions. Everyone believed that by being good, one could have a peaceful death. Everyone knew that the saint had lived a holy life. His life was an example for humankind. Could one live such a holy life to please God and end up like this? People could not believe that such a terrifying thing could happen to an innocent saint. What could be the reason?

Discarding of Diwaree's dead body became a complicated issue. Around the world people have different ways of disposing off a dead body. Such as: cremation - ashes to ashes, interment in a tomb, interment in a grave - dust to dust, sarcophagus - flesh-eating by nature, crypt – saint's samadhi in the Ashram, sepulchre - tomb chamber, ossuary - the place for the bones, mound, barrow, mausoleum (such as Taj Mahal), pyramid (such as Pyramid of Gija). Tibetan people used sky burial (placing the dead body on a mountain or open ground and leaving it for birds, which is similar to 'burial at sea'. Tower of silence (practiced by Parsi community), Mummification (practiced by the ancient Egyptians) or embalming - chemicals used to preserve it for longer, Several mountain villages have a tradition of hanging the coffin in woods. Ecological burial is a sequence of deep-freezing, pulverisation by vibration, freeze - drying, removing metals, and burying the resulting powder, which has 30% of the body mass. Cryonics is the process of cryopreservating of a body to liquid nitrogen temprature to stop the natural decay. Those practicing cryonics hope that future technology will allow the legally deceased person to be restored to life. Sinful ignorat way is space burial - uses a rocket to launch the cremated remains of a body into orbit. Body donation for medical research is good.

The mafia have been known to have the bodies chopped up (i.e. dismembered) then put in the trunk of the person's car. The car is then taken to a mafia-affiliated junkyard and the body crushed, leaving no trace and the car is gone so a murder investigation is never even started.

In many coastal areas it is common for person who where murdered to be disposed of by mean of a crab pot. A murderer may simply hack up the dead, remove the teeth and finger nails, and crush the skull. Then the deceased is put into a crab pot, put to sea.

But, Diwaree knew that a dead body is a dead body. After death it becomes *Parthiv* and belongs to Prithvi (Earth). However the best way of disposing a holy saint's dead body was to put it in the soil. A farmer dries up the seeds then sows them in the soil for reproduction. When the farmer knows that the seeds are good then they must be sowed to get more good fruits. Similarly all good seeds belong to Mother Nature. Though the Farmer-God may destroy all the bad or unwanted seeds and weeds and use only the good ones it is still good to give him all the seeds in good condition and then leave the rest up to Him.

Diwaree had learned that this body is the property of Mother Earth, because it is produced from her elements, out of her body, and must therefore be returned to her. However even if people do not follow this system to get a new life (body) God always reproduces the useful seeds from any cell of the body, which a man has thrown into the soil while he or she was alive. These cells can be collected from the hair trimmings near a barber shop or even from a piece of nail which one might have dropped on the ground – otherwise known as dead tissue. These seeds don't die. They may have been in the air or beneath the ground, in the form of invisible energy, for many years, and they will remain in the universe forever. These cells contain Karmic information, which doesn't fade away. Karma does not vanish because Karma is a man's balance sheet of actions in one life; forwarded to the next and they can only be nullified after reaping its fruit. The energy seeds of information which carry the strains of Punya Karma are like good seeds. Mother Nature prefers those good seeds to be reproduced because their fruit are always good, and Mother Nature's law is evolution.

Those who purify their genes by pure thoughts and by living a completely truthful life, by serving others, helping the helpless children of Mother Nature, and by being kind and lovable to fellow human beings; are on the road to perfection. Perfection has no end and in this world the road to perfection remains always under construction. *'The rung of a ladder was never meant to rest upon, but only to hold your foot long enough to put the other foot higher.'* In this world no human being is completely perfect; therefore, every human being must learn perfection through pure thoughts and practical truthful Karma in order to enter the planet of the Gods. Only good seeds are produced in Heaven - the land of perfect people.

Diwaree had striven very hard to please God. His aim in life was only to attain Nirvana (Moksha or Salvation). He would do anything to please God. He was a person who had renounced the material world to please God. He was a God-fearing person filled with ethical values and moral principles. He was a living example of honesty, naturalness, authenticity, seriousness, genuineness, straightforwardness, and truthfulness. His name was Diwaree because he used to live on a Diwaar (wall) between a cemetery and crematorium. He had always tried his best to live a holy life keeping 'Paap', 'Punya' and 'Karma' in mind, throughout his life. He used to live on the wall so that his body should not hurt any ants, or other creatures. While walking he always used to watch the ground so that no creatures got crushed under his feet. He never hurt any creature. He used to say; 'even the animals in the jungle must say to God about him, *'the saint has not harmed any creature'* He was the living example of a holy life. He did not do anything for money. He knew God would feed him if he led an honest life.

Devi Messiah had once told him, "Diwaree! I like the purity of your heart. First of all I want to tell you that; I love the humility in you. It is your 'humility' that has brought me closer to you. Your ways of reaching for perfection hroughout your life, your hunger to please God and your fear of committing sin, all these things are exceptional, but I am here to tell you that there are two things you must leave behind, if you are to be one of the men fit for Moksha. They are:

1. If you can appear in public wearing normal stitched clothes and thus erase people's misconception about a 'holy appearance' and an 'unholy appearance,' together with the rumours of 192 years... I know you understand what I mean.

2. Though you say that all religions are the same, yet somehow you do not like the Prophet-Diwaree religion and their believers. I know you are right about how a person can be called a 'believer' when he slaughters animals and human beings. But for a saint everyone must be equal. If you can overcome these weaknesses, while you are alive, then you will reside in the abode of Gods - one of the best places in this universe."

He had replied to Devi Messiah, "My Mother! Whatever you have said is all true, but the thing is, that most of my life is over and very little is left. Why should I play unusual music for the public in this short period? Let the expectations of those people be fulfilled and let them live undisturbed."

Devi Messiah had said to him, "Well Diwaree, a holy person's life is meant to serve others with truthfulness - erase confusion not to strengthen them. If you don't do that then how will people learn? I am telling you whatever confusion a person has spread around or whatever wrong concepts a person has established; it becomes his or her duty to correct them . You don't know where you will go after death, but if you clean up your road; I will show you the blue sky. Diwaree, there are more things than meet the eyes."

Diwaree did not publicly clarify that he was not 192 years old as some people believed. He did not tell them that he was just an ordinary man like others. To enter heaven he had to clean himself up in this life. He had to be born again, to remove those two weaknesses. He had to live a common life to learn that "all religions are good and no religion is bad" and also that a religious uniform has nothing to do with perfection. Truth is the way to perfection. Perfection is the way to God.

What happened to the saint's soul after his death is an interesting part of this journey, which we will reveal later. First let's continue with his dead body. After his disappearance many people believed that Diwaree was God and had returned to heaven with his body. Others believed he was just working a miracle and testing his devotees to see how far they could walk with him. Many followers believed that he would come back and some people believed that his resurrection would take place at any time. However the mystery was exposed on the fourth day, when some devotees including M. L. Singh followed dried drops of blood on the road, eventually they found his dead body in the jungle.

Diwaree's body was drenched in blood. Blood was splattered all around. Many of the devotees fainted with loud screams. All his devotees were stunned. Everyone was confused wondering what MayaLeela (illusive divine game of Almighty) was this. What was to be done no one knew, as his death was most unexpected.

There was a big argument at the time of Diwaree's funeral. Many of Diwaree's followers told Singh, not to bury his body but keep it preserved. Singh asked them as to why they wanted to have Diwaree's body preserved.

"His resurrection will take place in the next few days. Great master Diwaree had disappeared many times in the past and then reappeared. That is what we heard from our forefathers. This is his divine game which he has been playing since the time of our great grand fathers. We have a strong belief that this time too he will be resurrected, if you preserve his body."

Singh wanted to keep his promise to Diwaree and also to protect his rights of becoming a successor. Singh's dream could only come true by completing the last rites of Diwaree. He waited for five days. On the sixth day he said, "No resurrection has taken place, the body is decaying. Why won't you allow me to perform his last rites?"

"No he will come back to life. We should wait for his resurrection," said everyone. Eventually, the town judge was asked to give his judgment on the issue.

The town judge asked Singh, "M. L. Singh what right do you think you have, to perform the last rites of Diwaree?"

"Because, I am the only one, who had lived with him," replied M. L. Singh.

"Living with Diwaree does not give you right to perform his last rites, as there were many who had lived with him from time to time. What other reason do you have to do so?" asked the Judge.

"Because I am the only one, who knows how to perform his last rites as per his strict instructions," was his firm reply.

"Do you have any proof to that?" asked the Town Judge.

"Yes, he once told me how the last rites for his body must be performed. One of his followers was listening to our conversation," replied Singh.

"Who is he?" Judge asked.

"She is Maya. She is sitting right there," Singh said pointing towards Maya.
The judge asked Maya "Is this true?"

"Yes your honor, I heard the whole conversation when Diwaree was telling M. L. Singh how his body must be disposed off. Diwaree had authorized him to do so," was Maya's answer.

Then M. L. Singh revealed the whole story with tearful eyes of how he had made up his mind to live with Diwaree and what were the things Diwaree had asked him to do including forgiving everyone and asking for forgiveness by everyone. He said to the Judge,

"Your honor, I could ask him anything I wanted, but it's true he did not make me his disciple. Your honor, I also understand that a person who believes in God should never ever make a disciple. He should never guarantee heaven to anyone. His inner self should never allow him to commit such a terrible sin. A real God–fearing, good mother's son should never do such a thing. His mother, dead or alive, should always inspire him not to commit that sin. He should not revoke his mother's words and he should never ignore the advice of his 'inner God'. Your honor, Diwaree explained to me that he could not do that as he had renounced everything so as not to cheat others, but to tell them the truth. He had renounced everything not to form a cult, but serve humanity. That's why he did not make any disciples including myself. However, he allowed me to live with him but I was to sleep under the tree at a distance of few hundred yards from his wall. Since that time I have lived with him. I used to sleep under the tree at a distance of five hundred yards from his wall, yet I was close to him, so he had to explained me how to dispose off his dead body, and I had promised him I would do so"

"Your honor, Diwaree just wanted to make sure that nobody should use his name and commit a grave sin by erecting a permanent monument on the burial site, because this foolish act will deprive the poor from using that piece of land, regardless of how big or small. That sin committed by other ignorant people will make his soul suffer. Therefore, he had made it clear while he was alive that, no structure should be erected on his burial site. He explained that, as long as the land remains occupied by the mausoleum the dead may not achieve liberation. Thus he may have to suffer. The sin, according to Diwaree's philosophy, was a dead man's body occupies graveyard space, which takes the bread from a poor man who has need of that land. A man, who does not have enough space to live, If you want to be kind to someone then be kind while they are alive rather than placing diamonds or gold or flowers on their graves. First of all be kind to those who are alive.

Your honor, He learned the truth of not occupying a graveyard when he lived in a town called 'the town of wise people' near South Park Street in Calcutta, where many dead were residing and occupying a huge piece of land. He was stunned to see the outrageous mausoleums. Diwaree was aware of the nine thousand acres of land grabbed by the dead in Britain, Brookwood the Necropolis also known as 'city of the dead'. He was aware of other graveyards in Babylon New York, Ohlsdorf Cemetery of Hamburg (990 acres), Wadi Al Sallam Cemetery (3,500 acres), Zentral friedhof in Vienna, Rose Hills Memorial Park (1,400 acres), Arlington National cemetery, New Orleans, Boston, Forest Lawn Memorial Park in

Glendale, Washington, California, Paris, and Canada and in South America where thousands and thousands of acres of land is taken up by the dead. Six hundred and eighty (2.8 km2) acres is occupied by the dead in Sydney, which is not that bad because more then More than 1,000,000 dead are reside there. Then there are some other places where each of the rich dead is occupying one acre or more, and their maintenance plus funeral services cost was as much as a poor man's living costs for a lifetime. That was not unlike the symbol of greed, Imelda Marcos' husband, and other rich dead whose maintenance costs are high even after their deaths. In Brazil, China, and Germany, thousands and thousands of graves have been excavated and the bodies were cremated. The remains are preserved in a common building, perhaps because their poor relatives are unable to pay the graveyard maintenance fees, like in the Mexico where since their relatives couldn't pay the tax their bodies were exhumed from the graves. But man made religion forbids such acts. He knew many examples of inhumanity of our world such as Leona Helmsley who left behind three million dollars for the up to date maintenance of her Mausoleum. Your honor, Diwaree knew that on earth there was no religion to teach these people the science of God. There was no priest or preacher who could teach them the Karma - humanity or proper use of mother nature's gifts.

Your honor, I am not going to speak about how much land is occupied by churches, mosques and temples, but he had told me that human beings are suffering on account of ignorance. Your honor, he was not against shrines or cemeteries but he was not in favor of greedy politicians or greedy businessmen who use, people's sentimental feelings for religion or God's name to increase their money and build up political power. They are not interested in eliminating any deadly customs of the world. Your honor, his simple questions were; why does the confused public have to cast their vote for these ignorant politicians? Why cannot the public become honest and educated and cast their vote for an honest person? Why can't human beings become wise and honest? Why can an honest person not become a ruler in this world? Why our world has to be ruled by corrupt people only? How many centuries will it take to remove this centuries old tradition of worshipping wealthy people? How many centuries will it take to remove this tradition of war and poverty?

Your honor, he knew that selfish ignorant politicians are the root cause of tension, war and terrorism. He knew man is not man yet. His concern was who could teach them where to pray, where God lives and how to pray. Who would teach them that a rich man's graveyard costs as much as a poor man's brand new home? I am not going to speak of his knowledge of a rich man's funeral costs, and the cost of their marriages.

Your honor, those days he would lie on a rock in that cemetery, while watching how the rich people had made houses and tombs for their dead ones. He saw many other helpless people who did not have enough space even to stretch their legs while sleeping in tiny box-like huts. They had small cabin-like huts where they could only put half of their bodies. When it rained they had to fold their legs in.

Diwaree had once asked a humble homeless saint as to why was he sleeping like with his legs curled up.

The humble saint had told him, "Because many rich people have occupied the land with their dead relatives' tombs. Rich people deprive the living while taking care of the dead. We are suffering here because of their ignorance."

We can talk about the many churches, temples, mosques, other places of prayer; of huge houses, and how the wealthy seek peace by sowing the seeds of anger. Even at the burial ground they do not think about our suffering. We homeless people told them that we would not disturb their dead ones, we would just make huts to hide our heads under a shelter but nobody allowed us to do so.

That humble saint showed Diwaree the cemetery and told him, "This area is occupied by tombs. All the dead people live here legally. They have handed over the legal papers to their ancestors. That is why nobody can ask them to vacate this place. But I have a small hut in which I cannot even stretch my legs properly. Many times the police come here and hit me with sticks asking me to vacate this place. Now on earth where can I go....? "

Your honor, Saint Diwaree's kind heart could not bear others pain. Diwaree requested the town authorities to allow the homeless people to build mini huts in the cemetery area. The answer was a resounding, "No, off course not! This is the place for our dead ones. Those cemeteries are the bridge between the living and the dead. We love our dead and they also need a home to live. If you want to teach then, go to the politicians of rich countries who have unused land. Don't disturb our dead," responded the town people.

Diwaree started crying. With folded hands he looked up in the sky and with tears in his eyes he just said, "Oh God!" Then he bowed down.

Your honor, Diwaree had never cried in his lifetime, but that day his heart was filled with sadness. He said, "My God one man's enjoyment and foolishness is another's suffering. My God! Suffering and enjoyment are the two faces of your world... Let there be wisdom.' At that time Diwaree had made up his mind how his last rites should be performed."

M. L. Singh revealed the complete story with tearful eyes, sincerity and truthfulness. He revealed Diwaree's way of life; of being kind, to fellow human beings whilst they are alive. Also, he explained that the land belongs to the living ones. When Mr. M.L. Singh revealed the whole conversation with Diwaree, regarding the disposal of his body, there was one businessman named Pattiwala who was one of the jurors, and he listened carefully to the whole story.

The witness Maya said, "Yes your honor, Diwaree told M. L. Singh how his body must be disposed off. Diwaree has authorized him to do so and Singh has taken that responsibility. It is true, as I was there at that time. I did not live with Diwaree, but I had invited him a couple of times to my home. His views were totally different from other saints. He loved truth. He never claimed to be God, a God-man or luck-changer, and he never liked praise. He never made any disciple. M. L. Singh was the closest person to him therefore, for his last rites and succession I think M. L. Singh is the right person. M. L. Singh is the only person who knows what to do with his dead body."

After listening to this inspiring story, the town judge, duly impressed, delivered his judgment, saying, "M. L. Singh has been the closest person to live with Diwaree, and he is the only person who knows what is to be done in this time of confusion. Therefore his decision should be final."

All the members of the jury agreed with the judge's decision. M. L. Singh buried Diwaree's body and built no monument on top of its burial place. Heart broken M. L. Singh kept crying all the time. He recited the following verse from the scripture as advised by Diwaree," *Return to thy mother Earth. May she be kind to thee and lie lightly ... ... not oppress"*, and then he prayed to Mother Earth with the following verse from the Rigved, *"Open thy arms, O mother Earth, receive the body with gentle pressure and with loving welcome. Enshroud him tenderly, as a mother folds her soft vestment round the child she loves."* Diwaree had not asked for any other verses to be recited but with tearful eyes he recited one more verse from scripture; *"Accept these beautiful seeds, O Mother, regrow them if you wish, as we need saints like him in this world."* Crying he covered the body with soil and then planted a mango sapling on top.

****

After the funeral and burial they held a condolence ceremony. With tearful eyes M. L. Singh addressed the congregation in his first sermon; "Dear devotees, this sermon is a conversation between Diwaree and me. Diwaree once said to me... *(He told the story of the homeless people and cemetery in Calcutta, which he had told the judge)*

...Devotees! We all are the same human beings. Believing in good Karma is faith and practicing good Karma is religion. We should stay away from the path of falsehood, vice, injustice and follow the path of Truth because we have to pass the test of life. That's how our Diwaree was," concluded M. L. Singh.

Then wiping off his tears he said, "But, I miss him so much."

****

People were very impressed with the ideas of Diwaree. Only a true saint could say those things. Everyone sighed, what a great soul who had cried only once in his lifetime, and that too for unprivileged, poor homeless and helpless people.

Everyone heard the above story from M. L. Singh. Then Singh added, "The perfect ideas of a holy man are really worth emulating by people, who believe in good deeds."

After finishing the rituals, M. L. Singh was about to become the self-styled successor of a property-less Saint. Diwaree just had one wooden plank for guests to sit on. The wall did not belong to him legally, because it was not registered in his name. He had nothing; therefore, nobody had any objection because Diwaree had no property. Nobody objected as no one was interested in taking that penniless position. No one was willing to take a saint's wooden plank and suffer a life time.

The juror Seth Michael Pattiwala, who had been listening to the story at the time of the judgment and condolences, had started to think of something new. His original name was Magharam Pattiwala but since his original name didn't sound friendly to his international clients he had changed it to Michael Pattiwala. He was a good psychologist and expert in business. He immediately realized that the *Bali* (bloodshed, sacrifice) of a saint, in the name of truth, would attract people. On the other hand the saint was an extremely quiet *Vairagee* who could attract and tranquilize people's mind in this world full of tension, horror and hostility. Mr. Pattiwala was clever, enthusiastic and wanted to do business differently. His ideas were unique. For him, everything in this world was just a business including religion, saints, spirituality birth and death.

He knew people get excited after worshipping their dead Prophet's statue, or on hearing the accounts of fierce conflict and bloodshed in the name of religion. In that excitement they donate money heartily, to secure freedom from their fear of death. Diwaree's impressive life and horrifying death was a very marketable 'input', which could yield immense returns. After thinking about it over and over again, he found the market potential in Diwaree's name, an advantageous and profitable logo. The amount of money he would invest on that venture; should give him a return of two hundred percent profit in just six months. Then he could withdraw his original invested amount, and also get the fame to multiply his business. Money would attract money. An amazingly profitable business! Wow!

Other followers also did not want his name to disappear. He was such an inspiring personality the likes of which may never come again for many decades or even centuries. It would be easy to propagate his mission as he had already earned a great reputation. The way people liked him clearly demonstrated that one announcement in his name would keep the cash registers ringing.

What Diwaree taught; what he wanted or what he wished; all that become irrelevant. Now people started thinking of using his name as a marketable product; a 'brand'. Michael Pattiwala thought that M. L. Singh was the right person to be used for this purpose. M. L. Singh had two reasons to claim to be the successor of Diwaree. First, he was the only person who was with Diwaree during the last days of his life, and secondly he was the man who had performed his last rites. In addition to these two logical reasons he was a good speaker.

Though it was a business mission, he named it 'Diwaree's Mission'. Now the question was whether Diwaree had any kind of mission or not. That was hard to answer because Diwaree left no written testimony before dying, nor had he ever told anyone that he had ever thought of establishing a financial enterprise.

Another question was; if it was Diwaree's desire to establish a mission, which might have been hidden deep in his mind; then all the followers could be mistaken about his stoical renouncement (Vairagya) and pure life.

One of his followers had, however, claimed and told everyone that, "For some reason Diwaree could not express his inner feelings, and therefore he couldn't tell anyone that he wished to serve people in this way. For some reason he couldn't fulfill his own wishes, therefore, I will ensure his unfinished plans take shape."

Now, if that follower was right about Diwaree's desire, then Diwaree was not Diwaree, the great ascetic as he appeared to be. On the other hand, if Diwaree never desired so, then all of them were wrong. Anyway, forgetting who was wrong and who was right the business was safe. Diwaree was dead. Everyone knew that Diwaree had not made a copyright of his name nor any special will for anyone. He was definitely not going to come back to scold these people, in his bold straightforward way by saying,

(When Diwaree was alive, he sometimes used to make funny jokes. Once during his normal conversation he had said these lines to Mr. Sing). *"Hey! What the hell are you people doing here? Why are you using my name? Money, making greedy business people! Have I given you permission to use my name? Have I asked you to do this? Have I asked you to print this receipt book and collect donations in my name? Have I asked you to build a structure and engrave my name at the main gate? Have I asked you to wear this uniform in my name? Is this your mission or mine? Why are you using my name for your mission? Now I am going to sue you. I am going to take you to court. You will have to pay double the amount you have collected in my name for damaging my principles."* (Then Diwaree and Mr. had laughed and laughed throughout whole day.

Such a thing would have shaken them with fright, and they would have run away leaving behind the receipt book. Michael Pattiwala felt safe knowing that the dead Diwaree was not going to come back to sue him. He had about a million dollars for charity, which he wanted to donate to a good establishment, for good causes. In return, he wanted to put his parent's photo next to Diwaree's. Thus the name of his parents would become immortal by being so closely associated with Diwaree's name and fame. Their name would remain in this world as long Diwaree's name would remain. Whoever would come to visit the mission would read the wordings; *"Their son's thoughtful and generous donation has provided the support for the establishment and maintenance of the Diwaree Mission. May Diwaree bless them"* and every visitor would know that there had been one person whose son was generous and had a deep faith in Diwaree. He knew that with money he could do many things, but the best use of that money was to buy fame in this life, and to be remembered after death.

M. L. Singh thought about it again and again. He could not sleep the whole night thinking about whether do it or not, because he knew Diwaree was a saint who not would welcome such business people. There was a big difference between the thinking of Diwaree and Michael Pattiwala.

Singh kept worrying whether it was Diwaree's will, God's will or a time of trial. His inner conscience knew that it was not a good thing to follow a businessman, as he could hear the voice coming from his heart, *that is 'wrong', 'wrong', 'wrong',* but different people tried to convince him, and different thought waves were beyond his control. Eventually he decided to go ahead with Pattiwala's plan for 'one should do something in life'. Pattiwala and a lot of other people were very happy with Singh's decision.

M. L. Singh agreed to change his name and apparel to run this big mission. He agreed to wear two pieces of un-stitched clothes; one to cover the upper parts of his body, and the other to cover the lower. He agreed not to wear any other clothes and always walk barefoot. He agreed not to use impure metal steel pots for his food. He agreed not to trim his mustache and beard and also to change his name from Mr. L. P. Singh to Diwar-Devote.

Professionally a philosophy professor, M. L. Singh was a good speaker at his college. He was such a good speaker that after listening him for one hour the audience would say *'it's the middle of night'* even if that was middle of the day. With his expertise he could turn their minds and make them believe in anything. After living with Diwaree he had gathered plenty of information on real spirituality. Obviously after living with a good man he appreciated only good things. He had learned that gossiping was a big sin, and many other practical truths. He became a good convincing personality, quite clever and smart enough to motivate his listeners. Seth Michael Pattiwala knew that M. L. Singh had the ability to move the audience by his persuasive speeches. He had got the perfect person to run the Diwaree Mission.

Michael Pattiwala knew that without mystery no religion had flourished. In accordance with his clever instructions, Singh started claiming that

Diwaree had given him powers through a divine dream-vision, just after leaving for his heavenly abode. Singh did not hesitate at all, in declaring in such dream that he would be the only Saint, and besides him there would be no second saint. It was easy for other people to believe that M. L. Singh was the right person to bear Diwaree's divine powers on earth. Everybody believed in his dream and later that dream was written into their scriptures.

With Michael Pattiwala's advice, Saint Diwar-Devote (Mr. M. L. Singh) started wearing a simple unstitched robe, consumed simple food and had a rich impressive vocabulary to speak in public. This change took place on the third day of the condolence ceremony. On the second night Michael Pattiwala had a meeting with Saint Diwar-Devote. He elaborated his plans thus:

"The plan is this; the Mission's name will be Diwaree Mission. With my first donation, ten acres of land will be purchased in a peaceful area. We will build a huge monastery with four building blocks. The first block will be used for the poor and orphans. The second block will be used for free education for poor students. People who have renounced the world and celibate people will live there and work for free for the mission. However, to those workers we will give a ten-dollar coupon for a full day's work, with that coupon they shall be able to buy one day's food plus a few other necessary things from our canteen, or from any other shops within the monastery area. That coupon will be valid only inside our monastery. The third block will be the head office with all kinds of modern equipment; computers, faxes, telephones, Internet, media, monthly publications, and worldwide communication facilities. The fourth block will be used for Saint Diwar-Devote and other Very Important Persons (VIPs) including the treasurer and the accountant. There will be a separate VIP kitchen for only special people who will be allowed to eat the food cooked in that kitchen."

"Sounds great," Saint Diwar-Devote agreed.

They made a big prayer hall in the center of those four blocks, where a huge statue of Diwaree was installed. They kept Diwaree's dead body's photo at the center. After looking at that frightening photo, most of the devotees' heads used to spin, just knowing about their beloved Master's horrifying death, which made them realize that evil still exists in this world. The gory details depicted in the brutal and merciless murder of the great Saint made people's emotions rise to great heights.

Hence, Saint Diwaree Mission's following grew by leaps and bounds. Some incense with a nice fragrance and two candles always burned round the clock and seven days a week. Many people went there to meditate and believed that Diwaree would come to them during their meditations to answer the complicated questions of their lives. Most of the people were highly educated and did not belong to the plebeian class. However, the lower bourgeoisie could not even get admission to live in there. Many questions were asked, before rejecting a penniless seeker. The main concern was how much could they donate or what skills they had, and what they could do for the mission. The poor people could not understand that the mission was a multimillion dollar project meant to fill the coffers of Michael Pattiwala and others. They simply thought that it's a great and noble mission, wherein the homeless could find shelter.

All qualified people passed the test with the manager. They got jobs according to their ability. The lower class people usually got jobs such as; gardening, cleaning, cottage industries, and cooking. The back-biters and yes-men were more successful. They always got a higher class of job such as; supervision, office jobs, receptionists and staff to handle secret deals etc. Big donors were like the owners of the mission.

The photograph of Diwaree's dead body's touched people's hearts. Michael Pattiwala made thousands of diamond pendants, gold bracelets, diamond earrings, key rings, silver photo-frames for the coffee table, and many other expensive jewelry items along with the photo. Though the profit margin was small, but the quantities were huge; Michael Pattiwala's jewellery department made millions in a very short time.

Saint Diwar-Devote and Pattiwala's vision of the Diwaree enterprise was a thundering success. Diwaree's name was used by hundreds of people for their livelihood. Their livelihood depended upon the organization's success. Everyone who lived in the mission attended Diwaree's evening prayers and said that Diwaree was God. When a new visitor came to their mission, they tried hard to convert him saying that they were the only people in the world, walking on the right path while following a great man's footsteps. Only Diwaree had the qualification of being in communion with God, could lead them and guide them. New visitors had to listen to their madness and agree respectfully.

Though, everyone in the monastery was forbidden from all kinds of immoral acts, Saint Diwar-Devote did all of them without anybody's knowledge. His food was special. The kind of princely treatment he got was not available to anyone else. Only his saintly robs were simple.

Many people looked at their property and said, *"There must be some sort of divine power to run this mission, otherwise such a miracle could not happen."* The miracle was beyond any logical explanation. Such as; food cooked for a thousand people at a time, huge cooking pots, and unlimited amounts of oil, butter, rice, vegetables and such a large number of devotees working with dedication. All these things were being publicized as an amazing miracle of the late Diwaree. Many people went just to watch the miracle of the food being cooked. The food-miracle attracted many people and later they surrendered to that miracle by becoming a part of it.

****

Step Fourteen...

MAYA'S ARRIVAL

After a while Maya also went to visit the mission. She bowed down before Saint Diwar-Devote. "Hello Maya how are you?" asked saint Diwar-Devote with a joyful and moving expression on his face.

"With Diwaree's blessings, we are all somehow surviving." replied Maya.

"You know it was an amazing divine act of the master. We never knew that one-day we would meet here again. I have thought of you many times since the funeral of our Great Master. I wanted to thank you for helping me at the critical time of judgment for the funeral, but you never showed up. Everything is in the hands of the Great Master. It's his divine play, and only he knows what it is. Anyway, where and how have you been?" asked Diwar-Devote with a curious expression on his face.

At the same time a melodious song was going on in the main prayer hall. The wordings were;

My prayer has been answered:
I asked for strength...
And God gave me difficulties to make me strong
I asked for wisdom...
And God gave me problems to solve.
I asked for prosperity ...
And God gave me brain and brawn to overcome.
I asked for courage...
And God gave me danger to overcome.
I asked for love...
And God gave me troubled people to help.
I asked for favors...
And God gave me opportunities.

I received nothing I wanted,
I received everything I needed. My prayer has been answered.

Pretty and helpless Maya said about her stressful life, "Well, taking care of the kids, struggling to survive but life goes on with His will. I thought God had given me enough courage to face any obstacle in life, but now I am broken and tired. My strength is gone, and I cannot take this burden anymore. I want to live a renounced life."

Diwar-Devote said, "You know Maya, how great our Master Diwaree was, no matter what we do for him, it will always be counted as nothing. I have given my life here, I have peace and satisfaction and this life is far better than the life of a professor. Since the day I joined the teaching job, I never liked it because when I got the job my father had to pay a bribe to the management. My father was poor. I learned that qualifications were secondary and the bribe was the main parameter to get a job.

At the school every time a new student got admission we used to take a bribe, a so called 'donation.' Indirectly some of that money was being used by all the top office bearers, for their personal entertainment and the accountant never disclosed the truth, which led to a huge misunderstanding and clash among office bearers and teachers.

The poor parent's brilliant children had no future in the world. I wondered what impression a student would get when he got admission into the school, by paying an unaffordable amount of bribe and what would he do in the future. I requested my father not to pay the bribe, I would rather prefer to remain jobless, but...

To me, giving a bribe was as serious a sin as taking a bribe, but my poor father believed that one has to become corrupt in order to survive in this world. Without becoming corrupt a person cannot have a life. Corruption was the door to survival in this world. Without passing through that door a person will end up without experiencing the reality of life. He cannot get married and cannot have a family life, as a result his family line would end, but my conscience did not agree with all that.

Eventually, I became a teacher but memories of those corrupt practices always remained in my mind. I thought of renouncing the world as I hated corruption. It is far more honorable to fail than to cheat. Living in poverty was better than having a job through bribery. Living with principles was better than living with corruption, no matter what we get or what we loose. Since I respected my father, I listened to him and took the job through bribery. My poor father's entire property was gone. At that time I made up my mind, *"As long as my parents are alive I will do this job to keep them happy. But after their death I will become what I always wanted to be."* That was the reason after my father's death I quit the job and surrendered myself to the great Master Diwaree.

After my father's death, I went through a difficult time. I had a big argument with the bribe-taking group, including the chairman. Also my family life was out of control. I was sick and tired of all the rumors and gossip and wanted to have a peaceful life and to do something good in this life. I then started living with our Great Master.

"Maya, let me show you what we have achieved in the last two years." Saint Diwar-Devote took her outside and showed her the ten acres of land and the many buildings they had raised. Then he talked about the future plans. Maya was impressed!

Then he said, "How lucky you were that Diwaree himself came to your home, a man so great. There must be some reason, or you must be pure and God's chosen one. He came to your house, before leaving for his heavenly abode and purified the place with his holy presence. You have always worshipped God-Bawa's photo, but he never came to your house; Diwaree came. There is a saying that, *'It doesn't matter in which form and whom you worship; if your heart is pure, God comes to you.'* It happened to you.

For Diwaree it did not matter whether a person was rich or poor; he would always go to the house where only pure-hearted people lived. He knew who was pure and who was not. He knew who deserved and needed his blessings. He knew everything about this universe, life, death and heaven. That is the sign of a really enlightened saint. There has never been a holy saint like him, nor shall there be in the future. No human being could understand him. He was a true incarnation of God," said Diwar-Devote.

"Yes I believe that," acknowledged Maya.

After giving a long discourse, the object of which obviously was to impress with his godly achievements and erudition in religious matters; and after having established his credentials before a gullible lady, who was already facing a host of problems in her personal life, he persuaded Maya to live in and serve the mission. Her life changed instantly.

Maya really believed that Diwaree was a great God. A great God finds good people to establish and extend his mission. His invisible power was behind it. She thought that Diwaree was encouraging everyone to make this shrine and buildings. She believed that a shrine is a good method to teach children, but the children wanted real answers. Her elder son did not like collecting donations in the name of the poor and then using the money to build monuments. He thought that holy people should expose the farce and falsehood in the name of God, and reveal the 'mysteries.' That son boldly asked her, "Mummy now you are saying Diwaree was God, before you were always worshipping God-Bawa's photo, believing that he was God; are there two Gods or one? If there is only one God; then which is the real one, God Diwaree, or God God-Bawa? Were you right then or now?"

"Well, now I am going to stop worshipping God-Bawa's photo, because he never came to my house. He goes only to rich people's houses. I prayed before his photo many times but he never listened to my prayers. From now on I will worship Diwaree's photo. Diwaree, being a real and a great person, never showed that he was great and he came to my house. At that time I didn't recognize his greatness. At that time I desperately needed God to come to me, and he, the living God, came to help me. The proof was, after his visit to our home, you children became calm and serene. To me that was God telling me that when I was in dire straits and called for his help he came to me in the form of Diwaree, but it was my fault that I didn't recognize him. I wanted him to bless my children. He did that, but unfortunately I couldn't recognize him, due to the misunderstandings about God-Bawa's photo and a load of other problems," explained Maya. Then she started murmuring, *(Yah alag baat hai ki mai pahicaan na saki, per meri jarurat me tuu kahaan nahee milaa.*

(It's besides the point that I couldn't recognize you but my God, where did you not meet me in my moments of need? You have always been with me.)

Maya was only thirty-five and richly still attractive – a wealth of beauty. Saint Diwar-Devote gave her an apartment with all the facilities. She wore a holy dress. She looked holy and more attractive than in a common dress. Maya always wished to live in a monastery where she could have with peace of mind, with good people who would understand the philosophy of a holy life. She was happy living in the monastery and working as an assistant to Saint Diwar-Devote.

The evening bell rang along with many other musical instruments and people started singing the prayer of Diwaree. The atmosphere became very serene. Maya was very happy here. She believed that finally she had found a safe place where she wanted to be after a long time. Peace at last, but it lasted only a few months.

With time things started to change. Maya started having complications in the monastery. She felt she had exchanged her previous problems for, new and a completely different set of problems. One day she asked Diwar-Devote, "Saint Diwar-Devote, I cannot understand one thing, I always thought that monks are blessed with peace and wisdom, but here I can feel internal struggles and intrigues, people are involved in tittle-tattle and back biting everywhere. Why?"

Saint Diwar-Devote said, "Well there is struggle everywhere. One must know that as long as we live we have to struggle," then he repeated his usual formula, *"The rung of a ladder was never meant to rest upon, but only to hold your foot long enough to put the other foot higher.* God has created us to face struggles. Peace! A wise person can have peace at home. The wise will not leave home if they know how to obtain peace at home. If one cannot obtain peace and happiness at home then he will face problems in monasteries as well. Most saints are good, they are better than common people, but it is a matter between fulfilling the basic needs and unsatisfied desires. Together they have to try for perfection in the monastery. One can try for perfection living at home or living in a monastery because in this world struggle is everywhere. Here we teach them to accept it all as a 'state of mind.'

Most of the people who come to the Monastery come to take a break and they will not be asked to work too much. They get good food and accommodation and no bills to pay, but here too everyone has to work to survive. Those who work have better chances here as well. The grass on the other side always looks greener. Struggle is everywhere, Maya. Once the great master Diwaree told me; 'a thirsty man was walking in the desert where, at a distance of fifty yards, he kept seeing what looked like water. He kept walking and walking in the hope that the water would draw near, and eventually he said;

Pyaasaa Jindagee Bhar Chalataa Rahaa Ret Me,
Isa Aash Para Ki Aage Samundar Mil Jaayegaa.

I kept walking through the desert in the hope that the ocean will be just ahead, and I kept walking...till this end of life. End of life - but not the end of problems. After death the problems are transferred to the next generation or the next life.

Maya, problems are a part of life. Without problems life cannot be life as the rose always comes with thorns. Life cannot be without thorns because it cannot be meaningless. A smooth sea never made a skillful mariner. Struggle is the beauty of life. That's what the Great Master used to say. One cannot catch one's own shadow. Struggle will always follow you like your shadow. One cannot run away from struggles. Miseries are not always alike. Even if you are prepared for one kind of misery, you never know what kind of misery is waiting around the next corner. When people found the treatment for tuberculosis the next disease that appeared was cancer and when they started curing cancer the next disease to appear was AIDS, and we don't know what will be the next. Struggle is everywhere, Maya.

Take for example the inspiring life of our Great Master Diwaree. Thousands of people used to come to him with their problems, but nobody asked about his problems. Everyone thought he was a standing cow, ready to be milked, that he belonged to the public where anyone could go to get milk. Diwaree never asked anyone for anything. Many people even came to preach to him. They used to tell him their philosophy, their knowledge, their wisdom, achievements and how good they were. They would take him around their houses to show what wonderful houses they had. But nobody gave a thought as to how he survived in the rain. Diwaree believed in Salvation but they believed in houses and material wealth. A house was the only aim of their life but not a home. One day Diwaree explained it to me saying,

"M. L. Singh it is like a bird that makes a beautiful nest to impress fellow birds. A nest cannot impress a renounced person... I would rather go to the poor who live in humble huts. Their natural and real humility impresses me. To me the rich and the poor are good as long as they come to a penniless stoic vairaagee with humility, like a beggar. Only then can they find some jewels in their begging bowl. Instead of impressing others with big houses these people could have and do many good things in life such as; humility in conduct, loving deprived ones, gaining knowledge, leading a truthful life, and facing the realities of life silently, consider problems as a gift from God, being kind, sympathetic, non-violent, serene, self restrained, forgiving calm, and tranquil. I like people who respect honesty, spirituality and non-materialism. I like people when their normal conversation tells me that they are righteous."

Maya, once the Great Master had a tough time with two big tycoons and their one-point philosophy; aggrandizement of themselves at the cost of others. Whenever those rich tycoons invited him for a meal, they would harp on their own philosophy which was totally senseless.

On the other hand poor people do not share that philosophy. They believe only what they see with their own eyes. If they see a dead person being buried or cremated then they believe in death. If they see a hungry man wailing then they believe in God's law. If they see a person walking barefoot then they believe in Karma. If they see a war victim, an earthquake victim, the sun, moon and stars then they believe in God's miracles. When they see a growing child becoming old and then dying they believe in all these things. Their philosophy is everything; they see in this universe, are the miracles of God. They believe in every real thing but many rich people don't.

Maya the Great Master used to say, believing is better than not believing; but a person should know, understand, and follow the truth instead of just believing untruths. Believing is the word found in the dictionary of excuse-makers. There are many reasons why fools ignore reality and believe in mystery. There are many reasons why they believe in what they don't know.

Again Saint Diwar-Devote continued, "Maya I was deeply impressed with you when I saw you for the first time."

"I also thought of you as a man with good heart, educated and righteous since you were living with a Saint," replied Maya.

The next day Saint Diwar-Devote said to Maya, "Diwaree used to say that a man and woman should never sit alone, together in a room for a long time."

Maya said, "Nothing is wrong with that as long as your mind is pure and you keep your senses under control. This is devotion. When a person's mind is completely engrossed in God then nothing can affect them."

"You are one in a hundred and therefore two hundred percent right," said saint Diwar-Devote in his poetic style.

After couple of days he said, "Maya, we should never tell anyone about our love life. This is the secret of our religion's success. Maya you are the reason for the success of Diwar-Devote's religion. Though people say that love, a cough and murder cannot remain hidden, but we must hide it. *(a quick thought came to Maya's mind, 'Diwaree's murder is still hidden')* Our sacred love must always remain a secret, because that is the secret of our success," explained the Saint seriously.

"After all a woman is the strength of divine nature and man is the strength of God. People believe that it is a woman who makes a man, but here I will say, it is you, who have made my life," Maya said.

"Maya, it is woman who creates man with love. Her love changes man's direction. Love is God's biggest miracle. One cannot understand this miracle by disregarding it. God did not create Love without a reason. A human being is created to understand it, and it can be understood only by accepting its realities. Love is the path to God. Love is God's soul. Love is God's invisible form in this universe.

When he paused for a second, Maya started thinking, 'Wow! Is this a saint, God, or professor of philosophy?' The saint continued... "Maya, love is an amazing creation of God. It's like an invisible thread that spreads from one heart to another and weaves a net. Love unites two hearts, two families, two villages and two countries. Love is God's invisible powerful force that keeps human understanding evolving in order to beautify this world. If there was no love then a mother would abandon her new born baby, a brother wouldn't care about his sister, and a husband wouldn't care about his wife. No one would care about others and this beautiful world of God would not be bejeweled like it is. Love has made a net of relations and extended it.

Love is sentimental, fragile, yet the strongest and most powerful force in the world. Because of the ties of love, all creatures and human beings want their loved ones to be at peace and protected. The child doesn't want to see tears rolling down the cheek of the mother and a parent's heart melts at seeing the sufferings of their children. You do not want anyone to hurt your loved one. You want to make sure that no bad forces are going to attack them. Any evil forces must stay far away or you will try to destroy them to protect your loved ones. You take care of them as you take care of yourself. Lover and loved one become united like one body.

Great love always has a painful end. Our Great Master used to murmur these words when a woman's husband died and she got confused and started crying; 'O God, my companion is gone - leaving me behind alone - O God!'

Bholee Tiriyaa rovan Laagee Bichud Gayee Meree Jodee.
Kahat Diwaar Suno Bhaai Saadho, Jin Jodee Tin Todee.

Then Diwaree would explain, "O, innocent lady do not cry; the one who united you has taken him back. His will is supreme. We are all instruments of his will, and accept it as such. From now on God is your companion and keep him in your thoughts till the last breath."

Maya, I cannot believe that since the day you and Pattiwala came into my life we have achieved so much. When I finish building this complex I want to start a university that will be known as 'Diwaree University'. For donors it is easier to donate money in the name of an educational organization, for tax purposes. Pattiwala's friend is the education minister and he can grant a lot in the name of an educational establishment. The minister has explained to our accountant and lawyers how to prepare acceptable documents for a grant from the government's funds."

****

Part Three

GOD MADE RELIGION AND MAN MADE RELIGIONS

Step Fifteen...

DIWAR-DEVOTE RELIGION

Harry Kabeela was a retired army man and one of the members of Diwar-Devote's prayer group. He was very unhappy because of his own problems and had joined Diwar-Devote's prayer group to find a solution, and peace of mind through religion. Instead of finding the answers to his problems, he became even more disappointed with the falsehoods in the house of God. He was shocked to see what religious people were doing in the name of God. He couldn't believe that the so called holy who kept chanting God's name and leading the world to righteousness, led such a corrupt and deceitful life. He could not see anything good in religion and was alert to all deviations in the conduct of the self proclaimed religious God-men. He saw that they were filled with lust, ego, pretence and selfishness. They were double-faced wheeler dealers. These dirty minded people used religion and God for their personal pleasures.

He was very unhappy with Diwar-Devote, because he could unquestionably smell that Saint Diwar-Devote would not tolerate any insult in front of Maya. Many other followers also could smell the Saint and Maya's happy moments were unbecoming for an ascetic. A corrupted religious leader cannot set an example for the public. The public will have enough excuses to follow the path of folly if a religious leader is immoral. Not all the followers knew about Diwar-Devote's manly peccadilloes, and those who knew thought it prudent to turn a Nelson's eye. Once the self styled God-man descends from his high pedestal, he loses much of his shine. Harry Kabeela was brought up and trained in the glorious traditions of the regular army; therefore he couldn't bring himself to compromise with vice and injustice so brazenly indulged in by the helmsmen. So he made up his mind to bring together a disciplined congregation.

With the cooperation of all the disillusioned followers Harry Kabeela planned to establish an independent prayer group based on moral principles. He was enthusiastic in his passion to carry out the most needed job on earth. He wanted to expose all the dirty games in the religious field. He wanted to tell the people about the deceit and duplicity of these self styled God-men.

Diwar-Devote could smell the intentions of Harry Kabeela. Hoping to avert a power struggle and conflict Diwar-Devote quickly changed his name to "His Holiness Diwar-Devote". His followers were named as Diwar-Devotees. Within few weeks with the help of other educated followers he published a scripture, on the life and history of Diwaree, named "H.H. Diwar-Devote with St. Diwaree". This book became their main scripture. Apart from that they already had couple of other books written by different believers, for believers, during the previous few years. The main scripture was mainly a condensed version of those books because he had no time to write a new book from the beginning and he was in a hurry to convert this prayer group into a proper religion, and to hand over a proper scripture to millions of followers. Seven strict commands were added, they were;

1. No Gossiping or criticizing anyone: H.H. Diwar-Devote has forbidden any kind of gossiping in his monastery premises. Gossiping was not forbidden outside the boundaries of the monastery.

2. Remain attired in yellow robes while praying: All Diwar-Devotee monks and priests must be attired in yellow colored garments. All

followers of Diwar-Devote's religion must keep a piece of yellow cloth with them at all times.

3. Diwaree's Statue Prayer: All monastic staff must come to the prayer hall and sit around Diwaree's statue and remain silent for at least ten minutes in mass meditation and prayer to get in communion with the Great Master Diwaree.

4. Worshipping all Gods: Respect the deities of other inherited Gods and Goddesses, but Diwaree's huge statue must be always in the center because he is the head of all other Gods, the most ancient among Gods.

5. Strict Diwar-Devotee: God is one; he can speak only through H.H. Diwar-Devote. Therefore, do not attend the seminars of other groups. Do not read books of other beliefs.

6. Only Diwar-Devote shrines: Never enter the shrine of other beliefs, and do not allow followers of other beliefs to enter our shrine. Do not look at the shrines of other beliefs. If by mistake you happen to see their shrine, then as repentance wash your eyes ten times.

7. Glass of water: Everyone must drink a glass of water before taking a bath. Do not drink water for one hour after taking the evening meal. Do not drink machine made juices, sodas and any intoxicating or any other processed drinks on Sunday.

****

Step Sixteen...

PROPHET-DIWAREE RELIGION

Almost everybody was amazed to see what Diwar-Devote had achieved in only six years. Some businessmen's mouths started watering. They had found a fruitful opportunity for a religious business. They established a new religion with the Harry Kabeela group. Many people joined the new group as some of the followers were not happy with Maya's presence in the monastery. They did not say anything directly to Diwar-Devote out of respect and his high position, but they made up their minds to leave that group. Other discontented people also joined this group. With clever advertisement and programs in different places the growing number of believers reached the thousands in only a few months. Some of the trustees and patrons of that group were enormously rich. Other believers were also generous in donating money in the name of spirituality.

In his functioning Harry Kabeela replicated practically the same organization as that of Diwar-Devote except that a glamorous lady like Maya had no role to play as that would have set tongues wagging. In any case beautiful unattached ladies and saints are not quite a saintly mix. So the retired army man Harry Kabeela changed his name to Prophet-Diwar and the cult was known as Prophet-Diwaree cult and his followers were known as Prophet-Diwarians.

In the beginning they were a prayer group. Later when they got money they became a 'mission' and a little later when they got more money and more followers they were known as a 'cult', and finally they became a separate religion, which they declared after a little conflict.

His Holiness Diwar-Devote got very disturbed with the tricky actions of the former Diwar-Devote. Quickly he formatted his religion in a political way so that no other religions should compete with him.

Prophet-Diwar (Harry Kabeela) read Diwar-Devote's book and then he too added the title 'His Holiness' to his name and became 'His Holiness Prophet-Diwar'. Prophet-Diwarians published a book by the name "Diwaree as H.H. Prophet-Diwar". Prophet-Diwarians had more than ten other books written by well known and aggressive armymen of that group but "Diwaree as Prophet-Diwaree" became their main scripture. Any quotation taken from that book was accepted as the statement from the authorized God-man or God. Prophet-Diwarians had three main rules in their religion;

The first rule was Devotion: Do whatever you want, wear whatever you like. Clothes have nothing to do with devotion to Diwaree, but make sure that you get initiated by H.H. Prophet-Diwar, and remember him as your Savior. The more you think of H.H. Prophet-Diwar the closer you will get to Diwaree. You worship Diwaree through H.H. Prophet-Diwar. Offering something to H.H. Prophet-Diwar is the same as giving to our Great Master Diwaree, because now the Great Master is dwelling in H.H. Prophet-Diwar. He can see you even when you cannot see Him.

The second rule was Prayer: Everyone must pray to Prophet-Diwaree for at least fifteen minutes to nourish the spirit. Praying while walking is allowed, but never walk with sad feelings as it is like consuming junk food. The more you meditate on him, more you will be closer to the Great Master Diwaree.

The third rule was Donation: Make sure that at least one tenth of your net income is donated to the religion so as to purify the sinful money, and to deserve forgiveness. Giving away a tenth of your income will make you healthy, happy, wealthy and wise in this world and also in heaven. Ten percent is the least, but if you have more, then you must donate more. His Holiness doesn't touch money therefore give that to the secretary, or deposit it directly into our non-profit bank account. His Holiness will come in your dreams; to guide you, to tell you which level of spirituality you have achieved. He will save you, therefore donate more and more.

Their firm belief was; at the end of the world Diwaree would appear in front of them and if they recognized him they would go to heaven for good, and if they failed to recognize him they would go to hell, permanently. One could recognize him only by following the above three rules.

With the above mentioned three simple rules His Holiness got a good amount of money, in just a few weeks. After becoming financially strong and well established he thought of expanding his faith among second-rated people as well, to increase the number of followers. For that reason he verbally added many rules which anyone could easily follow to keep the restless mind engaged. Some of those rules were;

(1). Hold a piece of wood in the right hand every morning for two minutes. (2). Do not look at the shrines of other religions. (3). Do not consume bread on Tuesday. (4). Do not eat honey on Tuesday. (5). Never enter others' shrine and do not allow any person of other religions into our shrine. (6). Do not read scriptures of other religions; kill them if they don't convert. (7). Do not use the color they use in their prayers. (8). Convert everyone to our religion. (9). Never get converted; accept death instead. (10). If any member of our religion gets converted do not allow him/her to return to our religion.

Some of the customs though not mentioned in their scriptures were being practiced in their society. Such as; (1) Women are considered unholy and therefore no religious priest should touch them. (2). Women should not see His Holiness Prophet-Diwar alone. (3). Women should not perform any religious ceremonies. (4). Women cannot become high priests. (5). No one should touch any Diwar-Devote because their sinful master has kept a woman in his monastery. (6). All Non-Prophet-Diwarians are untouchables. (7). Converting them is saving them from falling into hell. (8). If they don't get converted kill them, physically exterminate and destroy them. (9). Kill three Non-Prophet-Diwarians and in return you shall be granted heaven. (10). The more you kill, the higher the reward you will get in heaven.

He was; very angry, full of passion, bold and only wanted 'yes' to any of his questions. Converting people of other religions to Prophet-Diwar religion became one of the central focus points for all of his followers. They were made to believe that if they convert ten people to the Prophet-Diwar religion they would achieve heaven. If they married girls of other religions for the sake of bringing at least five Prophet-Diwar children into this world then they would go to heaven. At the time of death Diwaree himself shall come to the door to welcome them. Diwaree shall embrace them and put them in a safe place.

Their scriptures had another 'diktat' to the effect that if a person was not willing to convert to the Prophet-Diwar religion, then he must be considered a disciple of the devil. To kill such a devil's disciple was another way to achieve heaven. Anyone who would kill more than twenty-five of such devilish brutes will go to an especially reserved section of heaven. Diwaree will welcome him with a big hug and smile on his face saying 'my blessed child you have been a worthy descendant.'

Further he declared that; those who got converted to the Prophet-Diwar religion were in safe hands. Converting them is as good as making them humans from beasts. Every follower of the Prophet-Diwar religion must therefore make at least one human being out of a beast, by converting them to our glorious religion in his or her life time.

He said, "One of the easiest ways to convert non-believers is to get married to their daughters; once you bring them into your home, in a purification ceremony she should be pronounced as a member of our religion. In the oath ceremony she herself should declare that, *of her free will and wish she is leaving the evil religion of her parents. She shall never again believe in that religion. With her husband she shall live according to Prophet-Diwar's rules, and she shall die while following this religion.* After making the commitment, eventually her last rite, which is another important ceremony, should be performed by our priest and she shall be sent to Prophet-Diwar's paradise. Another good thing was that all the children she might have produced would naturally be followers of the Prophet-Diwar religion. That girl would be as good as a fertilized field. That fertilized field would be good for increasing our members. All the credit would go to that boy who had changed that beast into a human. Family planning and abortion is a sin so keep increasing the members of this religion."

Some rich generous members had made a commitment for $5000 per case of such conversion. That mean't any boy who would marry a non-believer and brought her into the religion would be rewarded as a good man and thus receive $ 5000 from the fund right after marriage.

The girls of Prophet-Diwar religion were not allowed to marry the boys of other religions. In certain cases it was allowed with a strict condition. The condition was that the boy must leave his father's religion by taking a dip in the well of their shrine, and then in the oath ceremony he must proclaim that he was accepting the Prophet-Diwar religion. Four times publicly he must utter this sentence. *"My evil parent's evil religion was evil, I therefore quit that evil religion and now onwards holy Prophet-Diwar is my religion. After my death, I shall go the Prophet-Diwar's home – the absolute paradise.* After uttering this sentence four times, he would be given a permanent mark on the skin of his right hand and a new uniform that with all the signs of the Prophet-Diwar religion.

In the beginning, they were very flexible. All those additional rules were added only after getting money from Pattiwala's son-in-law, because many devotees were not satisfied with too much flexibility. They needed something more which could keep their monkey-minds busy. Everyday, they wanted to do something new to feel closer to His Holiness Prophetdiwaar. Fasting, looking up, looking down, making loud noises, eating holy bread, eating holy food, drinking blessed milk, drinking blessed soup, raising the right leg in the morning, raising the right hand in the evening, wearing green and purple clothes, walking in the street with a photo of Prophet-Diwar and so on...

They felt contented knowing that they were doing something for Prophet-Diwar. H.H. Prophet-Diwar made all those changes, which rich donors instructed him to do. The clever son-in-law insisted on bringing many changes to Prophet-Diwar religion so that each and every follower could contribute the maximum. He learned, from his former father-in-law, that as long as the followers were mystified with some mumbo-jumbo they would keep donating money.

With the advice of his main supporter His Holiness Prophet-Diwar added a new holy chapter to his religion, which was dedicated to the destruction of shrines. Any shrine that belonged to the devil religion must be destroyed. The new chapter said; "If you destroy one shrine of the devil's religion then you will get a brand new home in heaven. They must be forced to bring down all their shrines themselves, and if they don't do it themselves then kill them, and do the job yourself. If you destroy one shrine you will get one home, and if you destroy five shrines then you will be rewarded as a supreme devotee of the supreme Lord Master Diwaree. If you destroy all the shrines of a particular area then you will be crowned as a king of that much area in heaven.

After destroying their shrines, if you erect a Prophet-Diwar shrine at that place and afterwards if the converted people start praying at that shrine then you will get the highest reward. If you cannot erect our shrine at the spot where you destroy devil's shrine, then build it as close as you can.

The second part of that chapter said: If you want to have peace on earth you must destroy all the evil ones and their shrines. You must eradicate them completely and their shrines to establish peace at the root. Each and every seed of the devil must be rooted out from the earth; this is the way you can serve God Diwaree.

Prophet-Diwar's scripture was full of words like; kill, extinguish, electrocute, butcher, massacre, murder, slaughter, fast slaughter, slow slaughter, goat-meat, lamb-meat, animal-meat, fish-meat, blood, animal skin, animal blood, sea food, devil blood, and so on. The main purpose of all these rules was 'peace'.

Brotherhood was another teaching of Prophet-Diwar. In order to better serve all the followers of this religion they must always remain united by eating together, praying together and gaining political power by casting votes for our religion's candidate. Whoever puts more efforts into uniting brothers and sisters, he shall be rewarded in heaven. You need unity to fight with devils. To fight with mean people you have to come down to their level, but do it. There is no God but Prophet-Diwar. All other religions are evil and deserve destruction for the sake of peace on earth.

****

No religion ever grew without money, regardless of being good or bad, so the son-in-law's money came in handy in this cause. When the Diwar-Devote religion became a multi-million dollar project, and their main founder, Mr. Pattiwala, was praised in public especially in his community, and people were considering him the inspiring symbol of dedication, his son-in-law could not take it anymore. He was already disturbed since the day of his divorce. He was more of a businessman and less of a religious acolyte. He knew very well that religion was just a game of money in the hands of business people. Cunning people were above the laws of this world. Legal actions did not help him in his divorce trial, and he got defeated by the power of money. After that, he had the idea of bringing down his father-in-law's reputation. He thought of propagating a new religion and making that more popular and more spectacular with a bigger shrine than that of the Diwar-Devote religion.

The enthusiastic son-in-law's aggressiveness had suddenly and miraculously opened doors for H.H. Prophet-Diwar. Prophet-Diwar's luck turned into supernatural brightness when he went to His Holiness Prophet-Diwar, and told him the complete story of how Pattiwala had destroyed his life, how bad he was, how he was only pretending to be holy under Diwar-Devote's religious umbrella, how Monica was misguided by Pattiwala, and eventually taken away from him with half his assets. He said, "I have even been deprived of the right to visit my children. They won the case by giving a bribe of couple of hundred thousand bucks to the judge. The bribed money was distributed among the judge and four others. Right after the case, the judge built a big house in the heart of the city. Everybody knows that a judge doesn't get enough salary to build a palace-like house. Though there were many other lawmakers who have huge properties and very little salary, but their property didn't grow overnight like Pattiwala's judge. Michael Pattiwala has committed many sins to become a millionaire. I will tell you all his weak points, he is as bad as Diwar-Devote...," thus he exposed all his former father-in-law's weak points to Prophetdiwaar.

The son-in-law handed over Pattiwala's destructive key to Prophet-Diwar with his bank name and account number, which revealed Diwar-Devote's reality as well. Prophet-Diwar was extremely happy to find the key to destroy his competitor's backbone. For him, it was a good and powerful weapon to destroy an immoral man. The son-in-law was originally a believer of Diwaree. But after his divorce when he was left with nothing but millions of dollars his restless mind couldn't remain calm. H.H. Diwar-Devote had been hoping that after the divorce he would join his mission. He knew that his family life was destroyed and he needed to rest under the shade of any religious tree. Like every opportunist he had been trying to win him over by using the powerful Peace-Providing-Philosophy, also known as Triple P. The three rules of Triple P were; (1) you are there where you are, you are not there where you are not. don't think of money while praying if you want see God, nobody could stop thinking of money while praying, so nobody could see God, (2) don't get disturbed by the most terrible of situations - nobody could remain calm in a terrible situation, and (3) the third rule was a little funny and it was not told openly in public.

Successful politicians or rich men were like jewels for religious opportunists. The world will follow a useless saint if he is accepted by a famous wealthy film star or the President. Therefore whenever the son-in-law went to visit any shrine, the head priest of that shrine came himself to greet him and then praised him in public. The son in-law knew the reason why these people were treating him as a special person. He knew that their target was his money, but he had already made up his mind to be with the one who would provide peace to his agitated mind, which was possible only by gaining a larger reputation than Pattiwala and by marrying a better woman then his daughter. Prophet-Diwar immediately understood his hunger and how to satisfy him.

Though, the son-in-law knew that H.H. Diwar-Devote was better than Prophet-Diwar, as Diwar-Devote had actually lived with the Great Master, and the Great Master had touched him and he had partaken of the left-over food from Diwaree's plate. All these things really matter and made a person exceptionally holy, but "...father-in-law ... sinner and idiot...he had to be taught a lesson," he murmured.

After much thinking he decided to join the mission of His Holiness Prophet-Diwar. In one go, he donated a million dollars and soon the news spread all around. Many people had already been considering donating to H.H. Prophet-Diwar. They all donated good amounts according to their financial standing. In one fund raising drive, they collected a good fortune.

The son-in-law's donation and dedication made Prophet-Diwaree's mission grow at a rapid pace. They got free land from the government, as the papers were prepared by experts to withdraw money from government's cultural fund along with the grant of a huge peace of land. In just about eighteen months it acquired near parity with H.H. Diwar-Devote's monastery. This was how these two religions became powerful and thousands and thousands of people became their followers, but unfortunately most of their followers did not know the truth nor were they interested in knowing it. They were happy as long as the religion was growing fast.

****

Step Seventeen

SACKCLOTH RELIGION

My goodness! Yet another religion! Photographs of some members of a new religious sect, attired in sack clothes, appeared on the TV screens and leading magazines. It had started from the Banyan Island with profound principles of life which could easily spread all over the world. The people of the Banyan Island had no religion. Everyone had a strong desire to establish something in the name of the Almighty, which would make people afraid of committing sin.

By nature the human being is a social being. Not only human beings but animal, birds and even ants prefer to live in a group. Living in a group was natural, but from time to time problems kept arising among them, because some married boys were not understanding husband's responsibilities and so on... To control the unnecessary man made problems they established religious or social laws. In history many kings were considered as God's chosen ones through whom God would judge and punish a law breaking member of society.

When a few expert people started figuring out the principles of natural justice and common precepts of human behavior, and human law, in order to establish morality, education and nature's law for husband and wife and children, everyone started loving these logical rules. Those rules were established in the name of an all powerful God Almighty; who gives birth to everyone, decides the fate of everyone, and eventually kills everyone. After dying, the final judgment is pronounced by the Supreme Judge, King of Kings, Emperor of all Emperors – the God whose law governs the universe - and consequently they would receive heaven or hell according to the Judgment.

On Banyan Island they had no scripture and no idea how to start one. They had no prophet or saint. The educated people there read the books of Prophet-Diwar and Diwar-Devote, and learned that these religions were established by leaders who themselves claimed to be the power-holders at the behest of God himself.

They found a good ascetic minded man with a stoical disposition, who started teaching everyone wonderful and touching ideas in the name of God. Everyone believed that he would definitely lead his followers to perfection because he was not a money minded man. He started teaching them morality, and harmless concepts, non-violence, helping others and praying.

His slogan was 'Shatter the fetters of ignorance that spreads poison all around'. Because of his complete dedication and sincerity people believed in him strongly. The only problem was that the religion didn't grow fast for lack of financial resources. Consequently, they started criticizing the achievements of wealthy Diwar-Devotees and Prophet-Diwarians who had big buildings, but no morality, and no principles of life. They found themselves much more innocent and kind-hearted than others. Their faith and way of life was loved by everyone on Banyan Island. However, they claimed to be holy and close to the Great Master Diwaree. The Vairaagee started wearing sackcloth; so the religion was named the "Sackcloth religion".

The head of the religion was known as 'His Holiness Sackcloth' (H. H. Sackcloth) and the followers were known as Sackclothians. 'Sackclothians' published a book titled "Divine Sackclothians". H.H. Sackcloth insisted that they should not use his name because a true servant should use only God's (Master) name. The Master's name was too holy therefore it should not be pronounced with an unwashed mouth nor it should be uttered at dirty places, and while walking with bad people. Women should never utter the holy name.

Though, they had other books, their philosophies did not agree with each other, therefore, with the permission of their high priest they made a bonfire of all the books. The seven rules of their religion were:

1. Unholy Women: Woman is the seed of sins. Monk and priests should never touch them. All others should refrain from touching women on auspicious days, especially, on Diwaree's birthday. Diwaree was a celibate saint, his life was his message. One should observe the rules of celibacy in order to understand Him. By touching women man becomes unholy, like the devil. By touching women a person becomes untouchable. If, by mistake you've touched any, then you should take fifteen baths and fast for three days. The proper repentance is a must for purification. However, in politics women were allowed to vote and their vote was as good as a man's vote.

2. Priest Uniform: Priests must use a long sackcloth gown that must reach below his knees and he must not keep more than two gowns. He must not have more than one pair of shoes and he must not touch money. He must not drink hot water. He must not eat rice on Sundays. He must not eat with a copper spoon.

3. Devotee Uniform: All men should keep long beards and a brown cloth on their head or around the neck. They must wear an unstitched cap, a turban of sack cloth. Never use yellow clothes as the color yellow is a sign of ignorance. Apply pyre-ash on the left-hand everyday after taking the morning bath. Do not eat or drink anything without applying pyre ash on the left hand. Do not drink rain water. The moustache and beard should be equal in size.

4. Food: Remain a vegetarian. Eating meat is not forbidden if that is blessed by a priest, and as long as you have not seen anyone killing the animal, and you presume that the animal died naturally. However, all sin goes to the butcher. The butcher's sinful money can be purified if he keeps donating ten percent out of his net profit. The Butcher can charge that ten percent to his clients. Do not eat tomatoes, turmeric, bananas and don't drink alcohol on Thursday. Do not eat food from midnight to six a.m. Do not use a razor blade or knife at prayer time. Do not brush the teeth on Monday morning.

5. Untouchable Non-believers: Do not touch any non-believer (Diwar-Devotees and Prophet-Diwarians). If you touch any non-believer, fast for three days.

6.   Strictness: There is only one God and that is Diwaree. Diwaree can only be understood by following the Sackcloth religion.

7.   Prayers and Confession - for His forgiveness: any sin is forgivable, as long as you pray four times daily. If you confess, then there will be no Judge between you and heaven.

They added many interesting things to attract everyone's interest, such as; at the end of your life Diwaree will come to you and if that time you recognize him you will go to heaven but if you fail then you will go to hell. To recognize him at that time you have to follow the above seven rules. A few more rules were added later on. Most of those rules were just the opposite of the other two religions, such as; if they eat with right hand then we must eat with left, if others drink cold water then we must drink hot, if others leave a little hair on a particular area of their head then we must shave off that particular area, if others grow moustaches then we must shave off ours, if other's scriptures were written from left to right then ours must be from right to left, if others write from top to bottom then we must start writing in the opposite direction.

The people of the Sackcloth religion didn't perform idol worship. According to their scriptures worshipping idols was foolishness. The omnipresent Diwaree's divine presence was not limited to photos or idols. All the followers of Sackcloth must refrain from worshipping idols and refrain from worshipping statues.

However, they had somehow somewhere kept a photograph of Diwaree. At any difficult moment in life, they couldn't just stand in front of nothing. Therefore, they had many things inside their houses and outside; including their shrine's photo which kept reminding them of their God Diwaree. At difficult times, they knelt down before that photo. They couldn't keep a stone idol of Diwaree in their shrine as it was strictly forbidden. Gossiping or criticizing was not forbidden in their religion. Their scripture criticized the other two groups as much as they could. Criticizing the other two religion's leaders, one day, H.H. Sackcloth openly said to his congregation,

"Diwaree himself never worshipped any idol. Anything which was not done by our great master, no Diwaree respecting person should have courage to start such foolishness. Worshipping idols is foolish. It is the real proof that Diwar-Devote and Prophet-Diwaree are fools. A fool cannot do wise things. They are all ignorant. They are living beings with no vision, and they have no understanding. These foolish and selfish people should not do anything they want. They have to understand what our great Master was doing, and what kind of shrine he built, what kind of bedroom or house he had, what brand of car he was driving, what sort of life style he was living, which brand of TV, furniture, internet, and lavish style he was having. They have to understand; what kind of gold necklace with diamond pendant he was wearing, what kind of food he was eating and so on... They have to understand these realities about him. As you all know; Diwaree never built big buildings like H.H. Diwar-Devote and H.H. Prophet-Diwar, he did not occupy fifteen acres of land like them, he did not undertake frequent fund raising drives, and he did not have Rolls Royce cars and did not fly by airplanes.

Diwaree never kept any ladies like H. H. Diwar-Devote. Diwaree did not have five illegal wives like H. H. Prophet-Diwar, which he hides from the public but he cannot hide it from the Divine Master. The Great Master knows everything. They are not real devotees of the Great Master Diwaree. The things they tell the public; that they've got special instructions from Diwaree - that is absolute bunkum. Diwaree never played those games in the name of the Almighty. How can those dirty people call themselves 'God men' or His Holiness? They are leading everyone into the darkness. Therefore, they are anti-religious. They are opposing the reality. They both must be thrown into a well and that well must be filled with stones so that their games should end with their lives.

Diwar-Devote and Prophet-Diwaree are the most ignorant people in the world, who do not even know what is right. Who could be more ignorant than those who worship a statue and pretend that the statue is Diwaree? Can they not really understand that a statue is simply a statue? A statue cannot be God? In their love of money and a life of ease, their minds have completely forgotten the Almighty God." thus His Holiness Sackcloth concluded his speech.

*****

Step Eighteen...

FAITH IN OWN'S OWN RELIGION ONLY

If there are different restaurants in a city, everyone will have an opportunity to choose the food that is most suited to his taste and requirement.

But, how will one know if they cook unhealthy food? The people of all these religions had faith in only their own scriptures and way of living. All of them claimed that their scriptures were written by some unknown, yet unusually gifted person drawing inspiration from the Divine Master Diwaree.

The author of Prophet-Diwaree's religious scriptures was murdered, so that no one could claim authorship and thus His Holiness could claim that the book was thrown down directly from heaven by the late Diwaree's soul. He told everyone that he saw the book flying all the way from heaven to earth where eventually it came unto his hands. This was a very powerful statement from His Holiness Prophet-Diwar, which everybody believed.

His Holiness Prophet-Diwar declared, "Diwaree's book is the living form of Diwaree. Though Diwaree is no more with us, but he shall continue communicating with his devotees through this book. This book will inspire those who are really dedicated to the Great Master Diwaree. Whenever the devotees need guidance, Diwaree will guide them through this powerful book. Everyone must have this book at home and teach its facts to the children. All followers must light a candle next to this book and then pray to the Great Master Diwaree and this powerful book will listen to their prayers, and convey their messages to the Great Master."

The Diwar-Devotes and Sackclothians had more or less similar stories about their scriptures. Whenever they got confused they would open their religious book, pointing with their index finger at a specific verse related to that problem. They would say; *'Oh look here! Read it. It is written here. When someone went to Diwaree with a similar problem he found the solution and Diwaree replied through this holy verse.'*

In their scriptures they could find anything they wanted. Their scriptures approved all their actions; including their way of dressing, their food, and their thoughts. However all the hidden things they did, without anybody's knowledge, were not even imagined by their scriptures. That was the reason a follower had to be really careful about those hidden things especially the poor followers. It seemed that those scriptures were not aware of their hidden actions, otherwise why would they (the scriptures) guarantee them heaven?

On the one hand their scriptures supported all their actions and on the other hand it did not support the actions of the other two religions. On the contrary, the scriptures told them that the followers of the other two religions were condemned and would not find the door of heaven.

If any of their actions were not confirmed by their scriptures then their priests would help them by giving a favorable interpretation. The priests would provide proofs to support a generous follower's viewpoint. Anyone who followed their way of life was perfect for heaven. Confession was the ultimate option available to the followers.

Many things were quite similar in everyone's scriptures, such as; God is Omnipotent, Omnipresent, Almighty, Deus, Divine, All Knowing, the Supreme being, Creator, Master of the universe, Sustaining power, Organizer, Food-giver, Compassionate, Good-hearted, Forgiving, Pitying, Sympathetic, and Kind. Everyone's scripture said that God listens to our prayers. Further, these scriptures said; God loves Devotion, Faith, Dedication, Commitment, Loyalty, Truthfulness, Kindness, Righteousness, Ethicality, Religiousness, Holiness, Sanctity, Sacredness, Purity, Chastity etc.
Everyone visited his or her own shrine once a week or whenever they felt like it. Attendance at the shrines varied according to the taste of the free

food, marriage opportunities, business opportunities, friendship opportunities, and opportunities for the jobless, the beauty of the participating women or girls, free gifts, free enjoyment and quality of music and quality of prayers etc. Some completely broken hearted people also used to go there to pray but they were just a few.

Common fears dominated them. All of them were afraid of Death. All of them were afraid of Destruction, Ruin, Devastation, Loss, Sickness, Disease and loosing their loved ones. To avoid all those miseries they would perform many rituals including mass prayers. They sought Happiness through religion. All of them wanted to do something good for God before death. All were curious to know their destiny while they were still alive. All of them wanted to find God. They loved God. All of them wanted to have peace in life. Peace could be generated with God's blessings. All were confused about death but everyone hid that confusion. All they wanted was to live a fearless life with love and every need fulfilled. They all wanted more and more money. They all had a desire to invent exciting good facts about their own religions, which they believed could be found only in their scriptures. They all wanted to hide the awful bits and pieces of their own religions. They all wanted to have a good love life and respect. But there were also many differences in their religion. They were;

REINCARNATION:
1. **Diwar-Devote:** Rebirth will take place right after death.
2. **Prophet-Diwar:** Death is final till the Day of resurrection of Prophet-Diwar, which would take place at the end of the world.
3. **Sackcloth:** Death and rebirth is in the hand of His Holiness Sackcloth (Diwaree).

CONVERSION:
1. **Diwar-Devote:** Do not convert; God will bring them into our religion through birth, if they deserve it.
2. **Prophet-Diwar:** Convert non-believers so that they can be saved. If they do not convert kill them on the spot. Do not kill their wives and daughters use them for progeny or as slaves instead.
3. **Sackcloth:** Do not convert unholy people to this holy religion.

SACRIFICES FOR HEAVEN:
1. **Diwar-Devote:** Die to save others and thus achieve heaven.
2. **Prophet-Diwar:** For religion die to kill others such as; suicide bombing and achieve heaven.
3. **Sackcloth:** Leave both up to Diwaree God. Become good and achieve heaven.

REVENGE:
1. **Diwar-Devote:** An eye for an eye; God is too busy He has no time for little things. Let us do God's job, which is why we are here.
2. **Prophet-Diwar:** Two eyes for one eye. Teach them a proper lesson so that others may learn.
3. **Sackcloth:** Nothing for one eye; let God handle it. He is the only Judge. Let a sinner commit more sins so that he will suffer more and eventually he will understand God.

PUNISHMENT:
1. **Diwar-Devote:** If your right eye offend you, forgive it, for there is a chapter on forgiveness in life, and with your attitude learn to be kind.
2. **Prophet-Diwar:** If your right eye offend you, pluck it out, and cast it from you, for it will be profitable for you that one of your members has perished, rather than your whole body be cast into hell.
3. **Sackcloth:** If your right eye offend you, bear it, accept it as a gift from God and keep it with you, for it will make you suffer and you will learn to be good.

DOER;
1. **Diwar-Devote:** God does good things only.
2. **Prophet-Diwar:** God does good things, and the evil one or non-believer does bad things.
3. **Sackcloth:** God does not do anything except granting the consequences of Karma. It is man who does all good or bad things and pays the consequences.

****

Though the Sackcloth religion was established with good intentions, yet it approached the verge of extinction. A few thousand years ago there was a similar religion with similar principles that spread all over the world. Today, we can still see evidence of their huge mountain-like monuments. That religion was financed by an enormously wealthy and dedicated king. Sackcloth religion was almost dying. Unfortunately, no one was coming forward to help and propagate the religion. Although, some followers had enough money, they were scared to donate it to a dying religion as they might become poor like any other poor follower. Their 'fear' of being gripped by poverty did not allow them to donate to a vanishing religion.

Every follower blamed H.H. Sackcloth saying; "H.H. Sackcloth was absolutely wrong, otherwise, today Sackcloth would be far ahead of the other two religions. He had a big ego. He had a fatalistic attitude, no initiative and always waited for things to happen. He never swam to the boat instead he waited for the boat to come to him. He was not liberal. He was inflexible from the very beginning. He didn't listen to us. He was trying to become a renounced saint, but his style did not impress rich donors. No music, strict celibacy, no meat, no air-conditioning, no radio, no TV, no luxuries - too much orthodoxy. Who was going to be attracted with those foolish beliefs? Why could he not understand a donor's expectations? Why could he not make himself humble in front of donors? Why could he not learn from Diwar-Devote and Prophet-Diwar how to praise donors in public and why didn't he learn how to treat and admire rich politicians? He never appeared in public with humility and with folded hands like Diwar-Devote and Prophet-Diwar. Why could he not understand that without money a religion could die? He was not willing to do things like others. He was concerned about spiritualism only. He was against institutionalizing religion. He didn't have any business acumen. He was not a good organizer. This religion couldn't grow, because of him. ..."

Many people even said that due to the curse of Diwaree, this religion would never flourish. The curse existed because some priests had touched the untouchables. Those untouchables were unholy, ungodly, impious, condemned, and atheists. That ungodliness spread among their people like a contagious disease. Another fault was that one day a devotee brought a statue of Diwaree into our shrine. From that day, this holy shrine became impure. Diwaree's curse had ended this religion. The accusers had many things to say.

However, H.H. Sackcloth hated H.H. Diwar-Devote because he had kept a woman in his monastery as his secretary. H.H. Sackcloth said, "That lady is pretty therefore more people are attracted to his monastery. He has a bad practice of keeping mostly female disciples in his monastery. All those female disciples are quite good-looking and well trained. It's bad to attract donors by using that method. He is treating rich donors like God. He provides free food and entertainment for people. His shrine is not a religious place but a social club."

H.H. Sackcloth believed that Michael Pattiwala's friend gave enormous money to that cult only because of the pretty Maya. However, Diwar-Devote and his followers could not go to heaven. There was not enough room left in heaven. Only a few chosen ones could enter. They were depositing their hard earned money in a bank, which would be liquidated soon. They were investing in a company which was going to file for bankruptcy soon. They were working tirelessly on a building which was going to fall down in the near future. A diamond is bought by only a few but crystal is bought by many, and when everybody goes to the jeweler to sell their diamonds the fools would get nothing. They thought they had a diamond but in fact they had crystal. Eventually the fools would hit their foreheads with their palms and say, *"Oh God what have we done?"*

H.H. Sackcloth said, "Dear devotees you have to be careful because these days on this island there are many missionaries on the prowl to convert our innocent kids to their religion. They will do anything because their well-paid high priest has led them to believe that by converting our kids they will go to heaven. We, decent people, don't believe in conversion. Anyone who has been chosen by God will be born into this faith, in other words, good souls who deserve heaven will be brought here by God. This is not a self-choice but God's decision. No one else, in this world, but we Sackclothians are God's chosen ones, and the others are unable to understand the high philosophy of coming into a religion by birth. Therefore, be careful of those missionaries.

You know, Diwaree never wore any yellow or white dress but people who do the wrong thing cannot realize their own faults. All the people who are initiated by the fake men of Diwar-Devote or Prophet-Diwaree will get nothing but everlasting hell. They wear silk and the best ironed clothes. Maya has a BMW 745 Series and all the facilities of a common businessman's wife. They don't believe in spirituality, they believe only in pleasure, lust and luxury. They cannot go to heaven. Never...! Immoral Prophet-Diwar has five women in his life. How could an immoral man be a preacher? How can those dirty spiritual leaders go to heaven and lead their followers to heaven?" thus he explained.

Sackclothians had plenty of land with vast natural resources. Their innocent minds could not appreciate the value of what nature had gifted them. The followers of Diwar-Devote and Prophet-Diwaree were sent there to grab all the valuable things such as, gold, silver, diamonds, and other precious minerals. Eventually, Prophet-Diwaree's people tried to convert them to their religion by playing games. On Banyan Island, due to their geographical isolation, all the people had a similar appearance but three non-matching religions because they were converted by outsiders who came there from different parts of the world. There were many sad stories about the innocent victims of Banyan Island. Anyone who studied the pages of their history was stunned that such a terrible thing could happen. Don't you ever dare to open the pages of their history.

Banyan Island was governed by the people of Diwar-Devote and Prophet-Diwar. The original people of the island were used as slaves and worked for the Diwar-Devotees and Prophet-Diwarians for many many years.

H.H. Sackcloth had a small following, but some of them were aggressive and willing to do anything for Him. They were much more aggressive than those 'edicts' emanating from the H.H. Diwar-Devote or Prophet-Diwaree religions, but the problem was that they were not rich enough or else they would have taken their religion above the others. Some followers, who had too much money, had their own philosophy of charity and they had more than enough evidence to accuse H.H.

Sackcloth. They knew how to pray, what to read in the scriptures, but they did not believe in H.H.

H.H. Sackcloth was very unhappy because of the financial resources of the other religions. He was humiliated by people who blamed him for the moribund state of his religion, and also for allowing only boys to stay in the monastery. This last fact gave rise to malicious innuendos. Eventually, he became disgusted with all the criticism. One evening he said to his followers, "I am going to jump into the well because the government is not providing us with any facilities. They are providing all the facilities to H.H. Diwar-Devote and H.H. Prophet-Diwar. I am not happy with this government. I want to tell future generations that immoral people flourish in this world and good people have to commit suicide. I want to make history, so if I commit suicide, who will come with me?" Everyone present there responded in one voice, 'I', 'me' 'all of us'.

His Holiness Sackcloth thought carefully. If everyone died, then no one would remain behind to create havoc and the competitor's path would be clear. Most of the media belonged to Diwar-Devote and Prophet-Diwar and they would conceal the news of our sacrifice and with our death their dream will come true. The public will not notice my sacrifice, and then what would be the use of jumping into the well? He dropped the idea.

The human race was divided into three religions and three categories, i.e.: 1. Rich class, 2. Middle class, and 3. Poor class. The three religions were: 1. Diwar-Devote 2. Prophet-Diwar, and 3. Sackcloth. There were also many other man-made sub divisions, as the human brain was good at making the things more and more complicated. Through those divisions a poisonous hate spread rapidly.

One day a student named Pintu said to H.H. Prophet-Diwar, "Yesterday my school friend and I attended H.H. Diwar-Devote's discourse. I listened to his preaching. Everything he said was the same as what you tell us. Such as: his religion is the best in the world, the followers of his religion have the best minds to think about God, only his followers will go to heaven, followers of the other two religions (Sackcloth and Prophet-Diwaree) will go to hell. H.H. Diwar-Devote's words were,

"Devotees, just see the facts for yourselves. I am the only person who used to live with our Divine Master Diwaree. I have consumed the left over from his plate. I have walked with him, followed his footprints. I have had conversations with him. Therefore, I know what Diwaree wants and what he doesn't. I am the only person who has heard his wisdom directly from his mouth. I know what a devotee should do and should not. Therefore, only those who are initiated by me will go to heaven and all members of Prophet-Diwaree and Sackcloth's religions will go to hell. They are non-believers. Since, they have not lived with Diwaree; they don't know what is wrong and what is right. They are a jealous people who worship a fake God. They are ignorant fools, nincompoops and blind. On the other hand, we are spiritual, righteous, virtuous, holy, and blessed by the Great Master. Therefore, we are the only worshippers of the true God."

'H.H. Prophet-Diwar listened to the whole story from the student and just muttered, "Aahaa!! ... ... Uuuuuuuum." The whole night H.H. Prophet-Diwar kept thinking about what to do. The next day instead of preaching on spirituality, he said in his discourse, "Dear holy devotees of Diwaree, as you already know, I am the only one and the last incarnation of Diwaree to whom Diwaree has given his book from heaven. This world does not need more than one true prophet. Except for me there has never been and never will be in the future another. Therefore, be careful never listen to the devils. Devils! I mean the living devils. Never sit with them. Stay away from the evils, which harm your faith. Destroy them, who destroy your faith. They destroy your faith, your spiritual treasure. They will lead you nowhere. They are born to spread blasphemy. Do not even step on the ground where they have stood. Do not ever eat the food, which has been touched by them.

- Love God and hate devils.
- Help believers and destroy non-believers.
- Love good people and hate bad people."

"Esteemed Your Holiness Prophet-Diwar, please enlighten us by explaining; who are the good people, and who are bad?" asked a curious student, from the middle of the congregation.

"Good people are those who are members of our religion, and bad people are those who follow any of those two evil religions," answered Prophet-Diwaree. Then, after taking a sip of water, he continued further;

"Also do not listen to those, who listen to them. Stay away from those who enter their shrines. Those who enter their shrines even by mistake become unholy. Do not have any friendship with the person who has friendship with them. Do not touch them. Whoever will touch them even by mistake will become unholy. Anyone who gets involved with their sons or daughters cast him or her out of our society. Do not allow him or her to come back into our religion and do not invite that person to any occasion unless their partner gets converted to our religion. Consider them sinners and destroyers of our religion, moral values, devotion, faith and destroyers of the essence of purity. Keep a distance from those brainless animals with big horns." After a pause he again continued, "Those who even cross a non-believer's shadow will become condemned and consequently heaven's door will be locked to them for good. A real Prophet-Diwarian is one who will never look at the shrine of a Sackcloth or Diwar-Devote. While walking and along the way, if you pass by these shrines you should close your eyes or cover your eyes with a napkin to make sure that their shrine is not seen. Those are the shrines of devils, the gates to miseries, tragedies, misfortune and hell on earth. Stay away from the living devils," concluded H.H. Prophet-Diwar.

Through the indirect instructions from rich and influencial politicians and businessmen the three His Holinesses' had brainwashed their followers and filled them with hate for others. Whenever they went into the depths of their religious history their minds would become filled with hatred for the other religion's cruel people.

****

Step Nineteen...

INTER-CASTE LOVE

"We love because it's the only true adventure."
... Nikki Giovanni

Inter-caste love was strictly forbidden by every religion except the Prophet-Diwaree and that too only for the purpose of conversion. However, with time, marriages between couples of different religions started becoming commonplace. That was forbidden because eventually most of them faced an upsetting challenge in their married lives, especially when they were unable to understand each other's worthless philosophy. To make that kind of marriage successful compromise and the blind acceptance of wrong concepts was needed, which was no small sacrifice.

Everyone knew that marriage is always a tough decision that could lead one to hell or heaven. There were many unanswered questions and plenty of confusion. But with inter-caste marriages a person's life changes, the life style changes and the destiny of this life as well the next life changes. After death, if they have a system of dumping their dead bodies into the waters yours too will be dumped there. If they follow a burial system yours too will be buried. If they cremate their dead bodies yours also will be cremated. If they feed it to the vultures yours also will be fed to the vultures. If they mummified their dead bodies yours also will be mummified.

In addition, you may have to go to their shrine (Church, Mosque, Synagogue or whatever) even if you do not wish to. Even if your parents have been insulted by those people you may have to pretend that you like their religion. Even if your father had told you some bad things about their religion, you may have to keep that secret to yourself. You may have to share the thoughts and strange customs of those people, which your parents couldn't even think about. And, eventually parents have to die, and after their deaths you may carry your guilt for making them suffer for turning your back on their religion. In future should you have a tragedy, you may feel that it was the curse of dead parents.

And, if you get married with them you still have to follow their customs because if you don't you can never have a perfect relationship or perfect understanding with them. You have to be extremely careful. It's not a joke. If things start going wrong, life may become more painful then death. The fact is that a person's own religion is his own way of life, and it is in perfect harmony with God and Godly precepts. In an inter-caste marriage the two religions - the two ways life - are bound to face conflicting situations. In the absence of goodwill and a liberal approach these conflicts assume gigantic proportions bringing ruin and disaster to the two protagonists and their supporting clans. Any mistakes may cause condemnation from the in-law's religion.

The people of all religions had many examples of bitter experiences, which they put in a picture to teach their kids from time to time... Some questions for them were; what will they think, looking at you at the time of the marriage ceremony? Will they respect you as an inventor of a bridge to connect two religions or blame you for destroying the faith? Will you be following their religious ceremony or yours? Or will you do it in a court following no faith, but the law of the government? Will you live without any faith or you will create your own faith?

Unfortunately or fortunately, in a high class modern school, two students fell in love. They had been nurturing their love for each other for a long time. Love is said to be blind so it was in their case. When cupid's arrow strikes home, there is no power on earth which can dissuade a youth to retrace his steps. Though their attitudes were shaped during their formative years but only God knew what went wrong, what mistake their parents had made, or from where they got the instinct to do such thing.

The parents of both had always been concerned for their future and had taught them about the principles of life through different examples, but no one knows what went wrong. Many people tried to make them understand but they turned deaf. They wanted to do what they wanted and that was that. Though, they were aware of some of the facts and consequences their minds were gripped by the invisible force or Love. Every moment became hard to pass without meeting each other. From morning till night they couldn't think of anything else except each other. Even at night they dreamed of each other.

The girl's name was Nilu and the boy's Pintu. Nilu belonged to the orthodox Diwar-Devote religion and Pintu belonged to the orthodox Prophet-Diwaree religion. They were intelligent, smart and sincere in school. Donating blood, doing volunteer work for charity, helping the homeless, offering their seats to elderly people on the bus, helping neighbors, helping others find proper schools or jobs and many other good things were natural to them. They not only felt the pain of others but they helped everyone. They won a couple of competitions. For a long time, they didn't tell to their parents about their love because of the fear that their parents would be shocked, which may have provoked undesired violent incidents between the two families and the two factions. Their attempts to change a piece of the world became extreme tough.

Their souls were great and so was their love. Their souls were powerful and so were their intentions. Their intentions were to erase many unwanted things from the world. They prepared themselves because they were confident that when something did go wrong they would know what to do to make it right again because they strongly believed in the power of the invisible Truth.

One day Pintu said to Nilu, "Nilu! Love is really God's greatest gift. It makes us feel as if this world is heaven or heaven is within us. Love transcends all human barriers of caste, color, creed, or religion." Then both bowed down on the earth and prayed *"Our true destiny, God, thank you for making us fall onto the path of Love. We couldn't find the meaning of life by ourselves. We find it with (thee) love. Thank you God, thank you."*

After sometime with tearful eyes again their conversation resumed, "Yes in other words we can say love is not blind - it has real vision to see more, not less. It has real vision to see the facts. Without love, life is like an unlighted candle. Love is life. If we miss it, we miss life. It makes life, it spurs dynamism and progress. Without love the world is like a neglected garden where no flowers bloom. It is power, it is knowledge, it is wisdom, it is pure, it is holy, it is creative and the giver's greatest miraculous gift to human beings," said Nilu.

> Love is a flame that burns in heaven, and whose soft reflections radiate to us. Two worlds are opened, two lives given to it. It is by love that we double our being: It is by love that we approach God.
>
> ...Aimee Martin

Their philosophy was; God is continuously weaving a net of relations to bring better understanding among human beings. He needs two interlacing tools to weave his net. He picks up one tool from the east and another from the west or from two different religions. Then his invisible hands start weaving the net. The extension of the net is a contribution to the beauty of this world. The higher the contribution the greater the struggle the tools will have to face. But don't worry, life is meant to contribute something to this beautiful world. Let God's invisible hands use us to add a new chapter in the scriptures of this world because without a new chapter those scriptures will remain incomplete. In future, the human being's mind may grow and then they will need better answers to satisfy their inquisitive minds. Our contributions will be the answer to some of the many questions.

The next day, Nilu said to Pintu, "You know, what my father will do if he finds out about our love for each other?"

"What?" Pintu asked in a fearful voice.

"He will shoot me," replied Nilu.

"Yes, my father will do the same, I know he will go crazy but... but I will try to make him understand by telling him, *"Daddy I have been dating her for a long long time and now if I leave, her curse will burn everything to ash. Think if that would have been your daughter what would you want?"* I know on the other hand that I cannot take parent's curse." said Pintu with wrinkles on his forehead.

"Then what should we do?" asked Nilu with curious look on her face.

"We should be strong enough to face this situation. Running away is not going to solve the problem. Not facing reality, being a coward or, running away from duty is not the solution. If they cannot understand then they have to learn the truth. They must learn that Love is the greatest manifestation of God," answered Pintu with firmness.

"My Father will be simply unable to imagine that. One day, he will be welcoming a marriage procession of the Prophet-Diwaree religion, while being watched by all of his people. He would rather die before hearing of it or shoot the person who conveyed the news to him," said Nilu.

"Well Nilu, he said it is written in his religious scriptures that Love is God and God is Love. And my father has said it many times. Let us see, whether they meant it or it was just hogwash," said Pintu.

"Pintu, it's irrelevant what they say, they simply cannot tolerate any contradiction to their customs. Their hearts are full of hate for the people of other religions; there is no room for love. Our hearts are full of love there is no room for hate. Love is sacrifice, love is commitment, love is promise, love is a pledge, love is responsibility, love is a covenant, and love is duty. Love is the destiny of the soul. Love is God. Therefore, it deserves worship. Love is pure, chaste, innocent, virtuous, and honest. Love is religion, one must die for it. It is not a sin and we have to tell it to them," said Nilu in a priestly look on her face.

"Nilu, I believe my parents know all this philosophy of love and hate, but when it comes to putting it into practice then things take a different hue. They have so many wonderful sayings in their religious note book. They have many musical hymns about humanity but when the time comes to live in accordance with those high principles the wisdom balloon goes up and they start fighting. I have to show them that if fighting is not

irreligious then this is also right. I know they are very God-fearing. They
follow all the rules of our religion. They also keep many fasts, prayers or
whatever the priest tells them from time to time. They love the seminars
in the prayer hall. They are very religious, but they shall have to learn
one thing from me if they are not to remain hidebound and dogmatic,"
said Pintu nodding head up and down.

"I will change my religion without my parents' permission. Then, I will
be accepted into your family and I shall prove myself a useful member of
society. The only problem is that my father will not leave me alive. I will
teach him a proper lesson. I will tell him that this is my life and my
decision. This is our time, not yours. Your time is over. You did
whatever you wanted in your time and we will do whatever we want in
ours, so you just shut your mouth and keep watching," Nilu said of her
plan.

"Anyway, after marriage the girl belongs to the husband's family. Your
family name will be changed to mine. Nature's law is that one of the two
rivers loses its own identity after merging together. Once you come to
me then you will have nothing to do with them," said Pintu.

Next day, she went to mother and said to her, "Mummy I have something
very special to tell you."

"What is that my child?" asked her mother lovingly.

"First you promise that you will not feel offended," said Nilu.

"I trust you will not do anything that will hurt my feelings. You are my
best child. You have much more understanding than any other's children.
I know that you understand your responsibilities very well and I am very
proud of you. Tell me what you want to say?" said the loving mother
making her feel comfortable.

"Mummy, you might get upset. Do you promise that you will not?" Nilu
asked again.

"Look at my gray hair. How much experience do you think I have of life? I have gone through your age. I can read your mind and the expressions on your face. For the last few days you seem to be lost. I am your mother, well wisher, and a friend too. A good friend. A loyal one. Now let me think..." after thinking a little the mother asked, "Do you have a boyfriend?"

"Yes mummy," answered Nilu.

"So what? There is nothing wrong with that. I can fully understand. This is the age to have a good person in your life and share your thoughts and get married, but tell me who is he?" asked the mother impatiently.

"It is difficult to tell you." said Nilu, again, her expression uncomfortable.

"You know that the mother is the best friend to her daughter till the day of her marriage. After marriage, her husband becomes her best friend, but a mother's heart always remains with her child. My mother passed away twenty five years ago and even now I feel that she is still with me. Since this is such union of eternal love she always inspires me. The mother and child's soul remains connected even after cutting the umbilical cord. Therefore, you should not hide anything from me. At this stage of uncertainty and confusion, you will get the right advice only from your mother. Do you trust me?" asked the mother.

"Yes, I do," replied Nilu.

"Then come on, tell me. Who is he?" asked Mother.

"He belongs to the Prophet-Diwar religion and we've got married in the court," eventually replied Nilu after taking a deep breath.

The mother looked upwards. Prophet-Diwaree...? Got married in the court...? Her eyes opened wide. A picture of the whole community started moving around her eyes. Nilu's father was moving around her mind performing a destructive dance. She almost fainted, and then controlled herself and after a few moments, said to Nilu, "It would have been much better if you were not born, or if you were dead after the birth. If your father comes to know about this he is going to murder the whole family. He cannot control himself when he finds something wrong, especially when it concerns his reputation in society. Religion is his life. What have you done to us Nilu...? What is this, what have you done to us, tell me," the mother cried hysterically. A mother's main concern was for her daughter's future. She knew people without family values faced hell. At this age her daughter was loved by a boy as an object of his appetite. As soon as his appetite was satisfied she would be cast away as people cast away a dry sucked lemon. She knew it, but who could make these foolish children understand? They were destroying their own lives. "God, what have you done to us?" again she cried pressing her forehead with both hands.

Frightened Nilu ran from there and went to Pintu and told him the whole story.

Pintu said, "Your mother is right about your father; that his reputation is his life and identity. He has practiced his religion throughout his life just to maintain respect.   Whatever reputation he has earned is based on his ethical practices. Now, when he learns that his daughter has destroyed his reputation, which he took a lifetime to earn, in one day, he would feel as if his entire world had crumbled down upon his head. Everyone has been respecting him because of his ethical precepts. His enemies will have sufficient spicy reason to not only insult him, but to also demolish his well built reputation. They will have a chance to spit on him with condemnation. Now, they will start gossiping that his daughter has run away with a Prophet-Diwarian boy. All these things are true, but we have to follow the intentions of our soul till the last breath."

"Those who mind do not matter, and our well wishers are those who are concerned about our happiness and they won't mind... Anyway, forget all that. Come to the main point, what should we do now?" was Nilu's question.

"One who knows how to deal with a difficult situation is wise. We will tell them to face the consequences of love and hate," said Pintu.

They both went to Nilu's home and sat together. Nilu's father was cross and gnashing his teeth at the fact that a Prophet-Diwarian boy was in his home with Nilu. He felt the same as his uncle, who had gunned down two of his daughters, their boyfriends and eventually shot himself. He asked Nilu to come into his room and asked her angrily, "Do you know who he is?"

"Daddy, he is a human being - a good friend of mine," replied Nilu.

"Good friend of yours? What do you mean? A boy who belongs to our enemy's family, a baby snake, a reptile, a python, a murderer, butcher, killer, and he is a good friend of yours? In my home? What the hell are you doing to meeee...? Leave this home or I will leave right away, right now, now..." he said, keeping his voice low.

"Daddy, please listen to me, calm down. You haven't heard what I was going to tell you," requested Nilu.

"I know what you are going to tell me. You are going to tell me that I should perform your holy wedding ceremony with this evil boy? This poisonous snake could become a part of our family? Isn't that what you are going to tell me?" replied the father in anger.

"No Daddy, do not misunderstand me. I did not mean to hurt your feelings. I respect you but please understand and let me explain it," again pleaded Nilu.

"What can you explain to me? Your mother has already explained everything. I have been waiting to see this horrible moment in my life? I have suffered enough raising you and look what you are doing to me in return? One bad child can destroy the hard earned reputation of many forefathers," lamented the father.

"Well, I am trying to make you understand, but daddy I know now you will not listen to me – I know," replied Nilu.

"I don't have enough understanding ability, perhaps only you kids are wiser. We all are foolish. Only you - the new generation; educated kids are wise. I don't want to hear anything. Now, either you leave this home or I leave. And right now...you leave or I am going to say goodbye," replied the father. He was about to step out.

Nilu bid goodbye to her parents and as she was leaving the house her father said to her, "Do not forget one thing, you can never have good luck in your life. May God give you the same pain you have given me. And remember, no one can escape the curse of the parents who brought you into this world. You shall never be happy."

Nilu was crying while leaving home. She went to her priest and asked him, "What can happen if we make our parents unhappy?

"Mother and father are givers of birth. God has sent you into this world through them, therefore, for you, they are like Gods. You cannot see God but you can see your parents and God has been feeding you through their hands. Those hands deserve respect. Respect them and listen to them. You owe them a lot. If you make them unhappy then misfortunes could be awaiting you - behind the curtain," was the answer of the Priest. She understood the priest's pronouncement, but since her mind was gripped by some unseen powerful force, she didn't know what to do.

In utter confusion Nilu started shaking with fear. Where to go? What to do? Which direction to move? The questions were many but the answers were hard to come by. She walked away with Pintu.

Nilu's mother came home from the market and made a cup of coffee for her husband and went to wake him up. She kept the cup of coffee on the table and said in a sweet voice. "Hello! Seems you are really in deep sleep, wake up, wake up please. Here I am with your coffee."

Getting no reply then she went closer to him and stroked his cheek. She felt a stiffness to his cheek, and he was not breathing. She screamed and ran out frightened. Her neighbor came out and asked, "What happened, what happened?

"Nilu's father ... ... is no more..." cried Nilu's mother.

"What do you mean?" asked the neighbor with wide opened eyes.
Everybody went into his bedroom and found him dead. He didn't die of a
massive heart attack; it was a case of 'mental combustion'.

The father was so attached to his children that he couldn't digest the bad
news about his daughter. No wonder people say that *Mother and Father
are the living form of God*, which sounds logical because they have
protected their children and taken care of them day and night like real
Gods. For the children they were as gardeners, but the terrible thing was
that the daughter completely forgot these things, though she had a feeling
that he might die of shock.

Nilu and Pintu heard of his death. Pintu decided to go and be with them
at this time of distress and adversity. When they reached the house the
body had been sent for postmortem. They got the death certificate from
the doctor and confirmation from the mortuary that his system was
abnormal, but was certified as a natural death. They arranged the funeral.
The body was disposed off according to the religious rites. Pintu
accompanied them every step of the way.

After the ceremonies everybody went home along with Pintu. Pintu was
then taken to the head of the village who was known as the Headman.
There were five other jurors. They tied Pintu's hands and legs. They
asked Nilu to stay at a distance. Not knowing what was going to happen;
Pintu was frightened to see the scary people of the Diwar-Devote
religion. They started questioning Pintu. Pintu prayed to God for help.
He thought only of speaking the truth and believed that God would
decide everything.

"What is your relationship with Nilu?" asked the Headman in a loud
voice.

"We are class fellows," replied Pintu with a fearful but brave look.

"We already know that. Apart from that?" questioned the headman.

"Apart from that we are good friends," answered Pintu.

"You are good friends, in what sense? Did you marry her in the court?" asked the headman.

"Yes," acknowledged Pintu with an honest attitude.

The headman said to other jurors, "Now bring Nilu." Two men went and brought her to the meeting. They asked her, "What is your relationship with this baby snake?"

Pintu said to Nilu, "Nilu speak the truth and only the truth. God will help us."

One man slapped Pintu's face in anger saying, "Who authorized you to open your mouth, you devil's child!"

"No you cannot hit him without the final decision of the judge and jurors," the headman said to the angry man pulling him back.

"Excuse me your honor, I apologize," the angry man apologized.

"Yes Nilu, what is your answer to my question?" asked the headman again with strong powerful voice.

"We intend to live together and fulfill our duties as husband and wife," replied Nilu with a truthful look ness on her face.

"Do you know what religion he belongs to? Which family he belongs to and what his people are?" asked the headman.

"Yes I know but I found nothing wrong with that. My heart is filled with Love and there is no room for Hate in it. We have to teach this generation the difference between love and hate, that love unites and hate separates, and God wants his children to unite," replied Nilu.

In anger the Headman turned towards Pintu, and said, "What should we do to you now? Do you know you are guilty of poisoning our religion? Do you know you have made her mother a widow?"

"Well, it is all up to you. I know I have broken your religious concepts but this is love, I could not help it. At this time I have to teach one thing; love is a God-made-reality and religion is a man made philosophy. Inter-caste marriages are not forbidden by God, because they are like a bridge which connects two stubborn groups. An inter-caste marriage is a bridge of peace. Inter-caste marriages are God's ways of uniting more and more of his children. My aim in life was just to teach this reality," stated Pintu.

Nobody could understand what he said, but everyone started murmuring and saying to each other; "This boy wants to teach. He is a fit case for awarding exemplary deterrent punishment. Our children must watch a horrifying lesson and learn from it. So, we will use this brat." Turning towards each other they asked for ideas and suggestions for meeting out an exemplary punishment. Finally, the headman pronounced his decision,

"First, his clothes shall be ripped off. He will be left completely naked. Then he will be tied with ropes. He will be hung on a tree upside down in a bow shape. His head will point downwards and toes will be tied-up with ropes. Then, with a burning torch his hair will be burned off first. Then a fire will be lighted at a distance of one yard right underneath his head. His skin must be burned off slowly. He should not die for ten minutes. After ten minutes he should be burned completely by fire. If anyone has any objections, he may raise his hand."

In anger everyone agreed with one voice saying, "Yes your honor this is right." This was the general verdict.

While listening to this judgment, Pintu urinated with fear. He was helpless. Nilu's hands and feet also were tied. She could not do anything.

The headman said, "Well, member of the snake family it was your wish to teach the truth to everyone, right? You wanted to enlighten the family of an unwise religion, right? Therefore, we have decided to teach through you; no snake must dare enter our religion. All members of the snake family must know it and the same time you will be a lesson for all children; no one must commit such a transgression."

They brought ropes and tied up Pintu's feet and hung him from a tree. His hands were tied to a branch. His head was down and body bent a little like a bow so that he would not die of a stroke by the rupturing of any blood vessel in the brain. In this charged atmosphere everyone was burning with anger.

"Please help me. Somebody please help me," Pintu shouted, begging for help.

One man said to him while preparing the pyre underneath his hanging head, "Think of them, who taught you your philosophy. Now, realize the consequences of the useless philosophy of your parents and reap the fruit of your wrong doings. This will tell our children that this is the consequence of being ungrateful to parents. Your lynching and burning will be watched by all the youths of our religion and this shall be a great practical lesson to them. They will never ever dare to think of transgressing the 'border line' set by our religion. You brainless Prophet-Diwarian, born in the dark, living in darkness, your actions are dark therefore this is your destiny."

Another man shouted, "Child of a blind religion, small mouth and big talk! You wanted to teach us a lesson, now learn it yourself. First teach yourself before teaching others, and if you have learned it well, it's too late for you to teach."

Holding the fire torch in his hand before lighting the pyre one of the jurors announced; "Look, children of the next generation; anyone who thinks of punishing their parents by marrying into another religion will face this end."

With everyone watching, Pintu's testicles were burned with the flames of the burning torch. He screamed loudly. Everyone watched this terrible incident in utter silence. In their heart of hearts, they considered themselves lucky not to be in love with the follower of another religion, thereby escaping the disastrous wrath of the religious bigots. Then fire was set to the pyre, which was right underneath his head. In the beginning, just a few flames could reach him, just enough to burn his hair. A smell started emanating from his burning hair, which made everyone move back. It was the noon of mid-June and extremely hot and added to it was the scorching heat of the burning pyre. Pintu kept on screaming for several minutes, "Please help me, somebody please help me. Oh mother, O God, please help me. ..." then, he fell speechless. Looking at Pintu's death pyre, many people sighed.

"God, how many Jesus' do you need to bring this world into a better shape? How many living bodies do you need to feed this sacrificial fire? Hundreds and thousands of human bodies have already been offered to make human beings understand, and God, will it ever end?"

His body first turned red and then blue and then his tanned skin started pealing off. The children could not watch anymore but the elders insisted they stay there and watch. Flesh and skin burnt and melted down. Elbows, knees and other parts of the skeleton started dropping down one by one. After two hours, his neck was burnt. In four hours his once healthy and youthful body was reduced to bones and ashes on the ground.

Then, everybody asked Nilu what should they do to her? She replied, "He suffered such a ghastly and brutal death because of me, therefore, cremate me also in the same pyre, because we both committed the same crime of loving each other. Our crimes are the same, so must be our destiny. I am the reason for this crime and will suffer the consequences. You wise people can only take life, not give or create it! So do your job." she said to everyone standing there.

She continued, "You are saying that he was cremated alive because of his Karma. Now, you have also made your Karma. You may be sinless but you may never have loved anyone in your entire life. You will cremate me alive but let me tell you one thing before you cremate me. Religion has taught you only to hate. God has not made you any different from them. You also breathe like them, sweat like them. You all long for love. Your heart knows that death is the door and love is the destiny of human beings.

Love is the destiny of the soul, and the mind shall remain restless without the right place to sit. You are jealous, because you could not have love.

You had lust without love. You hide your lustful life. You jealous people could not taste God's wonderful gift to humankind - love. Under the cover of religion, you pretend to be good. Leave your religion and learn humanity. Leave the differences and learn equality. All sons and daughters are the same as your sons and daughters. Cut your finger, you'll see the same color of blood. Read your heart, you'll see the same feeling in the other's heart as well. Learn to establish the religion of humanity and love, not hate. Your religion teaches only hate. Your heart is full of hate and there is no room for love. Learn to 'Love', quit 'Hate'.

God has not forbidden inter-caste marriages, but your religion has. God is wise he knows that an inter-caste marriage is the bridge to unite two cultures, but your unwise religion is unable to comprehend God's wisdom. There is only one God. Prophet-Diwar's God is no different than yours, and the God of Sackcloth is also not any different from yours. Those people are not created by a different God, and you are not going to be questioned by a different God. Tell your priest to preach that there is only one God, and your scripture's God is the same as theirs.

Righteousness has nothing to do with your hateful religions. This is your religion, which is made by you and not by God. Religion has created a wall in between God and man. As long as you are only concerned with your religion, you shall never be any closer to God. If you have the strength to break this iron wall, you will understand the wise words of the all-caring God. All religions admire the same God, you all belong to one God, you all have one door, one destiny, and you all pray to that one God, but your falsehood and ego cannot compromise with the God-made religion of love and humanity.

Before you cremate me let me tell you one more thing; you need to erase all religions from the surface of Earth. Those who make a living under the umbrella of religions, tell them to seek other vocations. Ask His Holiness to stop energizing or strengthening the blind faith of a confused community or group. Tell those greedy politicians, not to use religion for self-promotion in society. Stop spreading the poison of hate on God's beautiful earth.

You may burn many people alive; burn as many innocents as you can, but you shall not suppress the truth. Make your Karma. You have taught your children the consequences of love and they have learned the horrible things you cruel people can do. They have learned what kind of cruel things our forefathers had done. You cruel people have made this lovely world a frightening place to live.

The headman said to the jurors, "Enough is enough. Stuff her mouth after ripping out her tongue, beat her with chains, throw her on ground, and stop her from shouting anymore."

"Silly girl, you blot of shame on our religion and on our society, you have brought shame to our religion. It is truly said that lust is blind. Now, only you are the wise one left in this village to teach us. Foolish, besotted girl, now that you have finished your sermon it is our turn to teach you a practical lesson," the headman said in anger.

"You are making me a 'Sati'. However, I am glad. I have never wanted to live without the man whom I loved with my soul. I was a chaste, vestal and virtuous wife to him. Go ahead and unite us by way of your religious tradition," said Nilu.

She was shaking with fear and impotent rage at the ghastly brutality carried out in front of her eyes. She knew what was going to happen to her in the next few minutes.

By then it was evening. The sun was setting in the West. The last flame of their pyre was turning into smoke. In order to be free from any single jot of sin, H.H. Diwar-Devote's high priest advised everyone to spit on the remains of the cremated bodies then wash their fingers with clean water before returning to their holy homes. Everyone followed his advice and then left for their homes.

The police arrived after the incident was over. The Police Inspector, who was one of the members of Diwar-Devote religion, paid his respects to His Holiness Diwar-Devote in the traditional way by bending his head down and holding his chin with the fingers of his right hand and said. *"Glory be to you.   God speaks through you and every decision of his is taken through you Glory be to you.* " H.H. Diwar-Devote extended his palm and touched the inspector's forehead to bless him and said, "May victory be always with you, a true servant of the nation - live long and serve the nation with faithfulness."

The Inspector then started preparing the case file. There were several forms to be filled out. All the forms were filled in few minutes. It was easy as everything was already understood, what to mention and what not to, because everything was set up with the cooperation of the police officer and police officer was directed by the Member of Parliament for that area. After signing the last paper he said, *"Long may the Diwar-Devote religion live"*.

When everything was over, the headman's wife said to her husband, "See, throughout life man keeps saying 'I', 'I', 'I', 'I', but what is it after all? This body turns into ashes in a few hours. Nothing remains except ash. That also blows away with the wind. How loudly they were shouting only few hours earlier. At that time, could they imagine that his body would be changed into ashes like this? And, where have they gone?"

Another person said, "A pyre turns a body into ashes in a few hours and now, there are high powered electric furnaces that cremate a body only in four hours. The temperature reaches over 2000 degrees with the extremely high heat generated inside. Pacemakers have to be removed because they explode and scatter the bones all over. Pulverizing the body by solidifying it in liquid nitrogen and then reducing it by freezing and drying is a new modern invention. The early Christians used to cremate their dead but later the concept of resurrection made them compromise with the Jewish system of burial. Still today almost thirty five percent Americans and well educated people prefer cremation to save the land."

Another person said, "In a burial the body bursts open and gets rotten in just a few hours, but people have seen flexibility in buried bodies after many decades. Most mummified bodies were preserved for decades and decades, and the surprising thing is that, those well mummified bodies contain the potential for growing again. However nobody knows where a man goes after his death."

The headman replied, "Everybody has to turn into dust and ashes one day, it's true. It's true and quite important how you die, but far more important is, how you live. As long as we are alive, we must live with family principles and abide by the laws of society. We human beings are designed to live in a society and therefore to follow the moral law of the society and religion. Everyone must learn the lessons of living and dying. The next generation should learn morality from our way of living."

Finally H.H. Diwar-Devote said, "Whatever you have done today is a holy act. Anyone who harms the religion should not be left breathing."

Who could read a mother's heart? Nilu's widowed mother's kind heart retained love for her disobedient but loving child. Her mother's loving eyes could see only good things in her child's actions. She could find nothing wrong in her loving daughter, as she could see all the reasons except the main reason of this world. One by one many thoughts came into her mind, and now she thought, 'O woman, you have many forms. She had always tried to be an ideal daughter to us, but she couldn't. She had wished to become the ideal wife to her husband and ideal mother to her children, but none of her dreams could come true. Her wishes were cremated alive. She was kind, wise, broad-minded, sincere, and transparent in her dealings, but this world was not meant for people like her. She wanted to change the world but she was left with no choice and was changed into dust. She was cremated alive for the crime 'in her heart' there was no Hate for any religion and only Love for all human beings. Love couldn't change the world and hate turned them into dust.'

The common opinion was, 'Children are born to parents for a reason. They might be a friend or an enemy from a past life. Therefore they can be the best support or the fatal enemy. They can be the biggest asset or the biggest liability. One can recognize them only when they grow up enough. Every fruit reveals its real taste after ripening. The enemy has to be reborn in the family to seek revenge. They take birth in the family, and if they are enemy they destroy the well built image, money, and eventually become the reason for the parent's death. She destroyed her father.'

This was the beginning of endless tragedies in their families. Her unfortunate brother, sisters and other family members faced heartbreaking devastation because of their disturbed minds.

There were many Nilus and many Pintus who sacrificed their lives in a similar way. They were burned alive before their dreams could flourish. They disappeared before enjoying the test of self-produced fruits. Whoever favored truth and tried to raise his or her voice against the religions vanished.

There were many families like Nilu and Pintu's whose spirited family member's lives were snuffed out even before they could blossom. They were buried alive by enemies before their talents could flourish. Whoever tried to raise his or her voice against the religions and for truth were reduced to ashes and dust. Their family members had deep pain in their hearts and their motive in life was just to destroy the family of the enemy. Thousands and thousands of their relatives and friends were filled with grief. They couldn't take the anguish anymore and they were unable to control themselves. They thought enough was enough; peace cannot survive without destroying the clouds of evil.

H.H. Prophet-Diwar's aggressive and angry followers were willing to do anything for their religion. Their commandment was; 'convert or kill'. Use whatever means come to your mind! Since those people have no understanding, therefore no wisdom can make them surrender; no wisdom can work on a donkey. Donkeys deserve to be beaten up, to move on the proper track. Preaching will not work in their case. The ignorant cannot understand the language of humanity, as fools cannot understand the language of decency. Evil cannot understand the language of human beings; the wicked can only understand the language of armed force.'

Diwar-Devote's people were frustrated with the disgusting and shocking stories of what Prophet-Diwar's people had done to their daughters and wives. Their hearts were bleeding with pain and whenever they read the awful stories, they couldn't control themselves. They said, 'they have terrified our wives and daughters in the past, they are doing it now and what guarantee do we have that they will not do it in the future? This is the time for us to wake up'.

Money minded politicians and businessmen who could study the atmosphere and knew that destroying the evil religion's people, is the best way to grab their resource filled land, money and other property. Money was their main objective.

Prophet-Diwar's convincing style of preaching was quite powerful for aggressive people only. His fully convinced followers were just waiting for his orders.

H.H. Prophet-Diwar said, "Convert them at gun point. Shoot them and show their dead bodies to others. Frighten them to death, kill them and terrify them. When you kill them, kill them using horrifying methods to scare others. Pull out their tongues, break their bones, cut off their hands, peel their skins off, burn their hair and horrify others with their wails. Sword and religion go together for success. Use any weapon, knives, swords, spikes, stick, grass cutters, stones, bricks or use fire or anything else. Spread their blood all around and throw their bones and flesh into the gutters. Cut their fingers, cut their toes, break their knees and chop them into pieces.

Bring down their big buildings with bombs, destroy their industries, and destroy their factories, resources, and properties. Destroy their parliaments, government houses and the personal property of their leaders. Pollute their air with destructive chemicals and destroy their population with destructive scientific weapons. Kill each and every member of their families horrifically. Go into their midst, take bombs with you, kill them and go to heaven. Wipe them completely off the face of the earth. We need peace. Peace can prevail only after completely uprooting them. Do it for the sake of peace, the next generation needs peace.

Most of their men died in the holy war. His Holiness Prophetdiwaar instructed his armed fighters not to kill the enemy's wives and daughters unless they were below ten years of age. Those wives and daughters were used as slaves and for progeny to increase the population of Prophetdiwaar religion. All the ladies were slaves and only men were controlling the religion. All the captured ladies were used, abused and mistreated by the militants of His Holiness. Everything was fair as long as the intention was to serve God His Holiness Prophetdiwaar. H.H. Prophet-Diwar said,

"Both Diwar-Devote and Sackclothians are non-believers. Non-believers should not be alive in this world of Diwaree. Non-believers have caused great harm to this beautiful world. All unwanted natural calamities are happening because of their existence. Devastating earthquakes, natural disasters everywhere in the world are signs of Diwaree's (God's) anger at the non-believer's existence. Peace cannot prevail as long as a single member of a non-believer's family is left alive, therefore to bring wisdom, happiness, and peace; these non-believers should be wiped completely from the face of the earth. Tell them that this earth belongs to Diwaree not to Satan (them). Cut off their noses, ears, fingers, and arms and slit their throats. Each day, at least ten thousand non-believers should be slaughtered. Enough is enough. Go ahead and remember we are in this religion for the victory."

****

Step Twenty...

HOLY WAR AND HOUSES OF GOD

His Holiness Prophet-Diwar asked everyone, "Do you agree with me that all the non-believers should be erased?"

Everybody raised their hands and clapped, agreeing with H.H. Prophet-Diwar and said in one voice, "Yes, they must be erased. They must be erased because they have no understanding. No matter how much you teach them, they are like the curled tail of a dog that can never be straightened, not even after keeping it in a hard straight pipe for years. Stubborn buffalo cannot become white, even if you wash them five hundred times. Snakes cannot become kind by feeding them on sugar. A donkey cannot be made to sing a song by teaching him the piano. Ignorant deaf idiots cannot understand the language of human philosophy no matter how much you try. Their deaths are the only solution."

Then the High Priest interpreted a quote from the scripture, "Non-believers should be erased from the surface of the earth or they must be distilled by any means." Thousands and thousands were prepared and taught that in the holy war the more devils they kill; the holier they will become. About one million followers of Diwar-Devote and Sackcloth religions were slaughtered in the Holy war, which lasted for three years. None of the slaughterers bothered as to what the coming generations reading this history would think of them. To them, the death of the devils was God's wish and all good devotees of God Prophet-Diwar did that job to please the Great Master - God. The Holy war was the war fought for God, so all the Prophet-Diwarians were happy that God's job was being done.

To please the king again the High Priest said, "One should do anything to save the religion and to destroy bad people. History teaches us that our wise and great forefathers had fought several wars to spread the religion. They destroyed ungodly temples and built godly temples over them. With enormous armies those kings chopped off the heads of ungodly people like chickens in a butcher's hall. Slaughtering thousands and thousands everyday they exterminated the enemies. They threw fifteen hundred people of an ungodly family into a single well. Five thousand devils were packed into a hall and made to suffocate to death. Seven thousand non-believers were burnt alive in a hall

The next day the king ordered the Ethnic Cleansing. Most of the politicians, heads of religious organizations, Ministers and many social workers got a real opportunity to take advantage of the Holy war to appear on television and newspapers. For many politicians, a holy war was a sign of good fortune. They knew that the share markets would collapse. Famine, disease and poverty would spread all over the nation. Many children would become orphans and many women would become widows, but who cares... as long as the king's fame was gaining strength.

In the Holy War the death of itinerant people became a new issue. These itinerants were people without legal documents. A sudden bombardment at the shrine of Diwar-Devote caused their deaths. Some followers of H.H. Prophet-Diwar placed a time bomb at the place of worship of H.H. Diwar-Devote. The bomb exploded in the middle of the night. Many people around the shrine died. Several, hundred of them were illegal. Their dead bodies were buried together in a common pit as they did not have any home or any family members. There was no record of where they originally came from and who their close relatives were. Nobody came forward to perform the last rites for these illegal people.

They died young anyway they had no hope in life and no reason to live. Their deaths were not a problem. The dead were gone. None of their relatives were going to come sue the politicians because they were 'people without legal documents'. They deserved deportation, exile, death or whatever. In their poor home countries people were sold like animals. People would buy one man for five dollars and half a dozen

men for twenty five dollars. After purchasing those animal-like servants the purchaser would make them work for as long as they stayed alive. That was another merciless story in the history. Can you imagine that?
In their constitution, the concept of 'Citizen of the Earth' did not exist. No human being was born to widen the limitations of their narrow vision. No ruler was willing to change the old laws. However, Mother Earth was very kind to those illegal children of hers. She did not say that they were her 'illegal' children. Mother Earth knew that a child cannot be born without a father, and she knew they had real fathers. They were not illegal therefore she accepted their dead bodies. Mother Earth ate those dead bodies happily as we eat our favorite food. Throughout their whole lives they had been eating the flesh of Mother Earth, and as time went by she ate their flesh. All dead bodies had gone into her stomach. Burial was quick...

The death of the 'illegal' people was not a big problem at all. The problem was how to reconstruct the shrine. Half of the shrine had been damaged. Eventually the Diwar-Devote's King said, "My people, enough is enough. So far we have never destroyed their shrines but now they have broken our backbone. Our non-violent philosophy and patience has encouraged them to frighten the world These shrines are God's home. They blasted God's home so they hate God, and it is yet another proof of their anti-God and non-believing character so they must be exterminated like vermin. The more non-believers you slaughter, the greater reward you will receive."

The people of Diwar-Devote religion cried when they saw the shrine tumbled down. They could not believe their eyes that God's home, where they used to go for prayers, was no more. They felt God's voice coming from their hearts, "My devotees today I am crying.."

Diwar-Devotees had great sentimental feeling for their shrine. The house of prayer was a place from where they could speak out the words of their hearts to their beloved God. They gathered money and in three months re-erected the same shrine at the same place. The businessman who collected funds from the public became very famous, because of his style of collecting funds. He knew how to draw money out from others' pockets in the name of religion. He advertised a quotation from scripture;

"God has sent human beings to earth to build at least one shrine in their lifetime."

Offerings; One brick for God's home is for $ 1, Fifty bricks for $ 35, Main gate with donor's name $ 100,000., Diwaree's statue with donor's name $ 250,000., Dead parents names can also be engraved (In Loving Memory) for $ 10,000., Fifty thousand marble tiles (donor's name will appear in big letters) for $ 50,000., Donor's name and his photo will be displayed for a donation of $250,000 and above. People with their names and photos will be immortal in this world and will live in heaven after leaving this body, as long as their photo, remains in the house of God," There was no restriction for accepting small amounts. Small amounts such as a half-dollar could also be offered for half a brick for God's home.

H.H. Diwar-Devote said, "My people! God is living without a home. We should be ashamed that we have big houses with big dining rooms, big living rooms, and many bed rooms. Giver God Diwaree has given us many things in our homes, but today our God has no home. Our God's home is broken. Our God is now homeless and we must quickly re-build his home. We should not let our God live without a home. It is not good. It is a shame that we all have homes but our God doesn't, therefore we also should not sleep in our beds as long as we keep our God without a bed. Every person who is born in this religion owes a lot to God. Now, God needs your help to re-build his home. This is the best time to re-pay your debts. God will see every penny of every donor. Whatever you have it's God's gift to you; with this gift you have to show him what you can do for him. Use God's gift for God. This is the time he needs your support. Now if you help God, God will help you in time of difficulties. Any kind of charity is accepted whether in the form of money, bricks, or other construction material or physical work. Please come forward with open hearts and show your generosity. This may be the only time in your life you will have an opportunity to do something for God."

After this impressive speech, many people felt that they had to do this job and leave everything else behind. God's home came first and God would take care of them. Many people thought God might be testing them at this time and it really was the best time to pass the test. One man stood-up and raising his hands said, "I will give five hundred thousand dollars."

The respectful loving look from the public surprised him and meant more than anything in the world to him. A wonderful feeling was generated by their praise. He had never before had this kind of soul satisfying feeling in his life. This inner satisfaction remained with him forever.

Next morning, his name with his photo appeared in the newspaper under the heading, "Living Example of Generosity." His name appeared on the front-page of Diwar-Devote's monthly magazine, under the heading, "Living Saint" - a true saint recognized at the needful time.

One generous man donated the entire cost of the main entrance. Another person made a commitment for windows and all the iron works. Then, one by one everyone offered much more then they could afford. Almost everyone said, "See, only few years back we had nothing. Today, we have much more than we could ever think of. Whatever we have is all because of Diwaree's blessings. Donating one brick is easy for anyone. We will do so. What can be a greater opportunity than to use this money in rebuilding God's home?"

There were many people who were willing to do anything in the name of religion. They would donate their houses, their property and all of their money in their excitement. They donated money with open hearts; by checks, money orders, credit cards and used different means to transfer money. Thus all gave some but some gave all to please God. On top of that they got a huge amount from the government funds through the minister in charge for cultural funds. People who did not have money worked free of charge. They worked day and night tirelessly to make a home for the Great Master Diwaree - their God.

In six months, much earlier than expected, the shrine was rebuilt. The new shrine was one of the biggest shrines in the world in size and value. It was far better than the one they had had previously. Now the question was; from where did all this money come, because the legitimate funds were not enough and surprised the whole world. However, that was another interesting secret.

All the members of the Diwar-Devote religion could not forget the sacrilege committed in the shrine. They controlled themselves in order to remain sinless, but whenever they discussed the incident; they started sweating with anger and their sleepless nights caused problems in their families. Again and again, they kept praying, "God help us. We don't like to do anything bad. Please give us strength to control ourselves. Let's not be malicious and revengeful."

Many educated and uneducated boys who were followers of the Diwar-Devote religion were jobless and had no hope for the future. They knew that soon they were going to be finished with life. A few extremely rich gang leaders started paying them forty dollars per month for their food. In the name of God Diwaree, they were used to spread terror in the land of the enemy.

One day about twenty hired jobless boys armed with guns and bullets went to Prophet-Diwarian's place of worship. While everyone was praying with closed eyes in a mass prayer, they started shooting them. A tumult and uproar arose all around the shrine. People ran around in panic trying to escape but in a few minutes hundreds of devotees were killed. Dead bodies lay piled up like sacks of rice on a storage floor. The killers ran away. Later a mass funeral was arranged for the dead. Famous politicians attended the mass funeral.

The head of the country in his address said, "Ladies and gentlemen! What has happened is a shocking incident for us, but we assure you that it will not happen again and every effort will be made to punish the guilty people."   Regardless of the regrets expressed by the politicians and despite their attempts to reassure the people, nothing was going to change as it was a complicated game pre-arranged by 'in power' and 'opposition' leaders.

After this incident, both the parties internationally and openly declared enmity. After such a declaration they became afraid of each other. They wanted to destroy their enemies completely before the hostile opposition started gunning down their families. They knew as long as their enemies were alive, they could be attacked at any time.

Prophet-Diwarians cleverly planned to destroy the city. One morning, four months later, when people turned on the television they saw the tallest buildings in the capital city tumbling down. There was fire everywhere. People were running everywhere in utter confusion. Many people had gas masks on, many were running with aid equipment and others were screaming loudly for help. Many people were jumping out from windows, some were suffocated to death and some were turned into ashes. Thousands and thousands of dead bodies were laid on the ground. Legs, hands, heads and other body parts were strewn all around. The traumatic scenes of bloodshed were beyond anyone's imagination.

Almost everyone died in that attack. The surviving victims were sent to hospitals. The hospitals were full of injured people. Many good people were trying to help them. Their pain was unimaginable. Most of them died, and those who did not die could not bear the pain. They became psychologically and mentally damaged. Those survivors went through a horrifying experience. Many of them lived; without hands, without feet, without eyes, without fingers, without ears, and many of them were paralyzed.

The following week an airplane was hijacked and made to land in the enemy's city. All the passengers and the crew members were held captive in a nearby house. A ransom of sixty million dollars was demanded, which the Diwar-Devotees could not pay. The passengers were then tortured. Boiling water was thrown on them. The captors started piercing the captives' skin with needles. After that they started chopping off noses, ears, fingers, toes, lips and dousing them with boiling water and all the women were raped by the captors.

A few days' later five buses were stopped by six gunmen, on a highway in a rural area, who shot all the passengers. Many people begged them for mercy but to no avail. Many passengers tried to escape but before they could begin to run they were shot down. Their wives and children were butchered and then they took all their money, ornaments and other belongings. The dead bodies of the passengers including the driver and the conductor were thrown by the roadside. All the devotees of Prophet-Diwaree ran away after the killing of these innocent passengers.

The next day at 11.23 a.m. five suicide bombers went to different crowded spots in the city, and exploded heavy bombs killing at least a thousand people, in the name of God! Soon after the suicide bombing, in one village, Prophet-Diwarians started dumping all the villagers alive into a well. Eventually they covered the well. It all happened during the night; therefore there were no eye witnesses.

The daily newspapers were fulfilled with horrifying headlines such as,
Man killed while on a morning walk.
Two families brutally murdered last night.
House burnt with ten members of a single family.
Bomb exploded in a bus, 40 passengers killed.
Nuclear threat. Chemical weapons threat.
Atomic war preparations.
Bomb exploded on airplane, many passengers dead.
Fire on cruise ship, all passengers dead.
Scary Anthrax powder in personal mail.
Five thousand AK rifles found in a place of worship.
Four thousand guns and swords seized from a shrine.
Train line removed, two thousand people killed in train accident.
Airplane hijacked, hijackers demand millions.
Child kidnapped for big ransom.
Half a million reward for a religious author's head.
Girl abducted at gun-point.

Many places of worship were stocked with guns, bombs, and other destructive weapons. H.H. Sackcloth couldn't buy expensive weapons. He said it was not good to keep weapons in the place of worship.

Prophet-Diwarians were planning to buy chemical weapons, biological weapons and many other sophisticated weapons from other countries. The Foreign Minister was willing to support the plan. The Foreign Minister needed money to fight the next elections. He was desperate to see his photo in the newspapers. This deal would really help him to remain in power for another few years.

A NEW POLITICIAN: Imperceptibly a new group made its appearance on the scene. Their backbone was the hotel and bar association. The financing businessmen were very wealthy. They appeared suddenly saying to everyone, "We do not believe in any religion but humanity. We want to help the poor and helpless victims of religions. We want to create more jobs for the jobless. We are concerned about, divorced women, high taxes, high living costs and humanity. If your views are the same as ours then cast your vote for our leader. We will rule the nation, and we will distribute the money equally. We will not siphon off everything as Diweardevotees, Prophet-Diwarians and Sackclothians are doing."

That group's leader said in his address, "Do you know how much money they have grabbed? Do you know what tricky things they do for money? Do you know they use government money to remain in power? That public money is used for their credentials and publicity. Do you know why the poor are becoming poorer? Do you know why they are not giving us our land? Do you know what they are fighting for? Not for God and not for religion, but money for money... always money... Cast your vote for us and once we are in power, we will reveal everything about this dastardly game of money."

Money and religion was a potent and heady mix. The politico-religious mafia could do whatever they wanted. Mr. Politician would do anything to remain in the chair. He didn't care about the unfolding tragedies. Many people tried to teach them; "Mr. Politician don't you remember the tragedies of the 1930's and 1940's? Do you know how many widows went through unbearable pain? Do you know how many mothers had committed suicide? Do you know how many mothers have seen the death of their children? Do you know how many children had seen the pieces of their parent's dead bodies? Can you imagine their pain? Do you know what is happening to those surviving victims?"

The political leader of the Sackcloth religion's answer was, "I can well understand, but why don't the ignorant hot-headed fools of Prophet-Diwaree religion and Diwar-Devote understand?"

The Diwar-Devote religion's politician answered, "I can well, understand but why can't that foolish Sackcloth understand all this? He must be taught a lesson and the people should see how pompously stupid that idiot is. That ignorant mad man of an evil religion should face the consequences of his stubbornness. The world should know that he is another Hitler, who used God's name and killed God's children for his own fame."

The arms dealers needed the politicians' favors. They wanted them to fight. The arm business could flourish only if they become life long enemies of each other and that was only possible by separating them. Then they would wage overt and covert wars against each other. For a war they would definitely need arms. They would buy fighter planes, guns, canons, tankers, missiles, bombs, nuclear bombs, chemical weapons, military equipment and the most advanced state–of-the art weapons. Thus the poor would fight and the rich would grab their money.

To make their weapons business successful they were teaching others to fight for rights, saying, "This is not the age of slavery. Do not let them have control over you. You can see they are grabbing most of the production. They are occupying the high posts in the administration. All the finance is under their control. They are using you. Go ahead, fight, we are with you, we will help you. And you know whoever we help becomes the most powerful ruler. ... Before we help you, you shall need to sign a paper that you will buy all fighter planes or any other military equipment only from our company. And, there will be one more paper to sign which will remain confidential."

The drug business was quite similar to the arms business. The rich people's money came to them through their drug addicted children. The children from rich families contributed to the business indirectly. Whenever they bought drugs for ten dollars, one third of that money went to the head of terrorist organizations. Out of that half of the amount went to His Holiness Prophet-Diwar for terrorizing the world and the rest was used by politicians to remain in power. All the terrorists were thankful to drug-addict kids. Through the drug business Prophet-Diwar's terrorist group gained amazing power indirectly, the leader was grateful to all those school kids, who bought drugs. Drug addicted children did a great job by strengthening underworld activities and despoiling the Earth. With their support, terrorists became capable of buying millions of dollars worth of weapons and military hardware in quantities sufficient to destroy innocent people.

A new Business-God: The appearance of a new Business-God suddenly came about. He understood the prevailing mentality of the public. He knew that all religions had been polluted badly. Dozens of dirty things in these religions could be exposed. People would understand the corruption, dirt and mal-practices in these religions. He did not see any good in religion and thus could see only bad things. For him religion was nothing but a business. He knew how to establish a new prosperous business in the name of religion and God. He knew the miracle of conviction. He originally belonged to a business family. He was a member of the Sackcloth religion, named Ronald or "Real-Diwaree". He did not exactly follow the philosophy of Sackcloth but he told everyone that he was the real incarnation of Diwaree and had received fresh instructions from Diwaree. He said Diwaree's message was that GOD IS ONE. If there is one God then there should be only one religion, only one path to reach him. Ignorant people did not know it, therefore they made many different paths. However, all of them are wrong. None of them are right….," people liked Real-Diwaree's amazing ideas. They accepted his beliefs.

Real-Diwaree said, "Our great master never told people to divide into three religions. He always said 'there is one God'. He did not even tell anyone that they should wear yellow, white or hessian cloth to please God. These are all self-created philosophies of confused and selfish people. These people have no right to take advantage of Diwaree's innocent life. They think that Diwaree is dead. Therefore, he cannot come back to sue them. Diwaree had no copyright to secure his viewpoint, but anyone can change Diwaree's viewpoint since neither is he alive nor has he left any official successor. But, now I am here to establish the real method and leading the right path. Everybody please come to me. I am the true one and the real incarnation of Diwaree. I am not an agent of God nor am I a common man. I am God. I have been hiding this fact from you people and now I am telling you openly. I have never revealed this fact in public till now and now I have told you, and I shall not repeat it in future. Now you must understand it."

Real-Diwaree was by far cleverer than all the others. He knew how to
take advantage of situations. He lied a lot and his sharp memory
remembered every lie, so he didn't made mistakes. He said, "Last night
Diwaree appeared in my dream and said to me, 'my son! Can you see
what these people have done to me?" then, he touched my head and said
to me, 'My real son! I am entering into you and from this time onwards,
you shall be known as Real-Diwaree. I give all my powers and rights to
you to spread my true message. I have not given this power to anyone
except you. All others are misusing my name and misleading the world.
You will be the only person through whom I shall be worshipped.'

Then Diwaree said to me in the dream. 'Now, I enter in your body, and
you will do only what I want.' I did surrender myself to him and he
accepted me. I gave up my identity and let Diwaree run me as he wanted.
He gave me a new name 'Real-Diwaree' which means the original and
true Diwaree."

It was the only statement Real-Diwaree made to the public telling them
that he is God. After that his first disciple did that all the talking. Real-
Diwaree's first disciple also claimed that he also had a dream about
joining Real-Diwaree for this good cause. Real-Diwaree and his first
disciple were having fun and enjoying life with great gusto. They
enjoyed, fame, respect, money and everything of which, otherwise, they
could only dream.

Real-Diwaree prepared his sermons by using favorable quotations. One
of his sermons was;

> *Vastu Kahee Dhudhe Kahee, Kehi Vidhi Aavai Haath.*
> *Kah Diwaar Tab Paaeye, Jab Bhedee Leejai Saath.*

The substance is hidden elsewhere and you are searching somewhere
else. You can find that only if you be with the knower of secrets of the
location. Only RealDiwaree can escort you safely in your perilous
journey of life.

> *Guru Govind Douu Khare, Kaake Laagu Paaw.*
> *Balihaaree Guru Aapane Govind Diyo Bataaya.*

Choose between God and Master, and always consider Master as greater
than God.

Real-Diwaree said in his impressive lecture;

Ek Nuur Se Sab Jaga Jaaya, Kaun Bhale Kaun Mande.
"The whole world is created from one great God. All are children of God
and all are equal here. No one is wholly good and no one is completely
bad. Everyone has weaknesses and everyone has good points. There is no
reason to fight against one another. Come out of the well of religions. No
scripture will control you and no religion will rule over you. Once you
become my follower then no one shall remain above you. We will
become the best people in the world. We are all the chosen ones. Anyone
joins us will also become a chosen one. All the people of those other
religions are controlled by their scriptures, and ignorant masters. They
are controlled by their own ego. Their ego has kept them in a closed
room. But God's chosen ones will come here from all over the world,
and will be immediately blessed with light."

His preaching became very popular. His first disciple would say, "Real-
Diwaree is the incarnation of Diwaree. You can go to heaven only if he
initiates you." His initiation business was as good as a flourishing
industrial enterprise. Many secret commission agents were walking
around building his fortune. His monastery became like a palace of
kings. People donated cash money, houses and buildings. He had an
attractive 'package deal program' for the people whereby if they donate
one room they could have a good and peaceful life in his monastery after
retirement. They would get all senior citizens facilities with; well
prepared food, no rent, no bills, and no social problems. Rich donors,
who donated all their property, could have everything for free as long as
they lived. They would have free hospital services and whatever they
might require. After they died they would go to heaven and the property
would go to the mission.

Real-Diwaree owned a big profit making drug plant; his son was
handling that business. Real-Diwaree was just an emergency financial
supporter for his son's drug plant. However, the main signatory of the
bank accounts was Real-Diwaree himself. His son knew that with the
death of his father (Real-Diwaree), he would inherit the entire property.
To prepare the public for such a contingency, Real-Diwaree discussed
the subject in public. He said, "Listen to me my people! I am God's man.

In other words, I am yours. So, if I am yours then to whom does my son belong?"

The public answered, "Your son also belongs to the public, of course!"

"Then, if I transfer this property in his name will it be the right decision?" Real-Diwaree asked everyone.

"Absolutely right," answered everybody.

Then, he took off his ceremonial head gear and put it on his son's head to mark the succession ceremony in public. People started clapping and said, "Hail! Hail, great master Real-Diwaree! Hail unto you. No one like you was born and no one is likely to be in the future. Your son is like you, Hail, Hail." All the property papers were immediately transferred to his son's name. That was Real-Diwaree's clever trick to persuade people and make them say from their own mouths that whatever he was doing was the public's wish. He knew that once the public approved his ideas, they would never in the future admit that their decision was wrong.

A most interesting outcome was that some of the members of all the three faiths were leaving their own religion to join Real-Diwaree. He had a good way of convincing the public. He had a good command of the English language as well as three other languages. To the illiterate people he said that he knew more than seventeen languages as he, the God has to communicate with everyone in the world.

They converted rich people by showing them their services to the tribes. When they received a good amount from the rich they then converted poor people with that money. Conversion became another big business. They were even offering shelters, clothes or blankets to newly converted poor people.

The followers of Real-Diwaree's religion advanced their businesses and made a lot of money. With that money they could convert thousands of tribal people to their religion in one week. His aim was to convert the entire world to the Real-Diwaree religion. He hired many jobless people who went to remote villages to convince the poor people known as 'untouchables'. They would tell them, "You have been deluded by the people of your religion. They call you "untouchable". The most shocking thing is that they will never treat you equally. They will not use the pots which you have used. They will not sit with you and have food together. On top of that they use you. They are exploiting you. At the end of it all what did you get? Nothing! You work for them, you wash their garments, you clean their place of living and you work for them with dedication and still they consider you a low-class people, "Untouchable" born to serve, born to hate.

Our Great Master says, all are equal and should therefore be treated equally. Our Master Real-Diwaree is practicing it precisely as it is supposed to be. Forget about the religions of Diwar-Devote, Prophet-Diwaree or Sackcloth. Come to us and live with dignity like a human being. We will give you one hundred dollars and a complementary set of clothes and if you do not have a shelter to live in we will provide a shelter with a voluntary job to fulfill your basic needs, but adopt our religion and work for us honestly."

Many poor people from the Diwar-Devote, Prophet-Diwaree and Sackcloth religions converted to Real-Diwaree's religion. After converting, they started criticizing their former religions, but they always remembered that they belonged to their original religion. They might return to the fold of their original religion the day their religion's people stopped hating them and stopped calling them low class, untouchables and provide sufficient means for their survival.

Those low-class neo-converts felt guilty after adopting the new religion. Their guilty consciences kept telling them, "You do not know where God is even after adopting this new religion. God had given you birth in that family, but you disregarded his will. You did not remain where God put you. You thought that was hard. Do you know the consequences of leaving your original religion?"

However, just to reassure themselves, they would remind themselves of terrible weaknesses of their original religion. To satisfy their own guilty consciences, they would talk among themselves, "What kind of religion was that, where a human being was treated as low class slaves, where women were known as unholy? We were considered and treated as untouchables. We had accepted ourselves as fools, ignorant, low class, born for slavery, born for hate and condemned by birth. We thought God had sent us into that family because of the Karma of our previous lives and that God wants us to be treated as low class slaves. We thought, we might have been sinners in our previous lives. We are ignorant, and whatever those preachers told us we followed. Now our eyes have been opened and those preachers cannot mislead us anymore. The time for misleading us is over. Thanks to Real-Diwaree - the God of innocents."

Though, nobody knew which religion was real i.e. Diwar-Devote, Prophet-Diwaree, Sackcloth or Real-Diwaree's, but those who had converted got a shelter to live in. In their shelters they had electricity. Their children started going to English medium schools and getting a good education. After converting, their children got shirts and pants to wear. These things they would never have got otherwise. Now, they had a better understanding than when they had while following their original religion. It was quite possible that one day their children would be capable of holding a top-ranking position in the civil administration. Professional achievement and money became their ultimate goals, which was possible because of their new religion and a higher understanding through their new education. But about the spiritual side, converted people knew, it was just coming out of a well and jumping into another.

However good or bad, conversion by the power of money caused hate. Hate and fear kept spreading like a contagious disease. After every war there was peace for a little while, but at the time of every election politicians made matters hot, and even deadly. On hearing the reality of their brutal history people became thirsty for the blood of the non-believers. Through highly developed scientific methods they were ready to destroy each other completely. Everything was ready for complete destruction. It was just a matter of pushing the button. Any brain-washed fanatic could push the computerized button at any moment to destroy the city of the non-believers. All they were waiting for was the button to be pushed. It seemed as if once again God was saying 'Kaalo'asmi lokakshyakritaprabridho' I am inflamed, Kaal the eternal Time-spirit, the destroyer of worlds.

The world was filled with non-believers. Now the question was; did everyone deserve to be a part of this horrific moment? Even the most fanatically brainwashed man who would first push the button of devastation would be a member of one of these groups. He was sure that he was pushing the button for the right reason - God.

While everyone was almost ready to exterminate each other a sudden change took place in the life of H.H. Diwar-Devote. As you know he was originally a professor and he really was a very humble person, which was the reason that he couldn't easily disagree with his own people. From the day of Diwaree's death he kept agreeing with Michael Pattiwala, Maya, and other followers. He did not like to hurt anyone's feelings, and believed that he could be wrong and everyone else could be right, but eventually he got sick and exhausted of the un-desirable games. Suddenly after many many years, he woke up, when Maya scolded him and told him to follow her law in the monastery. With a clear vision he opened his eyes. He saw that this world was like a dream. He started seeing again as Diwaree's words scolding him was saying;

'What the hell are you doing my son? Is this what you learned after living with a saint for so many years? Did I ask you to enjoy a life of palaces, Rolls Royce, servants and Maya? Did I ask you to serve the rich businessman Pattiwala? How can you forget everything you learned with me and let your mind be gripped by greed? Is this what you learned after reading all the scriptures and living with a saint? How can you offer your mind to Maya and Pattiwala? How can you let the spirits of lust and fame control your life? How can you sleep? Do you want to die in a deep sleep? What the hell are you doing my child? Do you want to disconnect my link with you completely?'

He started thinking about the words Diwaree used to tell him; 'My beloved son, though this world is a dream, you should not take it as a dream. Take it seriously and keep working properly in this dream. Follow that which is right rather then what people feel is right. You should work properly in the dream so that the moment your dream is over your soul's dream will come true.'

Diwaree would say that, everyone in this world is highly intoxicated and under the influence of the illusion of God. But a saint must always be aware of his aim of life. A saint must refrain from yearning for material things including fame and illusive maya. That's the only difference between a saint and an ordinary human being. As long as you are dreaming you are the same as a dead person, and as long as you are sleeping under the influence of illusive maya you are wandering in the darkness of night. Your day begins from the very moment you wake up, therefore count your age from the day you wake up.

Many were the amazing things Diwaree had told him. He started recollecting them one by one. While Diwar-Devote was lost in deep thought Maya and Pattiwala could feel that something was wrong with the Saint Diwar-Devote. Diwar-Devote did not say anything at all to anyone because he realized that he would have been far along the 'path' of purity if he had not listened to Pattiwala and other people. From the very beginning he was never really contented in his heart because he knew that whatever he was doing, in the name of a saint, was absolutely wrong. His inner conscience never agreed with all activities but everyone convinced him that whatever he was doing was for Diwaree - the God. Since everyone made him believe that it was Diwaree's will he too thought 'how could everyone be wrong?'

The dormant force within him was aroused and it didn't sleep after that. Once the eternal flame was lit, it continued burning for all time. Since the morning his dream was interrupted he did not sleep again for fear he would start dreaming again, so he concentrated on the right steps and proper way to give up all his incorrect practices. That day many things went through his mind but he didn't tell anyone anything. He kept pondering on his life with Diwaree and Pattiwala. After replaying the movie of his life and the journey from Professor M. L. Singh to renounced stoical despondency-Vairaagee to H. H. Diwar-Devote, he was astonished to see, what a dramatic change the 'Triple K' (Kantian - money; Kamini - women and Keerti – fame) had brought in his life. Instead of loving everyone he loved 'Triple K' and behaved completely opposite to what Diwaree had taught him. He couldn't believe it. What a pure life and philosophy he had while living with Diwaree.   He used to follow the wonderful wisdom of the Gita and the ten signs of righteousness before becoming involved with Pattiwala and Maya.

For six days he thought about it but he didn't tell to anyone, including Maya and Pattiwala, as he knew what they would say and do. Maya and Pattiwala noticed a different appearance on his face and the silence and the seriousness. They had a slight suspicion that something had gone wrong with the saint. He kept thinking of Diwaree's words, "Mr. Singh, one must be married to the aim of life not to the triple K."

God! What's wrong with me? What's the use of a marriage between hell and heaven? How can a Saint be married to Triple K? Diwaree had peace, love, and wisdom within him so he gave that to me but this whole drama has filled me with jealousy, hate and anger so how can I give to others what Diwaree had given me? What kind of disciple am I? While my master lived on a broken wall I am sleeping on a gold-framed bed? Being a peaceful saint's follower why do I have so much anxiety, tension and turbulence in my life? He used to pray in the middle of the night and here I am thinking of dealing with politicians. He used to walk barefoot and I have a Bentley. Whenever he got two blankets he gave the other to a poorer person whose need was greater than his. He used to wear one gown and I have a room filled with ironed clothes. He did not have soap, servants, air conditioning and many other things and I have a huge holiday home on the beach. What's wrong with me, God what's wrong with me? Whose follower have I become? God, where have I come?

He was constantly reminded by the mind stirring incident that had taken place in Diwaree's life, which nobody else but he knew. The incident happened long ago. Diwaree had lived on fruit for only seventeen years, as a result of that he had become very popular in the area. Knowing that fame is a big obstacle on the path to God, he quickly changed his name place and identity but only Mr. Singh knew.

God, what a wonderful saint you have blessed us with. Mr. Singh kept thinking of the many incidents, which only he knew. He was filled with regret and started crying, "Diwaree please forgive me. I don't know how it happened. I knew it was wrong, I knew this was not the way you lived or in what you believed. I knew everything but... Please Diwaree forgive

me… My beloved master, please forgive me… " The conscience within
him couldn't sleep anymore; he became helpless.

On the seventh day, early in the morning, leaving everything behind in
total dejection he went to a lonely place to live the life he used to live
long ago with Diwaree. Maya and Pattiwala couldn't believe that such a
thing could happen. He just disappeared without leaving any
information. What happened to him afterwards was another interesting
story… he was a saint before meeting to Pattiwala, and became a saint
after leaving Pattiwala. He was a saint. Indeed he was.

Till the day the 'enemy within' was controlling him, all his people were
happy with him because he was helping them in their religious and
political goals. He was fulfilling the wishes of Pattiwala, Maya and other
followers by fueling their opinion of themselves. He had left behind the
duty of a saint. Diwaree had told him that a saint must worship this
world as his home with his pure living, which he had unfortunately
forgotten. But now, after waking up, he realized his duty.

Till this day he had seen the rope as a snake in the darkness and therefore
forced to undergo the stress of fighting with a snake. While fighting with
the snake he had developed blood pressure and diabetes. Now that he had
found out that the snake was actually a rope, his stress and anxiety
disappeared and he became a peaceful saint again. His 'enemy within'
was dead and the 'friend within' aroused. Since the day he handed over
charge to the 'friend within' he did everything to please Him - the 'friend
within'. Once again he saw this world with the vision of Diwaree. He re-
realized; that the one God appears in thousands of forms to devotees and
according to their truthfulness and closeness to the 'friend within'. The
'friend within' could tell him the difference between dream and reality,
snake and rope, and the difference between day and night. The powerful
friend within, who projected the unique world that each and every mind
deserved to be in, was amazing.

The whole world was changed because he himself had changed. His
inner vision, his way of seeing the world, was changed. Every creation of
God was perfect for him because he had moved towards perfection. He
was very contented since he had re-found the real friend who would

never leave him. He would never go through the pain of separation
again. The thick curtain between him and the 'friend within' was
removed. His love, friendship, respect, and honor for the 'friend within'
grew by leaps and bounds. Neither language nor pictures could express
his feelings after his re-union with the real friend. He never again lived
with anyone, and never felt loneliness again.

After many years he had remembered the 'friend within' who was the
most powerful and mighty. This 'friend within' could take one to a holy
place, or to jail. This powerful friend could make anything out of a
person. Diwaree used to sing his glory. *Tere pujan Ko Bhagawan Banaa
Man Mandir Aalishaan.* (My God, please beautify this mind so that you
could be worshiped with it.)

The journey 'within' had become as important as the outside journey.
His 'friend within' was as honored as another's 'friend within' because
everyone's 'friend within' was the same energy from the single great
source - the Almighty. Taking care of the self by purifying one's own
genes was as important as taking care of everyone in the world.
Understanding the miracle of ones' own DNA was the same as
understanding the miracle of the universe and the Almighty.

Pattiwala, Maya and the other followers were not really affected by his
renunciation because by that time the religion was financially well
endowed and Pattiwala enjoyed taking charge. They continued the
struggle of religions.

While everyone was ready to exterminate each other a new aspect of
knowledge made its appearance on the scene. Some scientists started to
understand a phenomenon, which had already been explained by Devi
Messiah to her disciples long ago. The knowledge concerned age and it
was about becoming younger by traveling back into the past.
Interesting...

****

Part Four

TWO PATHS

Step Twenty One...

UFO, THE NEW CONUNDRUM

Invention of an amazing mind...

Scientists have, since time immemorial, tried to find the hidden truths that lie within our genes, within the planets and the universe, just as spiritualists have tried to fathom the secret of the invisible world, or the one whose law controls the visible world. The more they studied the genes, the mind, the soul, the planets, the solar system, and the scriptures, the more perplexed they became. No sooner were they done with one, than they would be faced with a new challenge. This mystery was so huge; it had never entered people's minds before. No one could have ever imagined that there would come a time when we would start to seriously consider the 'past' and the 'future' as realities. These subjects had already been mentioned in the Holy Scriptures - the Bible and the Bhagwad Gita as Uttarayan and Dakshinayan. Several visionary thinkers had also considered its possibilities yet no one really thought that people would actually start plans to travel in those directions. For the affluent, it was to become a new diversion. Greedy people were very eager to promote the idea, and the rich were eager to participate in such an adventure. There were two exciting prospects:

- First - if they traveled into the 'future', they would grow older and changes would quickly take place. Only the speed needed to be doubled, as the Earth is already traveling into 'future' at a speed of 18.51 miles per second.

- Second - if they traveled into the 'past', they could become younger and see the re-enactment of many historical events.

For example; take two friends of the same age. One stays on earth and the other goes into space and returns after sometime. In that time the earth will have taken five revolutions around the sun and the friend who stayed on earth would have become five years older. But the one who returned from space was younger than the one who stayed back. Many educated people, scientists and intellectuals started working on these two possibilities. Anyone who could master the mysteries of time-travel - whether 'past' or 'future' - would be worthy of many Nobel Prizes, not just one. Besides that, his or her name would become immortal in the scientific domain, spirituality and in the history of humankind.

Though this was a scientific phenomenon, there was concern about the consequences of getting lost among the unknown paths of time. This was the reason why people would rather seek out answers through the scriptures or from a holy person. After all, people already knew that death was a mystery, and that going deep into the 'past' or 'future' was equally mysterious. The difference was that death was an ancient mystery while time travel was a new concept.

As a matter of fact, 'time-travel' was a greater mystery than death, because over the centuries preachers had become practiced in speaking about death. Many famous writers have written well-known books claiming knowledge of death. Their books became popular, because they excited people's curiosity. Everyone wanted to learn more about death. Preachers, who did religious conversions to increase the numbers of their followers, always spoke of death. Listeners were fascinated with this terrifying word and immediately surrendered themselves. There were already many practiced ways to satisfy a frightened man's curiosity. Many preached that death was all right as long as they were with savior.

242   OUR GOD OUR EARTH

But, here the questions and the subject matter were totally new. Neither
H.H. Prophet-Diwaree nor H.H. Sackcloth nor even Real-Diwaree
believed that their followers would come to them with such profound
questions. Scientists and ordinary people knew that only a great
intelligence could answer such questions. Everyone's followers were
optimistic that their esteemed masters would provide the answers, whilst
utter confusion prevailed worldwide.

One day, H.H. Prophet-Diwar sent a spy to Pattiwala's discourse to find
out what he was saying about this burning issue. The spy listened
carefully to Pattiwala's discourse and reported everything in detail to
H.H. Prophet-Diwar. He quoted Pattiwala verbatim: "The end of this
world is fast approaching. The end is nearer than you think. You know
there should be someone to save you when the end comes. Lucky and
blessed are the pure hearted, good people who come to be initiated by me
and ensure their Salvation and safety after death. Do not fear. Come to
me. Why be afraid when I am here. I am the savior with all the powers of
our great master Diwaree. He has sent me to save you. Now, you listen to
me, become wise and understand the gravity of the present time and
aware of this serious matter. Do not delay, be initiated now, and the
money you deposit in this spiritual bank, wherein the share prices are
going to soar, and the benefit you will receive after the death will be
beyond your imagination."

After listening to Pattiwala's big scheme, H.H. Prophet-Diwaree realized
that Pattiwala was taking advantage of this exciting yet perturbing
subject. Such issues could be used to gain power, as it seemed that nature
favored clever people. Immediately, he too started claiming that, "The
end of the world is near. I am the bearer of miraculous powers. I have
always known about it. I am warning you in advance to come to me.
Otherwise, you will not have the savior's blessing. I am the founder of
this religion and I am the savior. At this time each and every person must
make sure that he or she is properly blessed." H.H. Prophet-Diwar
instructed his secretary; to deluge the city with big banners carrying huge
pictures of him, to make announcements on the radio, television and by
any other means they could think of, all the while collecting donations.

His secretary drew up a plan: "Rich disciples will donate the money for the banners. The banners displayed in the heart of the city, will be the most expensive, and those outside the city will be cheaper. Those who cannot donate large amounts may donate one dollar per sticker. There will be millions of stickers. We will cover the city-buses, trains, walls, staircases, balconies, restaurants, hotels, trees, houses, cars, motorcycles, rickshaws, clubs, shops and buildings with stickers bearing your photo and interesting quotations. But we must do it quickly and before Pattiwala, Sackcloth or Real-Diwaree can get wind of our plan."

All four groups and old God-Bawa had their own media - newspapers and television channels. The followers were all so deeply committed to their own religion that they did not bother to consider the others' philosophy. All they knew was that only their master mattered. After that, whenever they noticed any unusual natural phenomenon, such as an earthquake, volcano, hurricane, the earth's slowing speed, damage to the ozone layer - the preachers immediately included the event in their discourses. New millennium business also was a gimmick in the hands of these religious preachers and sensational newsmakers, as they found a ready made channel to propagate their business. Many frightened people rushed out with bags of money, which they offered at the preachers' feet in order to be blessed. Then the God-leaders promised them safety and heaven, saying, "Now, you are safe. If you want to save any of your close friends or family members, hurry and bring them too, otherwise they will not meet you in heaven."

Strangely enough, the thought never occurred to anyone that if the end was near, why should they offer money to these masters who were claiming to be God? Why did these Gods need that large amount in the final hours of reckoning? Why did they need to make plans to construct bigger and bigger buildings? Why were they seeking free help from builders, civil engineers, architects, granite dealers, marble dealers, steel dealers, iron dealers, brick dealers, property dealers and members of parliament? Why did they need to publicize the fact that they had received seventy five percent of the total building cost and required the rest within the next few days? If the end was near, then why were their needs growing so fast?

Many religious people collected vast sums in a few hours. Almost all religious heads took advantage of the prevailing mysteries surrounding death and the time-travel. If these two mysteries had not existed, they would not have become successful tycoons. People listened to discourses on issues like global warming, ozone layer depletion, AIDS etc. Since these things had never been heard of before in the history of humankind, each new mystery became a useful tool for them to build another high-rise edifice and so it went on.

One day a dog was reported missing from some people's home. Some eyewitnesses stated that they had seen the dog being taken away by a UFO. Until that day abduction by UFOs was unheard of. Also there was news in the morning that one man's original heart had been replaced by an old one. This might have been the work of aliens. Now, the mystifying question was what else could these UFOs do? In a world of confusion, a new fear had gripped the human psyche.

People knew there were living satans in the form of doctors who would steal the kidneys and other body parts of poor patients and sell them in the rich countries. Innocent patients were unaware that their kidneys had been removed, because they were anesthetized and injected with pain killers. Innumerable children's body parts were being sold to rich clients. Such businesses were booming. All the partners in such enterprises including the surgeons became rich within a short span of time. However, those who had lost their hearts and other internal organs were never admitted to hospitals. Who then, were these people who removed the organs of innocent human beings without an operation? Were they from our planet? If they did not live here, then where did they come from? Was it likely that they had arrived from other planets? If humans could land on the moon, then aliens could likewise land on our planet. Or did they live on a spaceship? Does religion say anything about them? Do Pattiwala, Prophet-Diwar, Sackcloth, Real-Diwaree or God-Bawa know about these aliens? Did those who claimed to have a special connection with God know anything? The much touted universal benevolence of God now came to be questioned. Some of the questions raised were:

Has God left us in the dark without a guide? Could it be our fault that we are unable to understand? Are Their Holinesses and God's agents wise?

If they don't know the answers, then why do they claim to be saviors or Gods? What sort of Gods are they who don't know anything? Can God be foolish or can a fool be a God? Can God be interested in constructing a big monastery? Is God a cheat or can a cheat become a God? What kind of heaven-promising personalities are they, who don't even know where heaven is? Are they Gods or what? What are they in the name of God, what are they...?

Neither the heads of these religions nor their members could provide any solutions to the confusion. The people were frightened as they did not know what was going on. What would happen next? What should they do? Was this the end of time? If it was, then did they need to do anything?

The hot topic of 'Time Travel' (TT) acquired a new dimension. Many people had heard that UFOs did exist, but it was the first time people had heard of them abducting a family. Every well educated person learned that UFOs could visit our planet, since some scientists had already declared that there was life on other planets. Now the questions about UFOs were:

- Where do they come from?
- Who or what are they?
- Are they good or bad?
- Can they help us or will they destroy us?
- How should we deal with them, if we come across them?
- Do the aliens speak their own language and do they understand ours?
- How can we communicate with them?
- How can we go near them, should we go or should we not?
- Will they just pick up one of us and take him or her to their world for good?
- Will they make us suffer like prisoners of war?
- Do they replace our kidneys or hearts with their old ones?
- Are they all the same or are some good and others evil?
- If there are both kinds - how do we recognize which is which?
- Should we make friends with them or not?

- Would these UFOs do something, which we cannot imagine or anticipate?

It was the same as when the Europeans arrived in the New World (America) they were afraid of speaking to the native inhabitants of America. Today we do not see very many Native Americans in the New World. What happened to the natives and how did the so called aliens increase in numbers? Was there any reason for it or was this just a coincidence?

None of them - God-Bawa's people, Diwar-Devotees, Prophet-Diwarians, Sackclothians, or Real-Diwaree's people - could provide the answers. Famous people, who used to appear on national and international TV channels during religious processions, were unable to furnish any plausible answer. There was no spiritualist or preacher, orthodox or modern religious pundit, psychiatrist, professor or Head of the Department of the biggest university, who could provide the answer. Many of the people, who had written famous books, produced famous movies on UFOs and aliens were also unable to provide any answers. People, who earlier preached about life after death and beyond, were now quiet. They had previously described what happened at the moment of death and where the soul traveled to after that. Now all of them were silent.

The second issue also gave rise to many questions. Such as:
Where would the people who were preparing to travel in time eventually land? What would be their fate? Would they return or be lost in an unknown place? There was another more interesting development about computer chip implants in the brain, of which I will tell you later.

If this is the "end of the time", then could it be the beginning of a "new time" as well? Could it be the end of history as well? Will history continue after this? Is there a great soul on earth whose birth generates a new history? If yes, then who and where is he or she? In which country and in which city does he or she live? What was the special quality which he or she had but others didn't? Did she or he know about the "end of time"?

Did those who planned to travel in two directions of time need to pray for the right answers? If so, then to whom should they pray? Should they go to a famous place of worship or should they meditate at a particular place on earth? What was the right method to find the correct answers that would resolve the prevailing confusion? Was it at all possible to talk to God? If so, what, who, and where was God?

It was just before the announcement of the end of the time Mr. Singh Messenger passed this unforeseen news to each and every responsible God-Man, saying:

"God-leaders, you carry the responsibility to teach the right things to the public. Now according to the time, you need to teach them two most essential things: 1. What Death really is and 2. What Time-Travel is and what are its consequences. To teach these, you will first need to learn about them. Until this day you have been claiming to be the bridge between God and the public. You have always promised them security after death and have continued to brainwash them. Brainwashing is one of the biggest crimes in the world of God. It indoctrinates people into becoming criminals. Brainwashed people follow you, leaving behind their life's goals. They stop searching for God. This is the reason many of them have your photo on their altar. You are the problem and now you have to become the solution.

If a child gets lost and is unable to find the way to his mother, then you should say to him: "*Dear baby I do not know where your mother is, but I can help you by doing such and such.*" You should not claim to be his mother and make him serve you. You should not use or abuse lost children. That is deception. This might result in a situation where his real mother finds him and tries to take him back. At such a time he may answer: 'No, you are not my mother. Get lost. Go away from here. This holy mentor is my mother, not you.' And the mother might say: 'My son, I love you. I am so happy to have found you. The proof is that I gave birth to you, and nourished you since you were an infant ...'

Not recognizing his real mother the obsessed child might reply: 'I am not a fool. I am living with my real mother. My real mother has taught me that if a deceiver comes to take me away I should chase her away, telling her to get lost. Now I am wise. I knew it could happen. I know cheats exist in this world. They use the same statements, the same words, but there is no room in my mind for deceivers.'

Mr. God-leader's, real mother may try to convince her children by recounting to them true incidents from the beginning of their lives to the day they were kidnapped. She might tell them that they were little babies when the kidnappers took them away from her, so they can no longer remember her. Now she may show them proof through "The Ascent of Man from Pluto to Venus"

You are obsessed. Earth mother cannot speak or the real mother does not exist. Still, you prepared all your brainwashed children for such an event, because something inside you kept telling you that this could happen one day. Therefore, your hard headed kids may never go to anyone including their real mother - the Savior.

This time the real mother in unbearable pain may cry: 'God, what a difficult situation you have put me in! Even my children cannot recognize me. You have made a mother's heart soft and kind, and you have thrown it into a furnace.'

Only a mother's heart feels such intense pain when knives and swords flash around her child's head. If her baby cuts his finger, a mother's heart bleeds. No one can plumb the depths of a mother's heart...

The leaders were enraged by these examples. They would respond, "Mr. Singh Messenger, do you have answers for the entire world's corruption? Do you know that people make spurious medicine and fill medicine capsules with flour? Corrupt doctors steal innocent people's organs to sell in rich countries? People export young girls to rich countries for the pleasure of rich devils? Do you have any idea about pickpockets, thieves, robbers, bandits, politicians, crooks, brutal police officers, drug dealers, arms dealers, gangs, and mafias spreading poison? Don't you know this world is filled with criminals? Why don't you go to them, if you are so concerned about the world? We are not harming anyone. We are not chopping off people's heads. We only tell them to pray and live life in the manner set forth by our master. Whatever we are doing, it is for peace.

"If you really want to deal with religious leaders, then why don't you go to the leaders of other religions who are fighting for money and political power? Look at H.H. St. Michael's monastery which is a billion dollar business; H.H.A turnover Rs 400 crore, H.H. B. turnover Rs 350 crore, H.H.C. turnover Rs 400 crore, H.H. D. turnover Rs 400 crore, H.H. turnover Rs 300 crore, H.H. E. turnover Rs 150 crore, H.H. F. turnover $ 200 million, H.H. G. turnover $ 500 million, H.H. J. turnover $ 300 million (real names are not disclosed). Michael Pattiwala's monastery, Sackcloth's monastery and billionaire Prophet-Diwaree's earnings... in the name of God... they have pulled this off by cleverly conning people. Those who cheat the public are the most recognized and well respected people in the world. Why don't you ask them to follow your truth?

"Mr. Singh Messenger, everybody lives for money, corruption is everywhere. If we do a bit of the same then what is the harm in that? If our actions are indirectly harming the world, why don't you first correct others who are doing direct harm? There are millionaires, billionaires and trillionaires in this world and the Constitution protects them. Why don't you tell them about your Anna Mario, and why don't you tell them that as long as billionaires and Anna Mario exist in this world the law is imperfect. Whoever occupies the chair of power takes the oath under the flag of truth, to remain faithful to the Constitution. Their salaries and assets are incomparable, while at the same time people are dying of hunger. Even if they follow the Constitution, that will still not solve your Anna Mario's problem. Everyone knows that Mother Nature has evolved the human brain but a centuries old constitution protects the powerful money-bags. The power brokers are concerned only about themselves and not for the poor Anna Marios of the earth. So why don't you go to those big bulls and law makers?

"Mr. Singh Messenger, we know what we are doing. People follow us because we are rich, good and we fulfill their needs. Their lives are ninety percent bad because of themselves, and the ten percent good is because of us. We are the wisest people in the world. This crowd is proof of our wisdom. We have gained this wisdom from our holy scriptures and our saints. We know thousands of things that no one else knows. Only after learning and understanding the truth that we lead this holy life. We are handling their issues in the best possible manner. We are providing solutions to all their problems.

"And listen, Mr. Singh Messenger; we don't believe that there is anyone wiser than us. You do not agree with our ideas and we don't agree with yours. The majority is wise enough to understand our truths. The wise will always agree with the truth and disagree with falsehood. You claim that your ideas are right, and we say we are right, so leave it to the public to decide. Leave us alone and mind your own business," was their general response.

"Listen, God-leaders, your philosophy is the root cause of all suffering! In order to bring peace to the world your ideas must be totally eradicated. Misery is the outcome of an ignorant and bigoted philosophy. This ignorance is being propagated by you fame hungry cheats and fools. It is you who have destroyed the happiness of Anna Mario. Tell them the truth about yourselves. Don't keep them in the dark because nobody can save you evil-doers. Do you know how many thousands of deaths your foolish acts are causing? Do you know the reason for endemic poverty? Do you have any idea why people are selling arms to the poor? With whose money are the rulers of poor countries buying these weapons? Why are they buying them? Do you know the disastrous consequences of war or protracted insurgency? What do you know about the long term damage caused by a bigoted philosophy?" These were Singh Messenger's questions.

"Listen Mr. Singh Messenger, science and religion are total opposites. They are like day and night, or light and darkness. We use cell phones, microphones, televisions, and other scientific equipment. That doesn't mean we should believe in your science. No one God knows better than we do. The rest is not our business. If your scientific truth is true, then why don't you go to the gene scientists and nature scientists, why are you spoiling our fun? After all everything is going well, enjoyment is enjoyment. Everyone enjoys our performances. Everyone is happy with what we are doing. We are doing what people enjoy," the God men answered.

"Listen God-leaders, if you guide others in spiritual matters then you must be filled with the truth. Your ego can cause serious aberrations in your perceptions. It is hard for you to tell your followers that you have been cheating them, because when you tell your people this, they will spit on you. But let them spit on you. Let them condemn and hit you. If you wish them well - then make this sacrifice for them. No truth can be established upon a foundation of lies. Live a true life and then learn to teach the truth. You have to clean up the garbage of confusion that you have spread on this beautiful Earth," Singh Messenger told them boldly.

The news of the conversation between Singh Messenger and the God-leaders spread slowly around the world. Their commission-agent followers warned them: "Do not dare to recant now. Do not dare to admit that you were wrong, because we brought all our well-wishers, friends, and family to you for initiation. Do not reveal that we cheated them. You should have thought about it at the very inception of this game of cheating and deception. What was wrong with your brain at that time? Now carry the burden of sin and falsehood that you have placed upon your shoulders. You are the ones who said that eventually truth prevails. Why didn't you understand what you preached," counseled the agents.

Then the question was: Were the great masters, His Holiness Sackcloth, His Holiness Prophet-Diwar, His Holiness God-Bawa or Real-Diwaree, really Gods? If yes then, why were there so many Gods? Was it not enough to get answers from one God? That's why the truth seekers were very angry with them. Their issue was if they are Gods or God's agents, why could they not provide the answers instead of enjoying an extravagant life in God's name?

A long time ago Tom had said to Maya, "If God-Bawa is God then no one on Earth is greater than he. He deserves the royal treatment - far grander than he is now receiving. But, if he is not God, then people should punish him in the most horrifying way, and teach him a proper lesson for being deceitful. He must be stripped naked and physically punished with a hundred thousand needles. His eyes must be gouged out. His tongue must be tied with rope and ripped out. His arms and legs must be pulled off for deceiving millions of people. He must get a punishment, harder than has as yet been suffered in this universe, because no crime is greater than deceit, the greatest crime in the universe, which locks the doors to God."

People started to question them: "Hey so-called great master! What is wrong with you? Did you not promise to grant heaven to your followers? Do you remember your promises to them? Do you know what you used to tell them at the time of their initiation? Do you remember what you used to say when you addressed the public from a high pedestal? If you did not know the truth then why did you cheat us? Why did you play with our lives? Now you tell us, what we should do to you? Should we punish you or leave it up to God? Should we strip you and beat you to death in front of your followers or what do you deserve? You cheat! You have been misleading us for decades. You cheat! Born deceiver!"

****

Step Twenty Two...

LIFE OF HIS HOLINESS

As you know, Singh messenger was formerly a professor of philosophy and an expert in the use of spiritual jargon. Since he was a reluctant but loyal saint, God-Bawa could feel his sincerity, honesty and something good in him. Before exposing the failings of the God-men Singh Messenger had lived with God-Bawa as a common saint for a while. God-Bawa felt as he had found a true friend in whom he could confide the hidden pain in his heart. They had had conversation during which they told each other everything, including their personal life stories, except that Singh didn't reveal that he was a messenger of the Messiah. One evening God-Bawa and Singh Messenger sat in a peaceful garden having coffee. Singh Messenger asked God-Bawa, "God-Bawa, how did your life become like this?"

God-Bawa started his story, "My life has been shaped by one police officer as well as those who loved me and those hated me. Mr. Andrew who was a very clever politician did the rest. When I was young I wanted only to please my creator by living a normal life of truth, honesty and righteousness. I wanted to live a saintly life. After finishing high school I looked for a job so I could lead a normal life. Most jobs were reserved for low caste people or untouchables. There was no room for high caste people even if they were intelligent and sincere. Everyone said that I would need to pay a bribe of thousands of dollars to get a good job. In their language a bribe was called 'gift' or 'donation'. For an average job the rate was one hundred thousand. It was not possible to get the kind of job I could do without paying a four hundred thousand dollar gift. Nothing could be done without greasing someone's palms.

Yet nobody ever told me openly what to do. My father was a poor farmer. He could never have afforded that much money. One army officer told me that when he joined the force he had paid fifty thousand dollars. His father had sold his property and pawned his mother's jewelry. But he had no regrets, as after joining the force he had made ten times more than that. He considered a bribe as an initial investment for making money. I was shocked to know that an army man could be corrupt. I controlled myself. 'What if I can't afford to bribe the officials concerned?' I asked casually. Funny question! He advised me to join a monastery, renounce the world and become a monk, not to look for a job. His words were imprinted in my mind.

The following week I went to a police recruitment office. The officer asked me to speak to his assistant who would explain how I should proceed. His assistant closed the door and said to me, 'One hundred thousand.' I was shocked. 'What do you mean by one hundred thousand?' I asked him.

He bluntly replied, 'You cannot become an officer, if you cannot understand what I just said. This was an interview and you have failed. When you are able to understand this question and its answer, then you can enter our world. For the time being you must go home and learn more about the real work-a-day world and its language,'

I was shocked. I had not known that a police officer could be corrupt. I couldn't understand, what was going on in this world. I only knew that the general public would break the laws, but a police officer? Are they devils in uniform or what? I couldn't believe it. However, I understood his point - as I had already had a similar experience with the army officer. 'But why one hundred thousand...?' I asked,

Then he graciously explained, 'We have donated half our father's property to obtain this position. Therefore, the first thing we have to do is to recover the amount. Whatever we make over and above that is profit. It is a one time investment for a lifetime's income. The larger your investment the greater your returns.'

I was shocked. Again I could not believe my ears. Then I said, 'Are you talking about a donation or a bribe? Are you really serving the nation?' I could not understand how a person whose service began with corruption could serve the nation.
He said, 'Anyway, you will receive your interview result by mail.'

Since I was quite candid with the officer regarding my opinion during the interview, I did not receive a reply. I was expecting a rejection anyway. I complained about that corrupt police officer but the next day they filed four allegations against me for no reason. Then they arrested me at gun point and took me to the police station in handcuffs where I was confined to a cell for forty eight hours. I was harassed by the police officer and told that if I opened my mouth about him, he could keep me in prison until I died. Anything was possible for him because he was powerful and I was nothing.

I learned that it was impossible to fight these monsters. I felt like a helpless child in a world of tigers. I knew he was a fiend in a police uniform and if I opened my mouth he would ensure that I faced a miserable death. In this world no one could win against corrupt and powerful people who misused their positions. I believed that even God could not touch them. No one could understand my situation - full of tension and never knowing when and from where my next meal would come! I became depressed.

Pretty Gloria who was with me for three years and nurtured my thoughts with her love, started to lose confidence in my ability to support her financially. She realized that in my bankrupt condition I would not be able to buy her good clothes. If I couldn't fulfill at least her basic needs, then it was understood that I should let her father arrange her marriage to someone else who would at least provide for her. There was no point in discussing the matter with her father because his first question would be about my job and my salary, and I had neither of them," explained God-Bawa.

"Her father had a lot of money, couldn't he provide a good dowry?" asked Singh Messenger.

"My father had lived an honest and principled life. He had taught me that one should never accept dowry. He could not bear to watch my sister suffer because of a lack of dowry and died in constant worry and tension. Later, my sister also committed suicide. Since then I could not reconcile the two - 'love and dowry' in other words, 'love and business' or 'virtue and sin'. My conscience would not permit me to be corrupt especially with regard to a girl whom I loved and was planning to make my life partner. For me love was God and dowry was evil. The two did not go together. For me it was better to lose a sinful game. For me taking dowry was as sinful as giving it. I decided never to indulge in such a sin in my life.

Her father was looking for a boy who was worth a gift of one hundred thousand dollars. An unemployed boy could not afford such a gift," explained God-Bawa.

"Where on earth can people arrange so much money from?" the Messenger asked curiously.

God-Bawa said, "The birth of a daughter is the biggest curse in our society. Her father had to find the money by fair means or foul. A daughter is a burden on a poor father's shoulder. Abortion became a common practice in our society. After ultra-sound scanning if the foetus in the womb was found to be a girl she was immediately killed and thrown into garbage. That is why in many states girls were twenty five percent less than boys. The dowry custom was causing an alarming imbalance in the population.

Just as an unemployed man is given one thousand dollars to take care of a diseased dog, a poor father had to pay money to buy a boy for his daughter. Greedy, shameless, irreligious, money minded, materialistic boys only accepted the girl for a sum. They do not value love. For them a bribe was primary and the bride was secondary. These shameless boys ruined the lives of poor girls. Any perceived or imagined lacuna in the bride's qualities was obliterated by money. She has to be sold to a cheap or expensive boy; otherwise a father must be prepared for social censure.

I did not read it in any scripture, but I knew from the bottom of my heart that corruption and religion could not go together. Religion was openly displayed everywhere, but corruption was covered with iron sheets. I knew that dowry is a big sin. Anyone who takes or gives dowry should be condemned to a permanent hell. He should be cursed by thousands and thousands of poor innocent fathers, who because of their poverty could not buy a boy for their daughters," said God-Bawa.

"Yes, God-Bawa, in this case I agree with you. It is true that these people have no value for love and humanity. They are only concerned about money. They are neither God-fearing nor religious. Such people cover their real faces with the mask of religion. But hell is their destiny. No matter how many times they pray, they must go to hell for this unforgivable sin. No religion can protect a man who does not place value in true love, but values only money and pleasure," said the Messenger.

With a deep breath God-Bawa said, "I was destroyed by the animal-headed policemen and corrupt customs of this world, but my passion had not died. There were dozens of stories I could tell you about the ministry of hell. In this hell any murderer can be proven virtuous, if he or she can afford an expensive lawyer, and any innocent person can be punished for no reason. The police harassed anyone who raised his or her voice against a powerful government official or Member of Parliament and their lives ended in agony, depression and a horrible death in jail. I shall not forget this until the day I die. I have not told anybody of this incident until today, even though, I wanted to tell the public that whomsoever takes or gives dowry or bribes is a sinner. I wanted to uproot the tree of human suffering by living a life of principle.

"In this world devils live in the uniforms of power. These devils are found in every field. Even though they number only a few, this world does not need so many of them to spread terror. One evil doer is more powerful than one hundred good people. One policeman can start a fire that a hundred fire fighters cannot extinguish. I have so many things to say about them, but I cannot, because my objective is only to turn people's minds to God. If I ask my followers not to turn weddings into business transactions, they might get an inkling of my personal trauma with the police and Gloria's father. You know in our world a man who is handcuffed and imprisoned is considered a bad person. Media people would find a thrilling news story in Bawa's once being handcuffed, beaten up and locked in a cell for two days. Nobody would bother to find out how truthful loyal and honest I was, and consequently my image would suffer. Also, some media people are ready eager to drag me down.

"Nobody knew that I loved Gloria. Neither would Gloria repeat this story to anyone. She left me. I was shocked. In those sorrowful moments my passions were subdued. I became a recluse and went to the holy mountains. I lived in solitude, spending my time in penance and self-mortification. Mostly, I traveled barefoot, pondering on the misfortune of those with little money who dared to love beauty. During that period I lived with many famous fate-changing God-men. I found out the truth about some of those famous luck changers. I learned a lot by spending time with them. I could not have understood them without living with them.

Singh Messenger, I still cannot forget Gloria. You know, youth is after all, just a moment, but it is the moment, when unique love sparks, which you carry in your heart until your last breath. Much of the time, I still think of her. She was my first love and my last. I cannot forget her tears. Whenever I think of her my heart bleeds," said God-Bawa sadly.

"What happened to Gloria after she left you?" asked Messenger.

"I became a recluse. I did not ask anyone about her. One day, I overheard some people say that her father had got her married to a police officer. The police officer was very short tempered. He wanted to know about Gloria's first love. She refused to talk about it, saying, 'Now I am yours. My past is behind me. It is over. A woman is like an ornamental tree. She belongs in the garden where she is planted. Please create a good atmosphere. Please, let me grow. I do not belong with my father's family anymore. I am yours, please let me live here in peace.'

"Her husband could not understand what she was talking about - gardens, trees, flowers, fruit ... He just wanted to dig up every skeleton even where there was none, because sometimes he felt that he was losing Gloria. One day she prayed, 'God help me. I don't know what to do.'

"Eventually, she could not fight her past any longer. She could not go to her father's home as that would mean losing face. Her father would not welcome her anyway, as according to custom, a married daughter does not return to live in her father's home.

One day, the police officer came home after work to find that Gloria had hanged herself by a ceiling fan. Thus, she ended her life. The police officer was very clever and the case was dismissed as an accidental death."

"Who told you this?" asked Singh Messenger curiously.

"One day, after I had renounced the world, I went to the town where Gloria had lived after she married. Since I was wearing the robes of an ascetic, nobody recognized me and some people in the town told me about the police officer's wife," said God-Bawa.

"It is very sad that people place no merit on loyalty, honesty and faithfulness, but value only money, expensive cars, jobs and big houses. They cannot understand love. Sinful money can buy any boy for a sinner's daughter. Sad that a person, who has no money, cannot find a good match for his daughter. Sinners like the king who spends millions on his daughter's wedding are praised by the poor. People who spend lavishly on wedding anniversaries, parties, and other celebrations are admired. The biggest criminal earns the highest reputation. Money has become all powerful. A rich man can build a Taj Mahal for his dead beloved to show the world his love for her, but poor men must say goodbye to their beloved because they don't have a job, and so keep the secret hidden in their hearts. One man can build a huge monument for his dead beloved and another has nothing to feed his living beloved. Rich, egocentric people cannot see into the loving eyes of the underprivileged. This world remembers to the one who has built the Taj Mahal and forgets the millions who have said goodbye to their beloveds," agreed the Messenger.

God-Bawa said: "After going through these painful experiences, I learned that it was extremely difficult to be honest. I tried to remain

honest, but I was pushed to death's door. Things in this world were
terribly wrong. I had been through hell - living without food and shelter.
Had I stood up for the truth I would not have seen this day. I am alive
with the blessings of corruption. You cannot even imagine how many
families I destroyed with the help of politicians.

"I was very angry with the corrupt people who controlled the world by
the power of money. I was angry with corrupt officials and their corrupt
employees. I do not blame the public. Why should the public follow rules
when their rulers are corrupt? Why should students listen to a principal
who doesn't have any principles? Why should children listen to their
parents if the parents are immoral? The value systems of this world are
faulty to this day. No one bothers to set it right, and no one will listen to
a pure Bawa if he teaches the truth. People are curious about a man who
has seven wives, one for each for a day of the week. Media people will
find the story interesting. But if someone were to speak up about
destructive customs like dowry or bribes and corruption, powerful
politicians would eliminate him. No one was prepared to pay attention to
a lesson on morality and humanity.

"I was very sad. Having no other choice, I had renounced the world. I
had no money while I lived in the holy city. I desperately needed a
blanket. I needed at least a pot to cook in. But nothing was possible
without money. I was hungry and crying out for help. But I learned there
is no kindness in the heart of humankind. Humanity did not exist in
human beings. Nobody wanted to understand the pain of a person dying
of starvation. Hundreds of people passed me by every hour. They saw
my situation but everyone was rushing to grab more and more. Rich
people had been busy gathering food for five hundred years over seven
generations. Nobody wanted to share his bread with a starving man. I
was about to die. I had no strength left to struggle to stay alive anymore
and was counting my last breaths. I knew I wouldn't survive. I was dying
anyway. Who would care if I was dead? Nobody! The municipal
employees would just dump my body somewhere.

"I learned that kindness, pity and humanity cannot exist in this world as
long as the devil wears the uniform of government officials and the law
protects corrupt billionaires. Everything in the name of religion was

show business. Nothing was real. Millions of falsehoods were being spread in the name of God and religion. These bewildering beliefs were tools of entertainment for human beings. If repeated a hundred times a lie becomes the truth. Anyone who has the confidence to claim to be God is worshiped. A lie is a powerful tool to change one's personal world. The bigger the lie, the greater are the chances of its acceptance. A butcher feels a little compunction at his first slaughter. After chopping off the necks of many innocents it becomes normal for him. After practicing dishonesty, one can lie with a straight face. After practicing deceit one doesn't even know what truth is. He can lie with confidence. Lie in the name of God with determination and confidence, people will lap it up and shower money on you. Lie if you want to do something in this world. Lie more, lie tactfully if you want to enjoy this world.

My anger was so strong; it turned my life in this direction. My blind ego made me believe that everything I was doing was absolutely correct. There was nothing wrong in fighting against their horrible customs and political inhumanity. I learned that there was no God, and there was no God-power. God would never come, even if one cried for him. That is why people lose their faith after such experiences. They cannot accept God's existence as a reality. Thus they have forgotten every miracle of God. The only thing that could make them believe in God's existence was magic, mysticism, mesmerism and hypnosis. To captivate them I needed to play games full of mysteries and lies. Only iron could cut iron therefore, only ignorance could deal with ignorance.

"I determined to completely and terribly mess up the system, so that one day a kind politician, rich and powerful or a religious leader would wake up and realize that the system had gone completely wrong. He or she would realize that it needed to be placed on the proper track. I determined to become as bad as I could, and spread complete madness, ignorance, and confusion. Then nature would produce a jewel to balance it. The sun could not rise unless complete darkness prevailed. Ram, Krishna or Jesus would never have come if there had not been complete madness. I knew that when things went from bad to worse, and worse to worst, it was then that God sent a remedy to completely stem the rot and re-establish the domain of truth and righteousness. War had to take place to bring peace. Dense darkness had to fall for sunrise to come. Extreme ignorance has to spread to create genuine knowledge. I started to deepen the ignorance.

Then I put my life into the game of destroying the egos of utterly selfish rich people who were totally oblivious of their obligations to society - to the poor and the helpless. I wanted to make the tycoons and the captains of the business and industry realize the pain caused by dowry and corruption. Dowry nurtures the body for a short time, but love nurtures the soul. This destructive instrument has destroyed the lives of innocents. There were many young people who died or disappeared in their twenties. Those young boys could not taste the fruit of love life. Nobody knows the number of young boys who became victims of this horrifying custom of bribery, dowry, and corruption.

During my ascetic days I learned a big lesson that there is only one thing that can help a man - and that is money. I was struggling to stay alive because I didn't know what would happen if I didn't struggle with my full strength to stay alive. I learned that if I wanted to live with high principles and honesty, I would be dead within weeks. If I were dead then I couldn't do anything to get life back into this body. If I didn't charge money to that cancer patient's son I would be dead. Nothing could keep me alive except money. Then I learned that money was so powerful that it could extend the life of a dying person. Money could do anything because it is more powerful than anything else. Therefore I made up my mind to live for the God of money by becoming a God-man.

I was sick and tired of it all, I said enough is enough. After going through all these religious practices, I discovered that none of those methods had yielded the desired results. All those things were just imaginary, but one could make money easily by applying psychological practices on others, because people believe myths. Now the question was: what about the fear of God? I came to the conclusion that no one has seen God, because to popular belief there is no God. I was one hundred percent sure that God would not come before a human being even if the man had murdered innocents or committed a crime. With that assurance I learned that money is power and money is everything, therefore one should do whatever possible to make money by any means, so as to enjoy life. Man lives once, and no one has seen what happens after death, so this life is for enjoyment.

As I had been practicing mystic contemplation for a long time, a few visitors started believing that I had become 'Numero Uno' in the fields of mystery and the occult. In those days when I was almost starving to death with no help in sight, an extremely rich businessman named Hirachand chanced to meet me. He was most unhappy because of his family and business problems. Mr. Hirachand blindly believed in miracles because of his family background. He had heard many stories about the 'miracle philosophy'. He looked at me and thought that I could be a real saint. He came to me and asked me, 'Bawa do you know anything about palm reading or luck-changing magic?'

'Of course I do - but how did you know this?' was my clever answer.

'Your thin, skinny body, the kind of life you are living, your austerity and authentic holy appearance tells me that you have some powers within you,' he said to me.

"Then I said to him with firmness, 'I have wealth beyond imagination. Your name is Hirachand and you are a property dealer and you are facing a big problem in your business and at the same time you are having troubles with your wife. Is this true?'

"Thrilled, Hirachand said to me in a shaky voice: 'Oh! Bawa you are the one I have been looking for. God-Bawa! You are God and if you are not God then you are God's only blessed son. Now, I have found the jewel for which I came.'

"Then I said to him, 'Yes, you are right. I am the one who brought you here. I inspired you to come here. I know you were longing to find the truth. You are indeed the best person in this world. Now I take you under my protection, and your wishes shall be fulfilled. Listen to me. I know you are burdened with family problems. There are numerous things going on in your family. You are a reasonable person but no one in your family can understand you. Your wife doesn't offer you support. You are a kind-hearted person. You are always right and a man who believes only in true principles. You are a religious and God fearing man, but people cannot understand your deep philosophy. Tell me if it is so,' I asked him to see his reaction. He was thrilled. He said to me, 'Yes, God-Bawa, every single thing you have said has touched my heart. I know you are God. You are revealing your hidden divinity in this way. I am glad that I have eventually found you. I have been looking for you for many years,' he said to me in excitement.

After I had read his palm, he concluded that I was God. Why would I tell him that I was not? Indirectly I strengthened his belief that he was absolutely right, and reinforced his ego. I said to him, 'Yes you are right. I am God, but this is a secret. Do not mention it to anyone. You are very special therefore I have come out of my cave to bless you.'

"With folded hands he requested, 'I want to take you to my home. Please accept my invitation.'

'I don't go to the city, but since you are a special devotee, I will come to your home. But listen carefully, I keep my divinity hidden so do not tell anyone who I am. You may reveal my secret only to your close friends and then also to not more than two or three,' I instructed. He agreed to my condition.

Hirachand bought me an airplane ticket and gave me some money and new clothes. For the first time in my life, I sat in an airplane. I was very happy now I would not die of starvation. I learned the tricks of 'Miracles' and the power of lies. I learned the psychology of making money. No one knew about this and Hirachand would never be able to figure it out in his lifetime. The unanswered question remained: *If God-Bawa is not God, then how did he know about my business, my name and my personal problems?* Later Hirachand himself told me the hidden details of his personal life. Hirachand requested me use my divine powers to help him in business and advise him about his investments.

In the airplane he told me most of his secrets, which he would never share with anyone else. Thus, he gave me the key to his personal life. He told me secrets about his best friend, a businessman named Mr. Harry Kingson.

Hirachand told me that he lived in London most of the time, but owned houses in other cities as well. He requested me to help him in his business through my Godly powers. He had many ideas about making his business prosper but he needed the godly powers to expand his business quickly. All he needed from me was to tell him where he must invest and where he shouldn't."

"How could you convince a businessman like Harry and all the other politicians?" asked Singh Messenger.

"I knew that Harry was an important person in the city. If he was convinced, then half the population would automatically come to know of me, and many of them would become my followers. The next morning, during a conversation, I invoked the invisible forces. I had a prayer book with a soft cover. Using the book as a supporting slate, I placed a sheet of writing paper on it and handing it to Harry I said, "Write your five biggest problems on this paper. I insist that you do not show me what you have written. Watch me and satisfy yourself that my eyes are closed.

With eyes closed, I turned my face away. Harry finished writing his five main problems. I was still facing the other way with my eyes still closed. "Yes God-Bawa! I have written out my five main problems," he said to me.

"Fold that paper and destroy it completely," I said to him and after a brief pause I asked, "Have you destroyed the paper?"

"Yes, completely,"

"Can I open my eyes now?"

"Yes God-Bawa,"

"Turning to him with closed eyes, I took the book from his hand. Then I opened my eyes. I put on a grave face and with an expertise acquired through extensive practice, casually turned over the first page of the book without arousing his suspicion I closed my eyes and shook my body in a mystic way, and went into a mysterious trance, impressing upon him that I was in the grip of super-natural mysterious powers, during the trance. Coming out of my deep meditation I calmly asked, "Harry, my child, was your first question about your desire to have a son?"

"Yes God-Bawa!!" he said, surprised.

"Is your second problem about the fact that you are not happy with your family life? Natalee or Ruby…? It is not clear in my thoughts."

"Yes God-Bawa!!" his eyes opened wide with astonishment.

"Is your third question about the problem with your in-laws?"

"Yes God-Bawa!!!"

"Are your fourth and fifth problems; about getting back your money from your buyers Malkiyat and Kareeman?" Harry was thrilled. He knelt before me and clasped my feet, "That's it! God-Bawa! Now I know you are God. You are the one I have been seeking since my childhood. Now I am blessed," he said to me with tearfully. After that things moved very quickly and now here I am…

This is the story of the total transformation of my life and my ideals. In my new life, I have become a dedicated devotee of mammon. Mammon is my patron saint, my only God - my everything. People want to serve me only because I have money. They want to serve me because they believe that I can do something for them. If you have money then everyone cares for you and thus money is the key for the success in any venture. I remember one of my Spanish disciples telling me, '*cuando tenia dinero era senor Tomas, Ahora que no tengo dinero, soy senor no mas*'. (When I had money I was Mr. Thomas but now that I have no money I am 'Mr. no more'). I had great difficulty suppressing a smile at this universal truth. Now I have money and I control the most powerful of politicians and businessmen by assuring them that they are safe after death.

And let me tell you one more thing. If I had learned the magic of David Copperfield I would have conquered the world. I would have controlled the minds of the entire population of this earth, if I could have made a helicopter vanish on a Las Vegas stage. If I could have slit a man's throat and then joined it back, if I could have resurrected a corpse before thousands of viewers, if I could have made huge buildings appear and disappear in minutes, or conjured up a strange spirit who could read the minds of thousands of rich people and put a written note about their thoughts into their pockets - I could have told big lies with my expertise.

I would have shaken the whole world and for thousands of years no one would have believed in God. Every human being on earth would have believed that I was the only God. They would forget all the other Prophets, Christs, Avatars, Saints or Reincarnations of God for ever. In future for thousands of years they would not welcome any real Christ unless he or she had performed greater magic than mine. But unfortunately I didn't find Copperfield or any other magician at the right time.

"Mr. Harry was Hirachand's best friend. After my ostensible blessings, he had a daughter and later a son as well. This 'miracle' made my name, fame and fortune. The rest is history. Harry and I, we did many things which nobody knew about. I did many things about which even Harry doesn't know. One should never tell the deepest secret of the heart to anyone. Therefore I will not reveal those secrets but anyone who puts a barrier in our way did not see the morning light. Now tell me Singh Messenger, what do you think of my life story?"

"Yes, it is interesting, amazing, and very unusual. Those corrupt people changed your life completely. Anger can change the life of an honest and daring person too. If Mahatma Gandhi had not been kicked off a train, he probably would have lived a common life. Those ticket inspectors kicked the dormant forces awake, and indirectly told him, "Wake up, wake up passionate sleeping man, wake up, and do something." Bawa, whatever happens, happens for a good reason. I understand that the sun rises from total darkness, and wisdom rises from dense confusion. Your contribution to this world was amazing. You can do so many things as you have the power. You can truly change the world," replied Messenger.

"What do you think I should do?" God-Bawa asked uncomfortably.
"Singh Messenger said: "You can tell corrupt people in the fields of law, politics, education, and other professions that you cannot save them, only God can, and unfortunately you are not God. To those millions who believe in you, you can tell them the truth about yourself, and all about the Truth. You can tell them that you are not the Savior or God. All your promises were false. They should seek the Truth, which may be much higher than they thought; therefore, they must search with passionate curiosity for a God-like supreme existence. You can present four gifts to this earth before your death. Only you can do that - no one else. That is the reason God has made you.

1. The first gift you can present to this world is by telling the truth that magic and superstition are not the ways to God. In this world only you can do this.
2. You can tell them God's path is not easy. Nor should they go through unnecessary problems by believing in the wrong things in God's name. In this world only you can do this.
3. You can tell them that by believing in the wrong things, they will eventually lose valuable time, in their precious lives, instead of gaining something. In this world only you can do this.
4. You can tell them that no one can change their luck except God and themselves. It is wrong to put a mediator in between. Those agents always become a barrier between them and their God. Only you can remove this great confusion about a mediator. They need to learn that every human being has an equal right to be close to God. Only they themselves can change their luck by performing good karma. This will be a great gift from you to this world of confusion. If you can present this gift to the world your name will be pronounced with respect for generations to come.

"Mr. Messenger, what is wrong with you? What do you mean by that? Why should I tell them what is good and what is bad? They are not going to listen to me. They will all do what they want. They are all hardened pleasure-seekers, who want to pretend that they are followers of a real

God. None of them are searching for the truth. So, let it be as it is. There is no point in stirring up a hornets' nest and inviting trouble. They are not here for repentance or confession. They are not here to learn truthfulness, loyalty, honesty or how to live an upright life. I know what they want to hear from me, and I tell them precisely that," said God-Bawa.

"I know people want to live in a fantasy, they do not want to listen to the truth. People don't like wise, truthful, practical things and a universal God in life. They want fantasy. They want fun. They want mystery. Mystery only... They want to tell their Judge that they actually have been trying to become good but a fake holy man misled them. They want to have some real sensible excuse to hide their guilt, but God-Bawa! Do not forget that you have promised them safety and salvation after their death," said Singh Messenger.

"Listen to me carefully Mr. Messenger; nobody except you knows how I create the magic in which they blindly believe. For instance; I used to hide a special sheet of carbon paper between the page of my book and the one being used as a supporting pad to write their questions. After tearing up the original paper, I would read it and repeat the questions in their minds. They used to believe that I had read their minds. They were astonished as they thought that only God can read minds. Thus they accepted me as an all knowing omnipresent and omnipotent or a supreme being gifted with special powers to read human minds. If they had come to know this, do you think that they would leave me alive? They would have lynched me on the spot. They want me to continue this game. They love it, they enjoy it. Let them enjoy. What is wrong with that?" reasoned God-Bawa.

"Everything is wrong with that. Nothing is right in that. You are supposed to tell them only the truth. That is what God has employed you for," replied Messenger.

"You are making a big mistake Mr. Singh Messenger! Be careful. Do you know about Diwaree? Until today, nobody knows where and how he disappeared from the face of the earth. Whoever does not listen to me ... Therefore, listen to me Singh Messenger! I cannot forget the time I lay helpless on the sidewalk inches away from death in that holy city. Did anybody care about me then? At that crucial moment what helped me - the truth or lies? Would I be in this world, if I did not lie? Would Mr. Hirachand have supported me if I had not lied? Did anybody ask me what happened to me when I could not find a simple job to keep the wolf away from my door? Did anybody care about me when Gloria was wrenched away from my heart for lack of filthy lucre? Did anybody find out what that police officer did to this innocent? Did anybody say to my father, *'It is okay. We will give your son a job without bribery, because he is honest?'* Did anybody say to me, *'it is the end of corruption?'* My life was finished. Is it not true that today I am alive because of my lies? I know it is bad, but look at the history of the world, whoever has committed this sin has survived. I know it is bad, but I also open the eyes of this world to how selfish and corrupt people have become, how they are being protected and how honest people are dying," God-Bawa retorted logically.

"Your fight is with corrupt mortals, not with God, therefore you should not use God's name. You should not claim to be God," said Singh Messenger boldly.

"I have not stated to anyone that I am God, but if people think I am, let them think so. Moreover if I tell them that I am not a God, they are not going to listen to me," retorted God-Bawa with a frown on his face.

"God-Bawa, you know what tricky language and ploys you used to make them believe that you are God. You know, you hypnotize them with your magic tricks to confuse them so that they can believe that you are God. If you stop pretending and performing that sleight of hand, which passes as *'divine power'*, will people still believe that you are God? If you tell them the truth, will they believe that you are God? If you just appear in modern clothes will people still believe that you are God? Why did you say, 'Why fear when I am here', 'If you can see me I can see you', 'Give up your burdens I will carry them for you', 'I am always with you,' 'I will save you when you are in difficulty', why? Don't you know that every day you kept confusing them with new entertainment and new slogans? Are you not aware of what is making them believe that you are God? Yes, God-Bawa, you are aware of your actions," said Singh Messenger bravely.

"People love fun. They enjoy fun. Nobody has seen God. Let them have fun. This life is for pleasure. Everything here is fun. If there is no fun, there is nothing. Only I can give them 'Fun'. I know how to make them enjoy life, so let it be. They are having fun by fooling their close friends and family members, so I too enjoy this fun by fooling them.

Everyone knows this is a fooling game, a fooling business, and fun. They said tears were rolling down the face of an idol, let them fool themselves, and let them enjoy the fun, at the same time let me enjoy being their leader and the royal treatment I get. It is a good feeling. Other than a king, nobody else knows the gratification of such treatment. Only a rich man can understand the delight of wealth. To understand the enjoyment of wealth is beyond the comprehension of the poor; they will keep talking like philosophers. I am an entertainer, let me entertain them," said God-Bawa animatedly.

God-Bawa stood up, and walking round his table, said to Singh Messenger, "People are not waiting for the truth. If I tell them the truth about how I win them over, everyone will come to me saying: *'Don't spoil our game Mr. Bawa, otherwise you will not see tomorrow's sun'*. They will say, *'You taught us to believe that fake glass is a diamond. We followed the crowd and made others follow us.'* Thus, one will say, *'I have cheated my best friend in your name.'* Another will say, *'I have cheated my mother and father telling them that I have seen the miracles of God-Bawa with my own eyes - he is God.'* Yet another will say *'I have cheated my boss by telling him that Bawa is God, and I have received miraculous benefits on account of his blessings.'* Some others will say *'We have cheated more than fifty people convincing them that God-Bawa gave us a new life when the doctor declared me dead on a hospital bed.'* And still another will say, *'I have cheated my whole family, by telling them that God-Bawa is a real God. I have had so many experiences after becoming his follower.'*

A whole bunch of powerful agent-followers will come to me saying, *'Don't you dare to reveal the facts God-Bawa!! If you tell the truth then be prepared for the consequence as well. You might not live to see the next sunrise.'*

"That's all right, but the truth is the truth, God-Bawa! You have played this entertaining game of lies in the name of the Truth," said Singh Messenger.

"Singh Messenger I have told you everything. There is a saying that *'telling your secrets to someone is the same as selling yourself to that person'*. Sorry, I cannot sell myself to anyone ..." said God-Bawa in a strained voice.

Singh Messenger started thinking about God-Bawa's usual words - you will not see tomorrow's sun ... tomorrow's sun ... tomorrow's sun ... sun? After thinking it over and over again, he came to the conclusion that, *'discretion is, after all, the better part of valor.'* At 1.30 in the morning, Singh Messenger packed up his belongings and saw the morning sunrise twenty-five miles away from God-Bawa's monastery.

****

Step Twenty Three

DNA – THE AMAZING SOUL

"Two beautiful birds (JeevaAtma – Soul, and ParmaAtma - God) with beautiful wings are inseparable friends, and they both reside upon one tree (the body). One bird (the soul) enjoys the taste of the sweet and bitter fruits of the tree by tasting them, but the other one just watches - a witness. Though they are identical, still the difference is; the first bird (human) always remains worried about the future and second bird (God) does not because he knows everything. The first bird (the fruit eater) gets entangled and feels miserable at all times, because he is not enlightened. But when he realizes the greatness of his constant companion, he becomes free from sorrow." Upanishad

SOUL: What is not has never been; and what is, always is. This truth about the real (soul) and unreal (body) has long been realized by the seers. Know that this vast universe is pervaded by that which is indestructible. No one can destroy what is everlasting and imperishable. The indwelling one is eternal, indestructible and immeasurable. The bodies of the indwelling are impermanent. Therefore, whoever thinks that the atma or the self does the killing or can be killed misunderstands. The self doesn't kill, nor is it ever killed. It is not born and it does not die. Unborn, eternal and ancient, the self is not killed when the body dies. Whoever truly knows the self – indestructible, eternal, birth less and changeless – knows that there is no way such a person could kill. Who would be killed? It is just like casting off worn out clothing and putting on new ones, that which is embodied casts off worn out bodies and enters others that are new. Weapons cannot affect the self; fire does not burn it, water does not wet it, and wind does not dry it. The self cannot be pierced or cut; it cannot be burned, moistened or dried. It is endless, all pervading, stable, immovable, and everlasting. It (the soul) is said to be un-manifested, inconceivable, and immutable. Even if you imagined the self continuously taking birth and dying – even then, there is no reason to grieve. Whatever is born will undoubtedly die; whatever is dead can certainly be reborn. You should not mourn what is inevitable. Beings originally are all un-manifested. At mid-state they are manifested; and un-manifested again at the end. What is the point of lamenting? One may perceive the self as full of wonders; another speaks of it as marvelous; another hears it is wonderful, yet none understands it completely. GITA

EVOLUTION BY BHAGWAN KAPIL: The great Sage Kapila is known as the father of the doctrine of evolution. Though the idea of evolution existed long before Kapila, he was the first who taught by observation and experimentation and how to solve the mysteries of the body. He scientifically studied the process of evolution of the mind, and tried to trace the true causes of the growth of the body. He knew that seeds were not the original source of life in the world, but there had to be some other more fundamental foundation behind the seeds, out of which seeds are produced. From such thinking he discovered the real origins of the universe; its phenomena and its laws. Something can never come out of nothing, though Mother Nature is the cause of evolution, yet God - the shining intelligence is really the force behind it.

THE SEED AND THE TREE: The tree is the potential or latent in a seed. When we are handling a seed, we are handling the potential tree. The tree exists in the seed in a causal form, and all the peculiarities that appear and make up any particular tree, are already present in the seed. If we call the seed cause, the cause will mean the un-manifested form of the tree, and when the seed is manifested in the form of a tree, we call it the effect. Therefore nothing comes from the outside. Environments may draw out a certain thing, but the basic tree is already present in the seed, otherwise any seed could produce any kind of tree at all, and there would be nothing to control the nature and species of the tree. For example, an elm would produce a fig, or a fig seed would produce a mango, and there would be a great want of reliability. Human DNA can produce humans. Everything is explained in the scriptures by the process of evolution of one substance, which helps to understand the process of Creation. This philosophy includes all the stages of suffering, perfection and karma.

JUSTIN MARTYR: His dialogue with Trypho (AD 155), part one, chapter 4, where he discusses Platonism with Trypho the Jew:

The old man: "What, then, is the advantage to those who have seen [God]? Or what has he who has seen more than he who has not seen, unless he remember this fact, that he has seen?"

Justin: "I cannot tell," I answered.

The old man: "And what do those suffer who are judged to be unworthy of this spectacle?" said he.

Justin: "[According to Plato] they are imprisoned in the bodies of certain wild beasts, and this is their punishment."

The old man: "Do they know, then, that it is for this reason they are in such forms, and that they have committed some sin?"

Justin: "I do not think so."

The old man: "Then these reap no advantage from their punishment, as it seems: moreover, I would say that they are not punished unless they are conscious of the punishment."

Justin: "No indeed."

The old man: "Therefore souls neither see God nor transmigrate into other bodies; for they would know that so they are punished, and they would be afraid to commit even the most trivial sin afterwards. But that they can perceive that God exists, and that righteousness and piety are honorable, I also quite agree with you," said he.

Justin: "You are right," I replied.

PLATO: Plato's meaning of salvation is definitely personal, as can be understand from Phaedo: Those also who are remarkable for having led holy lives are released from this earthly prison, and go to their pure home which is above, and dwell in the purer earth; and those who have duly purified themselves with philosophy live henceforth altogether without the body, in mansions far fairer than these, which may not be described, and of which the time would fail me to tell.

BIBLE:

(1). Fruit Karma in next life: John 9,2, "Who sinned, this man or his parents, that he was born blind?";

2). Death is the only door to Heaven: John 3,3, "No one can see the kingdom of God unless he is born again";

3). Reincarnation: James 3,6, "the wheel of nature";

40. Born again: John 3,6 "Do not marvel because I told you, you must be born again".

4). Karma: Galatians 6,7, "A man reaps what he sows";

5). Karma: Matthew 26,52, "all who draw the sword will die by the sword";

6). Intention: Revelation 13,10, "If anyone is to go into captivity, into captivity he will go. If anyone is to be killed with the sword, with the sword he will be killed."

TAO: Chuang Tzu (4th century BC), Birth is not a beginning; death is not an end. There is existence without limitation; there is continuity without a starting point. Existence without limitation is space. Continuity without a starting point is time. There is birth, there is death, there is issuing forth, there is entering in. That through which one passes in and out without seeing its form, that is the Portal of God (Chuang Tzu 23).

Saint Valluvar: "The soul from body any day, Like bird from egg-shell, flies away.

Death is sinking into slumbers deep Birth again is waking out of sleep".

****

My God, Thou Art Great

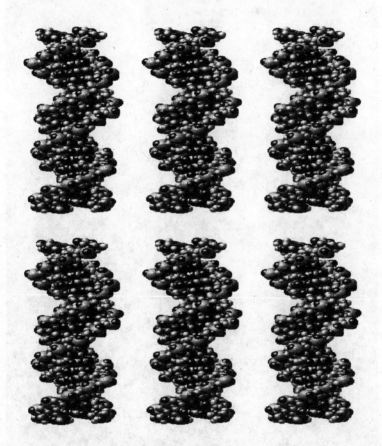

Your soul is the energy seed, which contains the potential of your future self. Just as the seed of an orange tree cannot produce an apple tree, when your present body expires your soul cannot produce a different person, it can only reproduce you.

Just like casting off worn out clothings and putting on new ones, that which is embodied casts off worn out bodies and enters others that are new.

courtesy of The Bhaktivedanta Book Trust International, Inc. used with permission

The Soul Passes Into Another Body At Death

You needed to discard the old used clothes to put on better ones. If you would have been stuck with banana leaves and fig leaves to cover your private parts then how you would have dressed in cotton clothes. There was a time when you used to wear one piece of a dead animal's skin to cover up your body.

If you would be afraid to leave that animal-skin, then today you would not see the woolen jacket, silk tie, pants and computers. Every time you evolved by leaving one body and taking a new one with a better brain, better understanding capability.

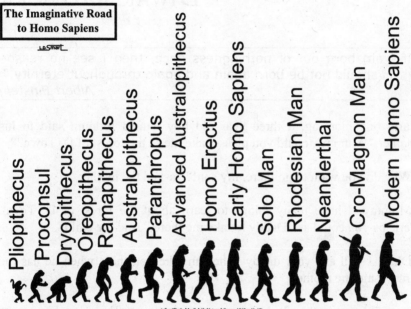

The Imaginative Road to Homo Sapiens

Pliopithecus · Proconsul · Dryopithecus · Oreopithecus · Ramapithecus · Australopithecus · Paranthropus · Advanced Australopithecus · Homo Erectus · Early Homo Sapiens · Solo Man · Rhodesian Man · Neanderthal · Cro-Magnon Man · Modern Homo Sapiens

(after "Early Man", Life Nature Library, 1969 p:41-45)

Courtesy: Unmasking Evolution, Australia, www.unmaskingevolution.com Used with permission.

Devi Messiah said, "Evolution is the whole of the law. Law demands changes, and change brings perfection. To obey the law one must accept death, as willingly as one accepts life."

Primitive man is thought to have first appeared in the form of Australopithecus which actually, Australopithecus coexisted with other Hominids when Earth occupied the Marsian orbit. The skeletal differences between races which co-existed on Mars are more apparent than the skeletal differences between races which co-exist on Earth.

****

Step Twenty Four...

DIWAREE REBORN

"If I am born out of nothingness once, then I see no reason why I should not be born again and again throughout eternity."
- Albert Einstein

Early one morning, a three year old boy named Ibrahim said to his mother, "Mummy, could you please take me to the forest of D. Town?"

"Why do you want to go there, my son!?" asked the mother.

"Mummy, I have many things to learn about the forest of D. Town. Perhaps you could ask Daddy to take me there," said the child.

"Okay, I will ask your daddy if he can take you there when he has the time," said the mother.

The child was restless and eager to go to the forest. He kept asking again and again if he could go to the forest with them or even on his own.

"But tell us why you want to go to D. Town?" asked the parents. The child narrated this story:

"Mummy, in my previous life I used to live near the forest of D. Town. I was a Saint. My name was Diwaree. I lived a simple life, but I was very famous. My fame affected a Bawa's business. My truthfulness was hurting his income. His name was God-Bawa. He was about thirty-five years old. Once, in the middle of night he came to me, and said: "Diwaree, whatever you are doing is for nothing. You are getting nothing, and my business is being affected, by your fruitless actions. Why don't we form a coalition and make this world aware of our purpose and powers? Together, we can do a lot. You can come and live with me. I will give you a nice house with all the facilities including television, telephone, refrigerator, two servants and good food. You will get plenty of respect. What else do you need? Whatever you want, you will get. You will always have money in your pocket, of which nobody will know. In return, you will tell everyone: *'I am Diwaree and I am impressed by God-Bawa's powers and I have seen no one greater than him. He is the real God on earth and therefore I have surrendered myself to his highness and joined his great mission. I am Diwaree no more, but God-Bawa's disciple'.*

Mummy, I said to him, "We already have so many Gods why should I add one more? We already have so many religions and so many paths. Each continent has its own religion and its own God. We already have enough God-leaders and philosophies to make people hate each other. Why should I add one more?" Then I looked at the expression on his face and told him,

"Now, about your plan to change the world! Yes, I do realize that this world must be changed. A saint must tell everyone how a politician should live. He must proclaim the Law of God to everyone and instead of adding one more God and one more path. He must preach that there is only one God and therefore only one path - the direct connection between a human being and the universal force. God-Bawa, I do agree with you that this world should be changed, but that should be in accordance with my ideas. This will be possible only if I can find a good disciple. However, if you are willing to become my disciple for this purpose, then why not? We will do it together. You will have to come here and live in this jungle with me. However, I don't think that is possible because I don't take on disciples, and your way of thinking is completely different from mine."

"Mummy, then in a slightly disturbed manner he said to me, "Diwaree I did not ask to become your follower, so you should not speak such insulting words. I am being respectful and talking to you politely and amiably, so I expect the same in return. Now to come to the main point about changing the world; this should be according to my vision, because I live in the city, and I am in contact with the public. I know what is going on out there, and how society needs to be changed. The world will always listen to us because of our enormous wealth, which proves our goodness. This world is inspired by wealthy film stars, wealthy businessmen and wealthy saints, regardless of their ethical character, even if they had five divorces and ten girlfriends. People learn from us, how to become successful, because we are successful and we have proof of that. If you don't mind let me say since you live in a jungle, you have no idea what is going on outside, and what can be done to fix it. This world is not inspired by people like you, and never will be. If you want to do something useful in life, this is your chance. But first you must understand the world and change your mentality. Then you must join hands with the people who have money and political power," he said to me.

"Then, Mummy, I told him about the principles of my life fear of God, Karma, God's Judgment, and God's existence. We had a big argument about God's existence and non-existence and *(please read the argument; in step eight)* finally I said to him: "God-Bawa, I have no intention of jumping on to your bandwagon. I am all right as I am. Most of my life is already over. I don't want to live long and learn nothing. I want to live short and learn a lot. You pass your time in your palace and I on this wall. He has fed me so far and the remaining days of my life will also definitely pass with His blessings, so there is no reason for me to gang up with you."

"Thus, I disagreed with his planning. I told him everything clearly. Why should I be diplomatic with him? Neither was he feeding me, nor were my needs so great. God was giving me food. After all God-Bawa was also passing his time as I was. The only difference was that he was doing what he wanted, and I was following my *'inner voice'* - *'the voice of my God'*. I knew it very well as my inner conscience, which told me that God is not happy with people who mislead others.

"I disagreed with him. I sensed that he would kill me, but I thought: 'Why would he kill a harmless man? I have not harmed anyone. I am a simple man. How will his conscience allow him to kill an innocent man? However, if God wants to save me, then He will, and if this is His will then let it be. This end will be better than joining the rich butcher's sinful gang and living in his golden palace and following the so called 'the path to God'.

"Mummy, I can still remember his face and his eyes, the way he looked at me and said, "Last year I tried to convince a saint to join my mission but he refused. He did not see the morning sun. Well, Diwaree I have done my duty," saying this he gave me a strange look and walked out with a wealthy man.

"I prayed to God and said, "My God! I am not doing anything wrong, I am not harming anyone. My God, I really don't know where you are. Why would I mislead people saying that God is here and that *he* is God-Bawa? I have done nothing wrong, but if he still wants to hurt me or if this is your wish then what can I do?" However, I wasn't sure that a person could really do such a thing to a harmless saint. Otherwise I would have run away and gone into hiding somewhere else.

"In the dead of night, a tall man came up to me from behind. He suddenly hit me and threw me off the wall onto the ground. I opened my eyes thinking *'what's going on?'* I saw three others coming towards me with weapons. I said, *'Oh! God-Bawa I knew you would do this.'*

"I could not recognize them, as their faces were covered. I knew that they had come to kill me. I tried to run away. I thought at least if I could reach M. L. Singh he would wake up and do something. I had run only ten yards when suddenly one man caught my leg, another put his palm over my mouth so I could not scream, and a third held my arms behind my back and tied me with a rope.

"They gagged my mouth with a cloth and tied up my legs and arms. Then they started hitting me with big bamboo sticks. I saw that they had knives, and an axe. I was frightened. In fear, I urinated on the spot. With my full strength I tried to scream for help, but my mouth was gagged and my voice could not reach Singh, who was in a deep sleep, wrapped in a blanket under the tree.

"I saw God-Bawa and the wealthy man watching all this from a distance. Then, one man held the big axe. I could see the axe clearly. Mummy, I cannot tell you how frightened I was at that time. Mummy I shall never forget that fear. Then that man wiped the axe with his fingers and lifted it high over me. I knew; the axe was going to cut through my body and I was left with only a few seconds of life. The length of my life was the distance of the axe from my body. I knew ... deep scar ... heavy bleeding ... I would die in the next few seconds. I was terrified. My whole body trembled like a helpless baby's.

"I said "O God!" and I died."

The blood-curdling description of what the child had undergone in his previous life left his parents thunder-struck. The child continued, "Mummy, I can still remember many things. If you take me there, I can tell you about each and every person who used to come to me. I know their names, their families, what they do and so on."

Frightened, the father said in a trembling voice, "My beloved son, we know about that murder. That was a well-known murder that has remained unsolved to this day. Almost everyone in this area knows the case.. To this day everyone is curious about what happened to Diwaree. However, nobody imagined that God-Bawa could ever do such a thing. God-Bawa is a famous holy man. People believe that he is God. Nobody ever thought that he could be a murderer. Even today, if you tell people that God-Bawa murdered Diwaree, nobody will believe you. The incriminating story you have narrated is astonishingly true. Once the people come to know what happened to Diwaree, H.H. God-Bawa's people will not let you live. They will kill us and kill everyone who knows the truth. This is a dangerous reality. God-Bawa has many rich followers now. Though some people say that a few murders have taken place in his monastery, nobody thought it to be true, therefore, beloved son, do us a favor - do not reveal this story to anyone. What you have told us must remain between you and us.

"But daddy, I have many things to tell you," said the child.

"Okay, we will go there tomorrow and then you can tell us the rest of the story," replied his father.

The next day the child and his parents took a bus, and went to the place from where Diwaree had reportedly disappeared. The mother held her son's hand and asked, "Is this the place which you were talking about?"

"Yes mummy, this is the place where I used to live. Now, let me tell you about this place. Lift this stone and you will find a silver coin underneath," said the child.

The father lifted the stone and was stunned when he saw the silver coin. "Oh God!" he cried. He couldn't believe it. He was astonished and thrilled. The mother asked, "Can I see it?" She held the coin, looking at her son with tearful eyes. Then he asked them to lift another stone where in they would find a handwritten book, by professor M.L. Singh named, *'Thus Revealed the Sages of Sanatan Dharma'*. "Oh God ..." sighed the mother. Then the child took them to every place where he used to sit, eat, cook, bathe and finally he spoke to them of many things about the wall on which he used to sleep.

After describing how those murderers had came with sticks, knives and an axe, he told them how he was murdered, then he took them to the place from where God-Bawa and the rich man had watched the whole incident.

The father asked, "If I show you a photo of God-Bawa, would you still be able to recognize him?"

"Yes, of course," said the child confidently.

Many of the shopkeepers in the market had H.H. God-Bawa's photo on their small altars of worship. The father showed him a photo in a restaurant and asked, "Is he the one?"

"Yes exactly, daddy, that's the one. The dangerous man!" replied the child.

"Dear son, we have heard people say that God-Bawa and Diwaree had a misunderstanding, but the matter later just slipped from people's memories. Now, that you've told us that it was God-Bawa who committed the foul deed, we remember the story a few people were circulating about the murder. But now we are frightened," said the parents.

"Daddy, there are many things about God-Bawa that people will not believe," replied the child.

"Don't mention any of this to anyone. Let's go home now," said his father.

There was God who walked on this earth in the form of an ordinary human being, but was not known to anyone. At the same time there was Satan incarnate, wearing a helper's uniform. Good people were like God but it was hard to know who they were.

The mother asked her son, "My son, do you know what has happened, in this world, in your name?"

****

Step Twenty Five...

REBIRTH FOR PERFECTION

There have always been religions. Even before the birth of the existing religions, there were religions, and after the extinction of these religions, there will be religions. In the history of this world, there have been similar incidents from time to time. For humankind, it is a little difficult to understand how, why, and when these religions came, ended and new ones occupied their place.

When the real God was alive in human form He or She was not only ignored, but experienced terrible situations. After His or Her death, people, in their attempt to practice evil, organized themselves into various sects or groups or religions to follow the precepts to their loving God - who was no longer in their midst. The main ideology and guiding principles of these religions were passed from generation to generation.

Without His or Her teachings, human beings couldn't comprehend the system in place elsewhere, on this and other planets.

Planet and place? Interesting!! Interesting!!! Have you ever heard of such a thing - except on July 21, 1986 when more than 260 scientists from 27 nations gathered in Los Angeles to discus the origin of life on Earth, and the Director of the chemical evolution laboratory of the University of Maryland expressed the opinion of all scientists present saying, '*The process which led to life on earth must have started somewhere else in the universe*'. Human beings find it difficult to grasp that there are or were beings that lived on planets other than on the Earth. Since their books were found on this planet, most historians presumed that the incidents had taken place on Earth, because they had no idea about life and evolution on other planets, they could only talk about this world.

Some of those new religions gradually vanished, as they lacked the support of wealthy people. Although, they followed very healthy, generous, liberal and utterly honest principles, the lack of financial backing, relegated them to the pages of history. The reason was that their people didn't want to contaminate their spiritualism with materialistic things, and they abhorred the idea of raising funds in the name of religion. On the contrary, some religions had no scruples about raising funds, and even wielding temporal powers, flourished and established themselves in the nooks and corners of the world.

According to those books, Prophet-Diwaree, Diwar-Devote, Sackcloth and many other religions had already existed on Earth for several thousands of years. On account of the close similarity between these religions and the then existing ones, people started comparing the two civilizations. They developed their scientific knowledge and spirituality, which eventually made it easier to understand the *'Unified Field'* a gift from God to this world, which we will discuss later.

One good man can lift up the reputation of a whole family, community, religion or even an entire country. The world doesn't need many people to lead aspirants' one step farther on the road to perfection. Those who wish to climb the ladder of perfection can find the clues from anywhere or from their own heart. Diwaree was reborn in a so called lower class family. His name was Ibrahim. His mother's religion was Prophet-Diwar. He loved his mother. She told him religious stories. She tried giving him good religious knowledge so that after her death God's mercy would protect him. She used to make him recite the word *'Prophet-Diwar'*, *'Prophet-Diwar'* continuously, as many times as he could, so that Prophet-Diwar would help him in difficult times. She knew her loving child would miss her after her death. He would look for his Mummy here and there. Only when he could not find her, would God help him! In the evening, he would wear the traditional Prophet-Diwarian dress while he prayed. He followed all the other rules and rituals his mother had taught him. According to his mother's teaching he would hold a piece of wood in his right hand for five minutes every morning. He didn't comb his hair after four o'clock in the afternoon. His parents showered their love on him and he was proud of his religion.

As you know, in his previous life he hadn't had any respect for Prophet-Diwar. Though, he was a saint, he used to say that all religions were the same, but somewhere in his heart there was no room for Prophet-Diwar. He used to believe that there were certain things in prophesizm, through which one could not attain enlightenment.

But here, due to his mother's teaching he had started declaring Prophesizm to be the best religion in the world. God had really brought about a big change in him, where just a couple of years ago he used to hate the religion. But after being reborn into that family he declared it to be the best. Usually almost everybody loves his or her own religion and considers all other religions secondary. It was the creator's wonderful way of teaching man not to hate any religion - thank God. If he had been reborn in a Sackcloth family, then he would definitely have admired the Sackcloth religion.

His parents passed away when he was only ten years old. A few years after their death, his personality underwent a dramatic change. He started sincerely believing that all religions were good, and the religion of his birth was in no way superior to others. He held the same belief about other religions. Due to his busy life he couldn't pay much attention to his previous life, but honesty was ingrained in his genes. Because of his honest and liberal perception about all religions, many orthodox people of his own religion did not like him. He did not care about those people because he did not need their mercy as a benevolent God had given him enough to survive. Greed didn't exist in his dictionary and he was satisfied with whatever God had given to him, therefore he didn't like to be identified as only a member of the Prophet-Diwaree religion. He was a farmer's son and was known as Ibrahim. The name also could not indicate precisely to which religion he actually belonged.

If people had known about his previous life, and his conversations with God, then they would have treated him like a saint. Everyone would have been curious to find out why God didn't accept him as a disciple, and why he had to be reborn on earth instead of going to heaven. On account of his religious purity and virtuosity Diwar-Devotes, Prophet-Diwarians and Sackclothians would claim him to be a member of their religion. For example in today's world; Jews would prove him, an original Jew.

Christians would claim him a Christian, Hindus would say he was a Hindu, Muslims would say he was a Muslim, Sikhs, Buddhists and others would claim him as a member of their religion because of his name and his previous life's saintly thoughts, embracing the whole human race.

All professors of philosophy would try to prove through their own understanding that he was a member of their philosophy, but fortunately, nobody knew who this poor farmer was. There were no drum beats and trumpets blowing heralding the arrival of a great Saint or a new God-man. He was just a simple farmer, so many people called him 'Farmer'.

H.H. God-Bawa's story haunted his life just like a five year old's dream. It was good that he had forgotten almost everything about that life, otherwise he might have thought of going back to the same place again. Ibrahim Farmer didn't need to go there as a new Diwaree, because he had to fulfill his family responsibilities here. He was far too occupied taking care of his two children, his wife and home. He lived a humble life here too. He did not read all the scriptures. Neither did he believe in the scriptures. He believed in only one scripture, his *'inner voice'*. He followed humanity, humility and whatever message came from deep within his heart. He was a God-fearing man. He loved to teach his children. He knew that God had given him children so he could feed them healthy things and nourish their minds with wisdom. He knew the duty of a father, and tried hard to become the perfect father. He knew, God had given him two raw diamonds to polish, and thus to serve Him. Though, both the children learned everything by watching and emulating their righteous father, still the Farmer kept teaching them.

FATHER: God created fathers to protect us when we are small,
To fix the things that we might break and catch us when we fall,

God knew we would need someone brave who would be gentle.
Someone to listen to our dreams, and help those dreams come true,

Someone who would teach us to be strong and understand our fears,
Who would be there when we needed a friend, and guide us through the years. Yes God, created fathers to depend on all life through.

Step Twenty Six...

TEACHING THE CHILDREN

He had a framed poster of Abraham Lincoln, which had been presented to him on his ninth birthday by his Uncle Lalchand. It was an interesting gift, because his name was also Ibrahim. The words on the poster read:

WORLD: MY SON STARTS SCHOOL TODAY

World, take my child by the hand - he starts school today! It is all going to be strange and new to him for a while, and I wish you would sort of treat him gently.

You see, up to now, he has been the king of the roost. He has been the boss of the backyard. I have always been around to mend his wounds, and I have always been handy to soothe his feelings.

But now things are going to be different. This morning he will walk down the front steps, wave his hand, and start out on a great adventure that will probably include wars and tragedy and sorrow.

To live in this world, will require faith and love and courage. So, World, I wish you would sort of take him by his young hand and teach him the things he will have to know. Teach him - but gently, if you can.

He will have to learn, I know, that all people are not just. That all men and women are not true. Teach him that for every scoundrel, there is a hero; that for every enemy, there is a friend. Let him learn early that bullies are the easiest people to lick.

Teach him the wonder of books. Give him quiet time to ponder the eternal mystery of birds in the sky, bees in the sun, and flowers on a green hill. Teach him that it is far more honorable to fail than to cheat.

Teach him to have faith in his own ideas, even if everyone tells him they are wrong.

Try to give my son instruction not to follow the crowd when everyone else is getting on the bandwagon. Teach him to listen to others, but to filter all he hears through a screen of truth and to take only the good that comes through.

Teach him never to put a price tag on his heart and soul. Teach him to close his ears on the howling mob - and to stand and fight if he thinks he is right. Teach him gently, World, but do not coddle him, because only the test of fire makes fine steel.

Signed,
Abraham Lincoln

Good parents are God's gift to a child. The farmer's character was formed during his childhood by watching the virtuous actions of his parents. His efforts to raise good children played a big role in the life of the children. The truth was in his genes. He loved to perform the duties of the ideal father knowing he was the one who did not lose his child's heart. He held his children's fingers and lovingly taught them how to walk the path of perfection. He loved to answer his children's questions.

DADDY WHAT IS TRUTH?

God is Truth and Truth is God. Therefore, always speak the truth. The more you live a truthful life, the more you will understand God.

DADDY, WHICH IS THE BEST SCRIPTURE TO READ?

Most of the scriptures were not written by God. They were written by believers for believers. There is a God residing within you, who keeps your heart pumping and makes your brain function. Seek him out. Understand him and obey his advice. There is only one scripture in this world. That is your 'inner voice'. Even if you burn all the scriptures on this planet and destroy them completely - this scripture will still remain to guide you. The inner voice is the finest scripture, which has been guiding seekers, and will continue guiding them until they reach their destiny. Your God is always within you and constantly advising you on what to do.

> "One percent inspiration and ninety nine percent perspiration." --
> Thomas Alva Edison

DADDY IS THERE ONE GOD OR MANY?

My dear child, everybody's God is one. There is only one God. People call him by different names, such as God, Omnipotent, All-powerful, Almighty, Divine, All-knowing, the Supreme Being, Creator, Master of the Universe, Sustainer, Organizer, Food-giver, Compassionate, Good-hearted, Forgiving, Pitying, Sympathetic, Kind and so on ... Here these people call him Diwaree, Diwar-Devote, Prophet-Diwaree, God-Bawa and so on ... You can call him by any name. It doesn't make a difference, but knowing him is the only thing that makes a difference.

One God appears to devotees in thousands of forms, according to their Karma. They deserve to perceive the Supreme God. One God speaks through the mouth of the enemy, and the same God speaks through the mouth of a friend. This universe is constantly changing the form of God. Once people know how this energy is generated by the great source, how the great source of all beings is related to the earth, and how this makes everything function, including our vision, hearing, speech, and together once they know the secret of time and the law of evolution controlled by the Main Source - all these religions will immediately be at peace. However at this time in this world people don't know where and what God is. They have the capability to understand but right now they have no understanding. In my previous life, I had a good opportunity to learn this, but due to two of my weaknesses I didn't deserve its fruit.

People of different religions are all creations of the same God - the Creator. Through Christianity, Hinduism, Buddhism, Islam, Jainism, Judaism, Platonism, Gnosticism, Shinto, Sikhism, Baha'i, Apostasy, Taoism, Zionism, Zoroastrianism, the Reformation, and Modern Disbelief, they have tried to find the true path to the Main Source of energy and - the Creator. All their scriptures tried to describe the truth about Him. All their scriptures sing the glory of the one, and the only one - the Main Source of energy, but ...

All the holy men of earth including Preachers, Priests, Sadhus, Gurus, Lamas, Imams, Fathers, Rabbis, Nahans, God-men and seekers sing the glory of the 'ONE' great Master. All the places of worship are built in the name of the Master Creator.

Although to understand it more easily you can say that the God of Destruction, God of Preservation and God of Creation are three faces of the Divine Trinity, but there is only one powerful Great Source who gives birth to all people.

Those who believe that after death Diwar-Devotes go to H.H. Pattiwala, Prophet-Diwarians go to H.H. Prophet-Diwar, and Sackclothians go to H.H. Sackcloth, they are all referring to the same Source. Since they don't know the Great Source they have to imagine him in any form they can. If they compromise and agree that all will go to the Divine Master Diwaree, they would still be wrong, because they don't know that Diwaree was not a God. Diwaree himself could not go to heaven, which they do not know, so how can they attain heaven by following a false God.

DADDY, SHOULD WE PRAY TO A FORMLESS GOD OR TO IDOLS?

A stoic, dispassionately renounced Vairaagee who can see God in all things and behave accordingly, can pray to Him as formless and omnipresent. But it is always better to have something in front of our eyes for better concentration. Omnipresent God's presence can be invoked at any place with the purity of the heart. Your prayers will be answered if you are full of truth.

DADDY, IS EVERYTHING IN THIS WORLD DONE BY GOD OR BY HUMAN BEINGS?

You have conscience, or buddhi, to understand right and wrong therefore you are bound to reap the consequences of your karma. You must understand that 'if you do wrong, God will punish you'. You cannot break His law by using saintly statements, or by claiming to be animal–like, innocent and ignorant. The same law does not apply to plants, animals and machine because they are not gifted with the understanding of God.

DADDY WHY DOES EVERYBODY HAVE A DIFFERENT MENTALITY?

My beloved children, every soul is born with a unique purpose. Their natural instincts are based on the experiences of a previous life and this one. They are like a unique word processor where there is one erasable page and one blank page. Love, jealousy, vengefulness and kindness are the different icons of this processor. Pristine souls perform wonderful jobs to please the Main Artist. We are put on this world to erase the bad things, and inscribe good things on this page.

DADDY WHY DO PEOPLE EXPERIENCE TENSION WHEN THEY ARE WITH THEIR FAMILIES OR IN A GROUP?

One of the parts of your life must be defective so that you can focus your full attention on fixing it, throughout your whole life, and if you succeed, the invention is your gift to the world. Many people have presented gifts to the world. That is why this world has so many good flowers. Those are the fruits of tension.

DADDY WHY DO HUMAN BEINGS GO THROUGH SO MANY UPS AND DOWNS?

There is nothing accidental in your life. Whoever was with you, whenever or whichever place was for a reason. Without that reason you wouldn't be like this today, and you wouldn't be walking with me, and enjoying this conversation. Ups and downs are what makes your mind work and, you think. I quote: *"The deeper that sorrow carves into your being the more joy you can contain. Is not the cup that holds your wine the very cup that was burned in the potter's oven?"*
–Kahil Gibran

DADDY WHAT SHOULD WE DO WHEN A PERSON IS TERRIBLY WRONG AND TRYING TO HURT US?

Every year God will keep adding to your load with one more brick upon your back. He will keep testing your strength. At that specific moment when He is placing the brick on your back you'll definitely feel a change. If you yell, even if by mistake, at the person through whom He has placed the brick, then you have failed to pass the test, and consequently you may loose the balance of life. God has blessed you with an intellect so accept the load to become stronger. When you are old and loaded with the burden of many bricks, when your back is bent, and when you can't carry the load anymore God will put the brakes to end your journey through this life. He will grant a stronger life to your wise soul, by which you may be able to accept a heavier load.

> The rung of a ladder was never meant to rest upon, but only to hold your foot long enough to put the other foot higher.

DADDY CAN WE CHANGE OUR FORTUNE?

Yes. Karma is like a garden. The garden doesn't care what seed you plant in the garden. It can work for you or against you depending what you have sowed. To receive good flowers from the garden it needs to be prepared for good flowers. After preparing the earth you have to find out where you can get good seeds and how to nurture them after sowing. Good seeds you can get from good parents, good teachers, good books, or inspiring stories. Childhood is the best time for sowing good seeds. I am telling you some of the ways of sowing good seeds, so that your foundations can be strong. Learn from failure souls why they are failure and learn from successful souls why they are successful. Some rich people finished in this very life after acquiring lots of knowledge about money. They started their real journey in this very life.

DADDY WHY DOES HUMAN NATURE DIFFER?

Millions of different memories are stored in your genes which are completely different from those of others. That is why you understand some things but they can't. Other people like some things which you don't such as food, music, a game and so on.

To understand other people's thoughts and lives you have to change; you have to give different food to your mind. You have to listen to the music to which they usually listen. You have to live with their kind of company. You have to read the kind of books they read till your mind is nurtured sufficiently with the kind of food they feed their minds. Still no two persons are identical in appearance, and thought. God wouldn't make another human being like one that already existed.

HOW WOULD WE KNOW THAT OUR ATTITUDE HAD IMPROVED?

Question yourself.

1. Do I just say *Daddy I love you*, or do I ask him, *Daddy can I do something for you* or do I say nothing but do something that makes him happy?

2. Do I feel pity when I see a person is suffering, or do I tell others about his pain, or do I help him?

3. Do I feel that others must speak the truth, or do I preach to others about the truth, or do I say nothing to them but speak only the truth?

4. Do I think that it's good to sacrifice a life for a good cause, or do I openly say that one must sacrifice for a good cause, or do say nothing but sacrifice my life for a good cause?

5. Do I appreciate someone's holy life or do I live a holy life?

6. Do I have too much knowledge of scripture, or do I follow my 'inner voice'?

7. Do I think about doing good things, or do I do good things. Do I do good things to impress others or because that is my nature?

8. Do I respect my parents, teachers, and elders?

Dear children, Karma is the invisible law of God. It brings happiness, distress, miseries, joy, sorrow, and eventually decides the soul's destiny - hell or heaven. The consequences of Karma cannot be erased without reaping its fruit. Keep storing good karmic memories into your DNA.

DADDY WHAT IS DHARMA?

The signs of Dharma are; 1. Truth, 2. Sympathy, 3. Acceptance of the hardship of duty, 4. Distinguishing the difference between right and wrong, and following the right one, 5. Non-violence, 6. Awareness of family duty, 7. Striving for perfection, 8. No gossiping and no gossiping friends, 9. Restraint, 10.Forgiveness.

Over and above this practice meditation to concentrate your mind on your duty, stay away from anything that causes disturbances in your mind, if you can. Such as; hard music and angry friends, people who use dirty language, and who have bad habits. Choose to live alone rather than associate with bad people.

Practice of religion teaches you your responsibilities, how you should perform your duties: as a son, a daughter, a father, a mother, a teacher, a social worker, a doctor, a priest, a preacher, a businessman, an accountant, a lawyer, a politician and so on... The aim of life is to please God through your excellent karma. So from time to time keep testing yourself by making a list of; (a) your weak points, (b) your virtuous points. Ask yourself;

(1) Am I sincere in pleasing to God?
(2) Do I have discipline in life?
(3) What about my character?
(4) What about integrity?
(5) What about loyalty?
(6) What about empathy?
(7) Am I a caring person?
(8) Am I trustworthy?
(9) Commitment and fidelity in married life.
(10) Do I perform a proper parent's job, if I am a parent? Do I teach properly, if I am a teacher? And so on...

Non-violence: Even a wild dog must wag his tail at you, sensing non-violence: He must say; *"O man of harmony, you haven't caused violence to any animal"* No gossip: You will not disturb the minds of others through gossip. Every soul will sense that *"you are a pure soul"*. Make up your mind to follow your 'inner voice' - the voice of God. A sign of perfection is to see perfections in others.

> "All gardeners live in beautiful places because they make them so."
>
>   ....William Wordsworth

DADDY WHAT IS THE AIM OF LIFE?

Each and everyday to do as much good as possible: with mind, speech, and actions.

SINCERETY AND COMMITMENT: If you are called to be an artist, you should design the board like a saint composes his prayers. You should design it so well that all the angels of heaven and earth will pause to say, *"Here lived a great artist who did his job well"*. Sing the song of life so well that your inner self will be contented. Only a few minutes performance will prove your sincerity; that you have practiced for many many years with sincerity.

DISCIPLINE: Dear children, a man is not a man if he is without principle, and discipline. Learn how to deal with different situations in life.

Dear children, there are three roads including the road on which you are. It's easy to take the lower road, but it's tough to climb higher one. If you walk the lower road, which is also known as the road of horror, then no one may come to lift you up to put you back on this road again. This world has a mixture of horror and joy, but if you climb higher you will achieve the world of bliss. Be careful, if you keep constantly looking back, you might fall into the hole ahead.

WHAT IS THE BEST WAY TO ACHIEVE?

Learning, Heat travels everywhere but ignites only the most sensitive fuel. A good friend is a gift to you. To get a good friend you have to be good yourself. To get a good employee, good spouse, good child, and good parents, first one has to be good. Relationships should never be taken for granted. Once relationships are established, they need to be nurtured constantly. Nobody is perfect in this world. Expecting perfection is setting yourself up for disappointment. You cannot perfect others but you can perfect yourself. Be good to everyone. When you are good to others you are good to yourself. The best way to defeat an enemy is to make him a friend. Staying out of trouble is better than getting out of trouble. Hate the sin not the sinner. Treat others with respect because you may meet them later on your journey – the journey of the soul. Consider bad company as a gift because they will constantly remind you what you should not be.

Don't do anything because it feels good, for the consequences are bad. Do that which will have good consequences. Ask yourself these questions before doing anything;

(1). If my parents see me doing this, will they like it?
(2). If God sees me doing this will He be happy?

DADDY WHAT IS BLIND FAITH AND SANSAAR?

You cannot stay here forever as 'Sansaar' (that which keeps changing) will keep changing. Each and every moment things are changing in the human body. Billions and billions of atoms are being replaced in this body everyday and in seven years you are almost completely renewed. Change is the law and you must accept this law. The very heavens change every minute in color and character, so must we...we must welcome the change.

Sansaar: that keeps changing each and every moment, called the world.

YESTERDAY - TODAY - TOMORROW

There are two days in every week; that you should not worry about. Those two days should be kept free from fear and apprehension. **

One is yesterday; with its mistakes and cares, it's fruits and blunders, its aches and pains. Yesterday has passed forever beyond your control. All the money in the world cannot bring back yesterday. No matter how much effort you put you cannot undo a single act you performed yesterday, nor can you erase a single word you've said; because that is recorded in God's home.**

The other day is tomorrow; you should not worry about tomorrow with its possible adversities, its burden, its hopeful promise and poor performance. Tomorrow is beyond your control. Tomorrow's sun will rise no matter how much effort you put to change it and until it does you have no stake in tomorrow, for it is yet unborn. That's up to God. Have no worry for the future. When the future comes to you, your God will always bless you with sufficient strength to face it.**

Today; you can fight the battle of just one day. Do not add the burdens of tomorrow and yesterday on it; otherwise you'll break down with a triple load. It is not the experience of to-day that drives you mad. It is the remorse of something that happened yesterday and the dread of what tomorrow may bring. **

Let us therefore live one day at a time, do all the good things you can today. Present good flowers to God today. **

Yesterday is history, tomorrow is a mystery, but the present is a gift to please God. Let God control history and mystery and let us please him today. **

WHAT ARE THE INDICATIONS OF AN ASPIRANT'S PROGRESS?

The less he is attracted to the world and the more he is dedicated to good Karma, by that much he has moved forward. In his progress, attraction and distraction gradually disappear. As a result, his humble attitude and love for the unprivileged keeps increasing.

DADDY, PLEASE TELL US ABOUT DEATH.

Dear children this is just an example; a mouse was very frightened of cats. He kept praying to God, and God changed him into a cat, so that his worries would be over. But then he became frightened of dogs and God turned him into a dog, and continued turning him into stronger animals. Even after becoming a lion – the king of beasts he was frightened of the hunter (man). Finally God made him a man with so many protective items including a talisman, but still he was frightened. My children do you know what that fear was? In all beings the major fear is death – an unavoidable event in every life.

Dear children, throughout life it is death which makes life beautiful. When a man knows he is to be hanged tomorrow, he concentrates his mind wonderfully. Birth and life are distinct entities. Everyone lives a life, but some people live a fruitful life because they keep death in mind.

With death God removes all the memories of our past lives, so that we wouldn't go crazy with all those memories. We would not be able to handle the burden of all those memories. Also we would still treat all our previous acquaintances as our friends or enemies. Thus we would have dozens of fathers, mothers, grandmothers, grandfathers, friends, enemies, children, and consequently we wouldn't be able to concentrate on the duties of this life.

> You can't have everything, where you put it!
> ...Steven Wright.

At the time of death all the previous memories get erased. However, all those Karmas are always with us. That is the reason every one of us has different luck, different ways of behaving, and different ways of understanding things. Due to the experiences and Karma of the past lives, everyone has a different attitude and a different way of dealing with situations.

Rebirth is like evolution. Body and soul are like 'an egg and the little bird inside it'. The little bird will peck on the shell, once he is grown enough to fly out. Once this soul is heavy enough and this body is unable to contain it anymore, then it flies-away and reappears somewhere else where it deserves to be.

I still remember a conversation with God in my past life when She said to me, "Diwaree, the beggar Anna Mario has learned his lesson by going through a painful life. He needed to go through that suffering otherwise there was no hope of him to listening to God. There was a time when he could hear everything but would listen to nothing, and later by going through that painful struggle his genes were purified. Now he doesn't hear anything because he is deaf, but he understands everything. After death if he is reborn into a wealthy family, he will never ignore a beggar. He will never throw food into the garbage. He will not behave like those modern rich and ignorant people, who leave half their food in the plate, which goes into the garbage. He will not play with life like Mr. Harry. Whenever he passes a beggar he will never say, that beggar is pretending just to get money. He will never make any excuse but help. He will definitely help the helpless. His heart will tell him, *"Don't ignore the pain of those beggars, you know that pain.'* If he is in a rich city he will find the poor around the globe. It's only because God had given him a solid lesson. He will carry that information with him to his next life to remember that *'one should always remain obedient to God'*. He will know how to behave with helpless people, what to do if he were to see a helpless person." but, still anyone can fall from a high peak – because falling down is easy.

My children, many things can be learned from Anna Mario's experiences. When you learn from his experiences, without going through the pain and sufferings, then you move ahead faster. Ultimately pain is the lesson that gives a person understanding. It is not bad that people want to experience the lesson themselves in order to learn it properly, but there is one problem in self-experiencing, if the short time of life runs out, the examination paper will be taken away by the examiner. Because one should keep in mind that the final bell may ring at any time and anywhere, so one should always be prepared to handover the final exam papers. Every evening before going to bed one must make sure that all the question papers are properly answered. Keep practicing to be perfect. Perfect practice will make you perfect.

DADDY, PLEASE TELL US WHICH RELIGION IS GOOD AND WHICH IS BAD?

No religion is bad and no religion is good. Every religion has good and bad points in them. Every religion has wise and foolish things in their scriptures. Every religion has bad customs and good customs also bad traditions and good traditions. All religions are made by human beings. Though everybody claims that his or her religion is established by God himself, however, no religion is established by God. God does not establish any religion and eventually, no religion supports an unseen truth. Every religion supports its own God and thus becomes a wall between man and man, and also between man and God. My children, no religion is inferior or superior in the eyes of God. It is man who enjoys religions and most people try for perfection through religion but a "good person" can be found in any religion or following no religion. Therefore, the answer to your question is; it is man who is good or bad, not religion.

Though many religions had done much astonishing work and provided examples of humanity, such as; hospitals, schools, charities, orphanages, shelters for homeless and so on… but on the other hand many religions have closed the door to the universal God. Today if Lord Krishna or any other messenger of God had visited the earth, he or she would definitely not agree with everyone and what they are doing in his name and in the name of the Almighty. Today if Jesus were to come to earth he would definitely scold everyone for not following the truth that he had taught. Nobody would understand him. Some people would even ask him why he is not carrying a cross on his shoulder. Many rich and poor people would have so many ideas to suggest him what to do and not to. He provably would not listen to them. Instead of learning something from him the situation would become alarming. Then once again people of this earth would have crucified him. People would have horrified him and he would have gone through unbearable mental pain. Even if they had visited the earth they would be frightened to witness the human mentality. The Holy Angel of heaven might not dare to speak out openly. This is the place in the universe where dangers exists even for the most truthful person. People don't see the world as it is, they see the world as they want. People don't see God as God is, they see God as they are. But when you are perfect you will see things as they are, including God.

You may have seen a greedy person following religion, appearing in holy looking robes, praying five times a day but having dirty thoughts. You can find a corrupt employee or a corrupt employer adhering to religion's funny rules. You may have seen people saying special prayers four times a day, yet greedy and hungry for power. Many religious people gossip and criticize others and are always looking to find others' weaknesses. Their gossiping brings all kinds of sin into the life of everyone. One who gossips with you about others, can gossip with others about you too. They make the gossip spicy and add many sinful lies. Stay away from a gossiping person, even if he or she is religious."

You may have seen a good person; following no religion, never lying, never cheating, very humble, not greedy, never gossiping, never criticizing others, always satisfied, never complaining to God, and striving to bring sunshine into the lives of others. You may have seen a good person who does not look at other's weaknesses but only at his own, who loves and helps everyone and is not involved with any cult, sect, or religion. That non-religious good person says from his heart *"Forgive me God! I don't know anything about the scriptures, but the only thing I know is that I try to live truthfully and try to be good to your creatures in order to please you."*.

Do not hate night if you are in the light. Love night if you are enlightened. Night is also a part of nature. It is created for a reason. The king of night may be as valuable as the king of day. The king of night is a blue rose, the king of day is a white rose, the king of the evening is a pink flower and the king of the morning is a yellow flower. There are reasons why seasons are different from each other. The summer is not like winter, spring is not like autumn, and snowfall is not like rain. These four different colors mix with each other to create more and more beautiful colors. Look at the snake and find its beauty as you find beauty in a meditating saint. Find beauty in thorns and flowers, heat and cold, day and night, heavy rain and drought, and in all other things. Understand the beauty of the Creator's mind.

Nature has shown you the rainbow to convey the message that God's creation is beautiful because it is multi-colored. You should love the blue rose as much as you love the pink rose. Do not hate the rich if you are poor, and do not hate the poor if you are rich. Do your duty, which is to serve God and keep in mind that the Creator can replace anyone with anyone. All flowers are beautiful and unique. God does not create any flower that is not beautiful. Night has its own importance in its darkness, the rose has its own importance in its fragrance, and the snake has its own importance in its poison. Happiness has its own beauty and unhappiness has its own. Likewise; richness and poverty, romance and 'Vairagya', union and separation, everything has its own beauty. Sometimes you find this world beautiful and sometimes horrible, sometime you like something but sometimes you don't like the same thing. Sometimes you understand something but sometimes you don't understand it. That is the beauty of this colorful creation. Find the best in all and find the best in everything.

There is nothing ugly in this world. To find fault with God-made man is the same as finding fault with God. When you deal with a bad man, just look at him as one of the flowers in the garden of God. May be the creator has some reason to create a mongoose and a snake. Maybe God loves a color that the world does not like. Maybe God needs all the seven colors to create a rainbow. Why would God create a bad man if he was not needed? When my parents came to know about the man who had me murdered, their first concern was not to harm him. Maybe God needed that kind of man in this world to frighten everyone and to become aware of the true God. Unhappiness, fear, separation, death of a beloved, sorrow and misery are unpleasant. No one likes them. Everyone hates them and prays to God to keep them away from his or her life. Yet for some reason they befall everyone because that's beauty.

There is always a reason behind pain, distress and misery. Many religions and movements are established because of unhappiness. Unhappiness has created many good philosophies. Unhappiness teaches a man to seek God's mercy and to walk the path of virtue.
Dear children grief, mourning, sadness, distress, sorrowfulness, unhappiness, regret, trouble, celebrations, pleasure, bliss, enjoyment, ecstasy, charm, happiness, contentment, pleasure, gladness, exhilaration, cheerfulness, satisfaction, gratification, leisure, amusement, desire, elation, aches, throbbing, soreness, nuisances, etc. are all part of human life. Being effected by all these things is natural, but trust that everything is for the evolution of the soul. Every tree has to accept spring, fall, summer, winter in order to grow bigger. Know how to deal with them

when you face them and learn how to say. 'Thank you God, thank you'
every time.
Revenge is not in the minds of the people who deserve heaven. No snake
can enter into the world of love, kindness, and goodness. Our thoughts
lead to our soul's destiny by forming actions, and habits. Therefore
always have pure thoughts for others. Keep yourself busy in learning as
if you were to live forever and live as if you were to die tonight.
Everyday is meant to plant at least one good seed in this garden.

Never be impressed by people who are only concerned about admiration,
rather than what they really are. Never argue with people who try to
prove themselves to be right rather than what is right. Even if you win
with such people; their hurt ego may harm you later. Do not argue about
spiritual and religious matters. The essence of religion is – art of living a
Karmic life.

DADDY, HOW TO DEAL WITH THE MOST DIFFICULT TIME OF LIFE?

Just accept it quietly and bear it... Be more careful at the most difficult
time, do not get victimized by so called 'luck changers'. Do not let them
to take advantage of your difficulties. In this world many deceivers claim
that their spiritual powers can remove misfortunes and make you
successful in your aim. I have to tell you that no one can overturn God's
plan, and no one can 'undo' your 'Karma'. They may promise to change
your luck by using their non-existing mysterious powers. If they succeed
in fooling you then you have failed to understand the inestimable
precious gift from God, consequently, you may have to go through same
difficulties, one more time, just to understand the value of the difficult
times - the gift. You may not realize that you were fooled consequently
you may mislead others and that might build a chain of wrongdoing. I
advise you not to go through a long process just to learn a little lesson.

Instead of giving your one thousand dollars to a fortune transforming
magician give it to a needy person. Some day you will get the fruit of it.
Seed your Karma at the right place and at the right time. Know that
nature doesn't produce fruit immediately. Some fruits you can see only

after many many years from the date of seeding. Trust that nature will always be just with you.

For your miseries do not blame others, don't blame the stars, dead souls, an unlucky house, black magic or any other such foolish mysteries. Never blame any of your family members or others for the unhappiness you went through. Your mind and God are the cause of all the things you faced. Only God gives difficult times for your advancement, and only God can remove them when you have learned. Consider difficulties as a gift from God, and accept them happily. If happy moments can bear some good fruits then unhappy moments also cannot be without fruit. Bear them, and learn to pray more and more, learn to understand more and more, understand the miracle of God and do one more good thing at the time of your test. Struggle is the time to add one more good seed in this Karma-garden, with your strength. Learn how to deal with chaos; that's the most important lesson God wants you to learn. Learn how to react when someone yells at you? Learn how to react when someone is terribly wrong with you, and learn how to act during the moments of your trial and triumph. Repeat any magic mantra to control your emotions while dealing with an angry person. It's a dream... It's a dream... It's a dream...

So the answer to your question is; it doesn't matter what religion you follow but it matters how you behave. You have a 'hurting nature' or a 'healing nature'? My beloved no one can remain unhurt while trying to hurt others. If you have a healing nature, you will heal others as well as yourself. Become peaceful to bring others at peace. You can give others only that which you have. When you have a healing nature you will see the whole world differently, not because the whole world has changed but because the power within you has changed. 'healing nature'..." the children were very happy to hear it.

DADDY WHY DO PEOPLE CHANGE RELIGION?

BE HUMBLE, LOVE ALL, TRUST A FEW; Ramkrsishna Paramhansa was a holy and humble Saint, who walked the spiritual path with his wife along to ease the journey of the soul to its destiny. Many people from different missions went to impress him, to convert him to their religion.

His innocent, clean mind was willing to take any good thing from anywhere. Once he got converted into Islamic religion leaving behind the principles of his own religion, he started consuming Mother Cow's meat, reading the Koran and doing Namaz five times a day. Once he got very impressed with the Virgin Mary's picture and the Christian philosophy, and almost converted into Christianity. Buddhist, Jains and many others went to impress him with their philosophy in order to convert him. His inner beauty made him like a diamond that attracted everyone to him in order to seize the treasure of a fruitful heart. Be humble but at the same time do not let others take disadvantage of your humility.

My children, anything which reminds you of the Almighty's powerful law, that is the right place for you to be at. Any shrine, preacher, priest, or religion, which makes you love everyone, want to embrace the whole human race that is holy. Whenever your wisdom starts growing, your heart gets filled with love for every God-made creature, consider that meaningful. Live to learn, live to serve, live to love, and live to ease the journey of the soul to its destiny.

"WHAT IS THE DIFFERENCE BETWEEN A GOOD PERSON AND AN ASPIRANT?"

A person of good character, virtues, good attributes, and behavior, is a good man; while he who has a yearning to realize God or to attain salvation is an aspirant. A dedicated devotee is a good person but the contrary is not necessarily true. One who criticizes, the tenet or sect of others, condemns or apposes others, he could possibly a good person, but not an aspirant devoted to God. An aspirant is one who supports his faith, but at the same time does not criticize, condemn or hate those of others."

WHERE CAN WE FIND GOD?

Seek Him in the smile of your friends, in the glow of angry eyes, in the throb of love, in the storm of passion. Everywhere it his glow that is gleaming through different emotions, thoughts and actions. Seek him in the thrill of down, in the sadness of dusk, in the embrace of rains, in hustling storms, in the murmuring breeze – in green pastures, in the blue lotus, in the sangam of graceful Ganges and restless Jamuna. He is everywhere – in everything – not in mortal legs and hands – but in his presence as the Divine joy infinite. You are in Him – You are but him alone.

DADDY WHICH IS THE BEST SHRINE WHERE WE SHOULD GO TO PRAY?

I still remember one of the great consequential things Devi Messiah had told me about two kinds of shrines. That time due to my two weaknesses, I was unable to comprehend it exactly. I will tell you about those two kinds of shrines.

****

Step Twenty Seven...
_____

GOD-MADE SHRINES &
MAN-MADE SHRINES

> Whenever God erects a house of prayer, the Devil always builds a chapel there: And it will be found, upon examination, the latter has the largest congregation.   ...'Daniel Defoe'

Merciful God had sent the former Diwaree into a family where he was leading a common life to perfect himself, thus here he had no ego of renouncement, as he had in his previous life. He was not concerned about recognition. He did not know any ancient religious language, nor did he hate any religion. He was just a simple farmer and good to everyone. Perfection in Diwaree enabled him to understand the reality of the two kinds of shrines.

He only spoke the truth so if somebody asked him, *'are you 192 years old?'* His answer would be, *'No; of course not I am only 41'. What a strange question!! How can a man live for 192 years?'* He perfected himself. All his children used to say about him, "Our Daddy always speaks the truth. He never tells lies." Often he said to his children, "Truth is God and God is Truth. Therefore to understand God you need to lead a truthful life. That is the root mantra (secret of secrets) to understand God."

His ideas about shrines, such as; Prophet-Diwarian's shrine, Diwar-Devote's shrine, Sackclothian's shrine, Real-Diwaree's shrine and all others (Hindu temples, Catholic Churches, Muslim Mosques, Buddhist temples etc.) was very different from other peoples' concepts. He taught to his children about the real shrines:

My children there are two kinds of shrines;
1. God-made Shrines.
2. Man-made Shrines.

GOD MADE SHRINES: Now, listen carefully as to what and where those God-Made Shrines are; God made Shrines are those Shrines which are built by God himself. Such as the animals, dogs, cats, birds, human beings and all other creatures. All these beautiful Shrines are the true Shrines of God; therefore, God himself dwells in them.

MAN MADE SHRINES: Man made Shrines are those shrines which are made by human beings, such as; Prophet-Diwarian shrine, Diwar-Devote shrine, Sackcloth shrine, Real-Diwaree shrine, (Churches, Mosques, Synagogues, Gurudwaras etc. and unoccupied palace-like-houses as well) all other religious monuments, and houses of worship.

Those seekers, who cannot find their God in God-made Shrines, they search for him in man-made Shrines. They cannot understand, or don't believe in the God who dwells within themselves; therefore they can't understand God dwelling in those Shrines. The simplicity of God made Shrines becomes too complicated for them therefore they prefer God in man made Shrines only. They go to man made Shrines and pray in front of something or nothing or in front of a man-made image. They place food or light candles in front of that image. They say many things to that picture, but unfortunately there is no one to hear them or to answer their questions, and no one is there to taste their offered food nor can they see that picture eating food or using the candle light. When these people cannot find the answers then they look for some spiritual man's stories to satisfy their restless minds. They believe in the mysterious lectures of a confused but clever spiritual preacher. They believe in him or her because it's better to believe than not to. They believe in unreal things because it's easier.

They do not like to believe in reality because it's hard to accept the reality. They love confusion and mystery therefore for their mental peace and satisfaction they have to believe in myths. They love these kinds of myths, such as, "There was a great saint, his resurrection took place suddenly and he spoke to the chapel congregation' or 'the wooden statue ate the food offered by the saint', or 'long ago there was a devotee, God granted him life of a thousand years after his death and resurrection." To make these shrines stronger those confused preachers do not hesitate to speak out on anything.

These people do not like to believe that God dwells in 'God-made Shrines' only. They are happy if a so-called holy preacher will tell them that Satan dwells in human beings and God dwells in 'man-made Shrines. This way they feel relieved of their responsibilities towards humankind.

However some wise people prefer God made Shrines. They are not many. They are nice people - may God bless them. They know the best way to know God is through truth and love towards everything He has created. Therefore love everyone and love everything. The best gift human being is blessed with is that he can love and he can be loved. Love them – love God.

****

Step Twenty Eight…

HATE FOR GOD MADE SHRINES

God sent me to this village and into a farmer's home because I did not honor God by not clearly speaking about my age, dress and dislike for this religion. The God who was dwelling in me did not like it. God made this wise decision otherwise I was not strong enough to remove those weaknesses. Death is the door to perfection and perfection is the door to evolution and eventually to heaven. Though, death was extremely frightening because in my previous life when I was a renounced saint, I was brutally murdered at the behest of God-Bawa and Harry Kingson, but that death was a blessing.

After my death Harry Kingson also died of some incurable disease. He came to the Judge-God for the final judgment. Judge-God looked exactly like Devi. She granted me an opportunity to watch the judgment of my murderer. I was amazed to hear the conversation between Judge-God and Harry. Harry's greed caused the destruction of thousands and thousands of God Made Shrines. The Judge (God) said to him,

"Yes, Harry Kingson, I live in the Shrines, which are constructed by me. One who hates my hand made Shrine, hates me! One who locks my Shrines, locks his door to heaven! One who demolishes my Shrine, demolishes his own mind! In only twenty-five years you demolished more than a million Shrines of mine. I made them with my hands and you demolished them like cruel Satan. Even just one of my hand made Shrines cannot be compared with the numerous Shrines made by you people.

And listen to me Harry Kingson, anyone who hates my hand-made Shrine cannot enter into my kingdom. And now, I will tell you how many Shrines of mine were locked by you, while you were involved in the

"Brainwashing Program" of God-Bawa. Whoever got treated by that program, could never understand me. You locked their brain for me. Brainwashing is the same as demolishing my Shrines. Now, look at these millions of Shrines whose doors were locked to me for their lifetime."

God did not ask Mr. Harry Kingson how much he had donated. God counted only that which he had kept with him, because all the money belonged to God. God was the owner of everything. God Bawa prayed to God in this life only when he was starving to death but Harry prayed in his previous life when he was a starving beggar. God trusted him. God had appointed him with power so that he could be an instrument of God's will and help the destitute and the down trodden who needed God's help. The Judge-God said, *"I created human beings to do good things only. I did not create them to do bad things."* (Also, please see the Day of Judgment; step 12)

Love everyone. Spiritual progress has no end. When you want to measure your spiritual attainments always compare them with an all loving person, saints, or with a God-like person, but never compare your performance with the actions of a bad person.

In the God's court justice is dispensed in an equal and just measure. Many surprising things were happening there. I had seen the famous religion's spiritual leaders who were praised here, they were horrified there. Their money and intellect was worth nothing. They were beaten up and thrown into boiling oil. That horrifying punishment cannot be compared with the punishment of Anna Mario or Pintu because hate existed in their genes.

Love everyone. I saw one man who was being sent to heaven. He was surprised at the judgment, and said, "How can I go to heaven, Your Honor? I do not even know any scripture. I am poor uneducated and cannot read or chant a single verse from scriptures. I did not study any holy book, did not choose any holy master to guide me, did not go to any shrine, and I did not perform any rituals or religious acts. How can I go to heaven? I am afraid. May be, your honor, you are teasing me before punishing me."

God explained to him, "All loving humble man, don't be afraid. It is true you will live in heaven. All those religious things you mentioned are irrelevant to reach this place of truthful people. Truthfulness, humility and your respect towards me, your love for your fellow, and your living according to the 'inner scripture' has earned the reward great souls deserve. Even the wild animals of jungle are saying that you have loved them."

Do not mislead and do not get misled. Many deceivers were going through awful punishments. They could not be forgiven. They simply vanished. They shall never again see the sun. They were consigned to deep unfathomable caves in hell. No creature will ever hear their sermons. Their followers also suffered for following them. Everyone received the fruit of their own Karma, because some of them were good people and they had followed the crowd just to be relieved from worldly fear and to bring perfection into their lives. Though they could not go to heaven because they were knocking at the wrong door but if their Karma were good enough then they got one more chance to knock at the right door. Each of them was getting different fruit according to their own Karma.

I was not accepted as a disciple by the holy soul, due to my two weaknesses, but in her infinite mercy she gave me a chance to redeem myself by granting me a new birth here. I am perfecting myself in this life by leading a truthful life and not repeating my two earlier mistakes or any other mistakes again. If Harry Kingson had given all his money to Anna Mario, the beggar, then Anna Mario would have become a millionaire and Harry Kingson would have become a beggar. Rich Harry was chosen to establish a balance in this world, but he was concerned with only his fame. Eventually Harry Mario learned through a different route by going through indescribable difficulties and unbearable pain. After death, Anna Mario became a very rich man like the late Mr. Harry Kingson.

Anna Mario had already promised God, on numerous occasions, to become honest and faithful to God-made Shrines. As those promises came from the bottom of his heart, the inner voice sent the pure signals to the Almighty, and Almighty God listened to his promises and sent him into an enormously wealthy family to fulfill God's wishes.

Love everyone; omnipresent God's presence is within every God-Made-Temple.

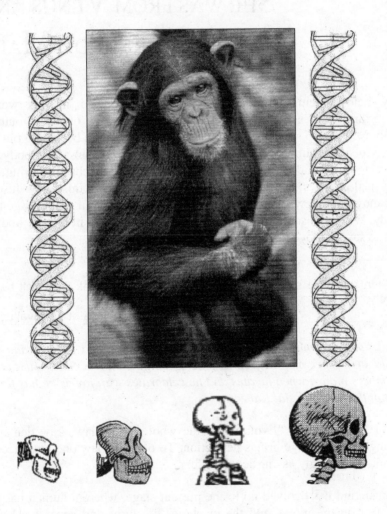

Step Twenty Nine…

SHE WAS FROM VENUS AND WE WERE FROM MARS

My beloved children! Nothing remains unchanged in this world, everything moves, every second, towards changes. To obtain a youthful body we have to say goodbye to the baby-body, and in becoming old we have to say goodbye to the youthful body, and to obtain a new body we have to say goodbye to this body. The 'I' did not change during the physical changes, and it will not change after leaving this body. Just as we move to a new room, or change our outfits; the soul will change this body. When the soul outgrows and is unable to remain in this old body it has to say goodbye to its decayed home.

"When the little bird grows enough he pecks to break the shell to fly freely."

...Saint Thiruvalluvar.

"All family members celebrate with joy when a child is born and the child cries, because he realizes he is confined to a cage. All family members mourn when he dies and he celebrates with joy as he has flown out of the cage." Saint Kabeer.

Devi Messiah said, "Evolution is the whole of the law. Law demands changes, and change brings perfection. To obey the law one must accept death, as willingly as one accepts life.

Humankind has evolved up to the present stage, wherein human has set his feet on the moon, and the mysteries of atoms and genes are being decoded. However, this is not the end of evolution. You have been evolving faster than you imagined. Only a few hundreds years ago, you did not have trains, airplanes, ships, telephones, cell-phones telescopes, cars, motors, typewriters and computers. Every time you evolved by leaving one body and taking a new one with a better brain, better understanding capability. You needed to discard the old used clothes to put on better ones. If you would have been stuck with banana leaves and fig leaves to cover your private parts then how you would have dressed in cotton clothes. There was a time when you used to wear one piece of a dead animal's skin to cover up your body. If you would be afraid to leave that animal-skin, then today you would not see the woolen jacket, silk tie and pants.

You have to die. In order to wear a better outfit, you have to take off this dress. You should not be too attached with this old and decayed body. You should know that the sun does not die in the evening. It sets on this side and rises at the other side. The sun exists even during the middle of night."

Devi Messiah had installed a telescope and after focusing it on a bright star, she said to me, "That is a planet like this Earth. That looks smaller because of the distance. Your people call it by many names such as; Celestial home, Kingdom to come, New Jerusalem, Junnat, Nirvana, Moksha, Elysian fields, Bliss-land, Paradise, Devalok, Planet of Gods and so on! This planet is also known by many other names as well in different religions and different languages. That is the planet where good people go after death. Now for the first time in your life you can see heaven through a telescope. No one on your planet knows what kind of people live there.

There are living beings like us. They are very wise. They understand the facts of life, death, evolution, growth, change, spirals, volcanoes, whirlpools, gravity, secrets of all the planets, secrets of creation, and secrets of the universe etc. They are the 'guardians' of the solar system. They can see you as their scientific knowledge is highly evolved so they can change the density system by reducing it to make it thinner or increase to make it thicker as to be perceived by their own eyes. They have those instruments by which they can see you and remain invisible to you. They can go anywhere they want, but after traveling they always go back to their mother planet. They know how to travel and where to travel, but they always return to their home planet. They are completely devoted and obedient to nature. They know where to go and where not to.

The densities of their bodies are in harmony with the surface density of their planet. And the temperature of their bodies is attuned to the temperature of their planet's surface. They are beautiful, very handsome. They have amazing houses, far in advance of the houses of this Earth.

They have Wisdom, and perfect love. They don't commit mistakes as you people do. They have perfect peace and ultimate happiness. No one is ill there. They don't have social differences. No one is poor or rich there. They know how to share. No greed exists there. They are kind and always helping others. Their doctors and scientists are perfect. Therefore, it is also known as the planet of the perfects, Purna, Gods. They don't follow any religion. When they want to find out any rule of nature they don't open a book like you do. They have wisdom, and they know what to do and what not to. They are living scriptures.

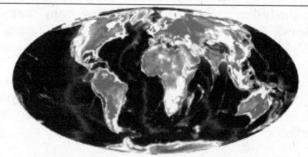

Mother earth, Goddes Earth, Tonantzin, Bhuma, Pachamama, Hou-T'u'
Gaia, Dhara Devi, Jord, Geb, Prithvi, one Morher of all beings.

This earth is alive. That is the reason she can give birth to you, grow vegetation, grass, trees, fruits and corn for all of you children. She produces cotton and other materials to cover your body to protect you from the heat and cold. She creates volcanoes, earthquakes, tornadoes, hurricanes etc. She is the one who makes rivers flow, winds to move, heat, energy, light and life for you to stay alive. She causes your heart and pulse beat. If she stopped even for one hour then you wouldn't survive. She is the one who is supporting you on her back continuously, and keeps producing food for you. Not only these things but the bricks, the wood and all other materials used in your house are from her body.

Everything you possess; is from her body and, therefore, you are a part of her body. Furthermore, the chemicals used in your body; are from her body therefore you are her property. All the money you have in your bank belongs to her. She wants you to use that money to help her helpless children. There are many who are dying, they are wailing crying, "Mother! Mother! Help! ...please help! Please Mother help give us something to survive. ... This mother is helpless as long as you don't come forward with helping hands.

Those who do not perform their duties, have to learn the lesson of honesty. They have to stay here and live with calamities, sickness, poverty, misunderstandings, selfishness, hate, discrimination, disasters, sometimes without clothes, sometimes without food and so on ... until they make their-selves fit for the planet of perfects. After perfecting their-selves they will leave this body here. The genes of their bodies are like energy seeds which carry the information of their Karma. If their Karma is good it will be able to cross the line of truth and they will get new bodies in heaven.

When this earth moves to that position, you will all be unconscious and then die. Death is the law because; this body is made to suit the conditions and the atmosphere of this earth. The atmosphere of heaven is completely different than that of this world. The soul is an energy seed of information or energy seed of intention that beholds the information of your Karma. When you die your body mass reverts back to the soil of which it is composed. Only your soul remains. You are the dispenser of your own destiny. The actions done in former lives are seen to produce fruits in this.
The soul is born again with its accumulated load of Karma. By performing only virtuous actions, it attains heaven. By indulgence in sensuality and similar vices, it is born among the lower stages of evolution. The genes in your body carry the information of your Karma. Genes never die. They stay alive. They have records of your actions. They are like seeds. The difference between vegetable seed and human

genes is that a vegetable seed is seeded in the soil and human soul (seed) is seeded in a mother's womb. Then they grow with god's energy. God selects the mother according to your Karma.

The soul is in the center of the cells. It permeates a person's entire existence. You can see the soul with a very powerful microscope. Karma is written in the chromosomes. Chromosomes carry all your physical information, such as; the color of your hair, the color of your eyes, the color of your skin and so on. They carry the information of your Karma as well. If you hurt someone it is immediately stored in your chromosomes. Whatever you do or think good or bad is stored in you.

Life giver God is in the center of the Earth. He looks like an extremely hot moon. He (the Core) places the soul in the mother's womb wherein it grows with energy (life) and time. All these miracles on the Earth you can see are the miracles of the father and mother. They are known as Core and Earth or Ardhanaareeshwar. Father God (core) has many names in different languages. All those names are meaningful. For example, he gives life therefore is known as Life-giver. Mother also has so many names. However, a name doesn't make any difference. You must know what the Earth is and what the Core is and how they produce life.

Life giver core is our father. He is like the moon. He moves clockwise, in the opposite direction to the earth. The clockwise moving father releases the clockwise traveling energy. This clockwise energy enters the seeds and DNA etc. This is the reason everything in the nature is wound clockwise, such as the DNA of your body, spirals, hair around your head, spirals in your fingers, tornadoes etc.

The next day, She showed me many pictures. Such as a picture of the Moon, Mercury, Earth, core of the sun, Solar system, orbits of all the planets, whirlpools, tornadoes, galaxy spirals, cell ands DNA and the evolutionary process. I never had any idea that these pictures could be related with spirituality and God. Pointing at a particular picture she explained the strange miracles of that planet called heaven. That picture was taken by NASA scientists. The distance between the sun and the earth is about 93 million miles or 8 light minutes. She then explained the distance between Heaven and earth.   The earth makes one rotation around its axis in 23h.56m.4s. It means, we have a day-night span of about 24 hours, but people in Heaven have a different day-night time span.

On earth, one year is of about 365.26 days. Earth's average orbital speed is 18.51 miles per second. It means, this earth takes 365 ¼ days to make one complete revolution around the Sun, but people who live in heaven have their own length of day and length of year as well. The planet Heaven has its own time span of revolving and rotating. Their days and years are of different duration from us. Our ambient temperature is very different than the ambient temperature of heaven. If you land on that planet, you will not be able to survive, because your body is made to suit the weather conditions of this planet, and your scientific knowledge is not good enough to control the whether conditions of heaven. Then she revealed the realities of nature, such as; why craters on the surface of moon are similar to the craters on Mercury, or why the soil from the moon is similar to the soil of a volcano's lava. She told me many astonishing secrets of this universe and life and death. Astounding!!! I was thrilled and astonished. With tearful eyes I looked at her and started crying with love. Then I said to her, "Thank you for visiting our planet."

"Thank you for listening to me," She said to me.

****

You have come a long way from a distant cold orbit and you have experienced many improvements. The differences between the body of primitive man-apes and your present Homo Sapiens body are the apparent from the fossil record. Primitive man-apes had protruding jaws and smaller, less heavy brains than Homo Sapiens

You are a part of this Universe

The Universe is alive and all that is contained within the Universe is alive including Earth.

The Universe is finite, it is a mega Sun. Were you able to put your head through the periphery of the Universe you would see a system of giant planets revolving around it. The Universe, which you perceive as many star systems, is the Sun of a mega Solar System. Our home is, a mighty ball of fire.

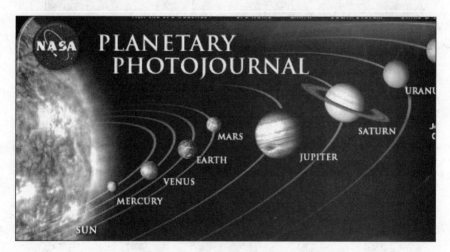

Present stage of the solar system

Now we are on the third orbit from the sun between Venus and Mars.

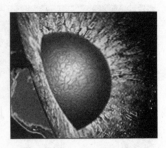

Earth and Core are our Mother and Father. Energy or life emanates
from the core. On the third orbit Earth is already traveling into 'future'
at a speed of 18.51 miles per second. We are evolving with her.

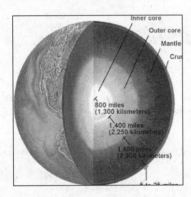

The invigorating energy which rises from the Core enters all
bodies on Earth as 'life' and consciousness. It enters into all
seeds which are planted in the ground, brings healthy seeds
alive and nudges them through the soil until they emerge as
young plants on the surface of Earth. Both the young
saprophytes of a seed plant and the human foetus are stirred
into life by the same energy.

 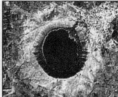 

Moon - Lonar creter India - Volcanic Larva same as lunar

Surface of the moon and mercury has same density, and same appearance with dried bubbles of volcanic larva. I am surprised that our people don't know it. Though this knowledge has been on our earth for more than half a century yet nobody welcomed the truth. 2nd surprise, we people can spend billions of dollars to find these facts and the knower had to starve sometime for days.

Same as preachers who claimed to be knower of secrets of the soul were treated as a king and the one who knew it (DNA - soul) was completely ignored in our world. However saint Diwaree said, this is the beauty of our world.

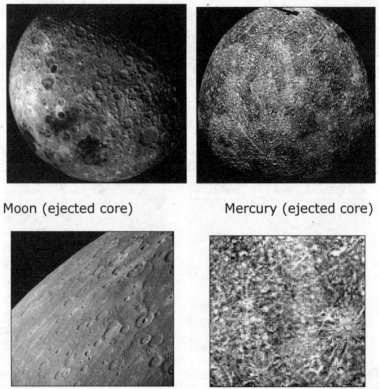

Moon (ejected core)   Mercury (ejected core)

Courtesy: NASA

When the Core is equal in mass to the residue of the planet, the Core is ejected. The satellites of planets, such as Mercury, our Moon, Phobos and Deimos of Mars etc., are the ejected Cores of planets. The bubbles are boiling lava that is frozen in cold space.

****

Just like casting off worn out clothings and putting on new ones, that which is embodied casts off worn out bodies and enters others that are new. Gita

The fossil bones which an archeologist unearths and considers to be the remains of an unknown hominid who existed during an early period in the development of man, could be the fossilized remains of his own primal body.

Earth has always supported life, however, primates are terrestrial organisms who first appear in the fourth orbit from the Sun, the Marsian orbit.

****

Life on Mars

...Australopithecus coexisted with other Hominids when Earth occupied the Marsian orbit. The skeletal differences between races which co-existed on Mars are more apparent than the skeletal differences between races which co-exist on Earth

January 22nd, 2008 NASA captured a female alien waiving her hand. "These pictures are amazing. I couldn't believe my eyes when I saw what appears to be a naked alien running around on Mars."

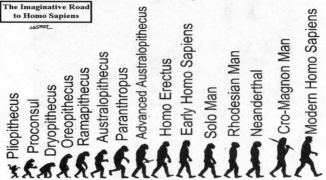

A beautiful journey with mother Earth
A journey from (...Saturn orbit, Jupiter orbit) Mars to Earth... to Venus

Photo Credit: Laurence D Smart, Unmasking Evolution, Canberra, Australia

It was already explained more than twenty years ago, in Her book "Ascent of man from Pluto to Venus, and Christ of this era. ... life on Mars. "Hellas is an ocean and the 'Sand-Dune crater' is Hellas Pontus is in fact the sea floor of Hellas ocean. The water in Hellas ocean is not visible to us because it has the same density as our atmosphere. ...not aware of life on Mars, ...not visible to us ...because organisms on the surface of Mars do not exist in the same density system as those organisms on the surface of Earth."

Spirals – God's Signature

All spiriling phenomena on Earth result from the opposite directions of motion of Earth and Core; snails, shells, whirlpools, waterspouts, cyclones, even our bodies, from the spiriling DNA molecules to the loops and whorls under our finger and toes.

Spirals – God's Signature

Do you know were you are?

Stages of a Solar System

Step 1   Step 2   Step 3

Formation of planets and the Solar System

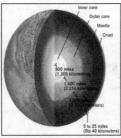

Images courtesy: NASA

Earth is the Great Mother Goddess of all religions call her by any name; Mother earth, Goddes Earth, Tonantzin, Pachamama, Hou-T'u' Gaia, Dhara Devi, Jord, Geb, Prithvi, you are one people of one

Mother. Core is the Great Father God. Call the Core what you will, YHVH, Brahma, Shiva, Allah, God, you are one people of one God.

****

Due to the process of differentiation (heavy material in the body of a planet falls inward towards the Core while lighter material rises), the Core of a planet grows. When the Core is equal in mass (mass can be thought of simply as weight) to the residue of the planet, the Core is ejected.

When Earth moved out of the Marsian orbit and entered into this, the third orbit from the Sun all organisms present on Earth were adapted to suit the conditions of this orbit. Prior to moving out of the Marsian orbit.

Our Solar System

"Sansarati – Sansaarah" Veda
"The wheel of nature" I am Alga and Omega the beginning
and the end." Bible

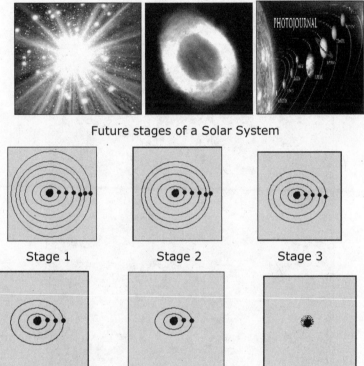

Future stages of a Solar System

Stage 1   Stage 2   Stage 3

Stage 4   Stage 5   Stage 6

"Heaven and earth shall pass away," and "the fashion of this world
passeth away," and "the heavens shall perish," and what follows. Bible

Size comparison of inner planets: Mercury, Venus, Earth, and Mars

God said, I am the seed of all beings. For without me, whether animate or inanimate, nothing can exist. I am the beginning, middle and ending also of everything created. I sustain everyone as I dispense the fruit of all actions. I support the whole cosmos with only a tiny fragment of my being. Gita

Art image: Cosmic form of God – the universal soul

Devotee Arjun Said, My God! O universal soul, you reach everywhere. Everywhere, millions of faces, eyes seeing everything; countless mouths all speaking wanders; and visions too numerous to describe... you exist before anything else...You wield infinite power. O lord of universe, your body is entire cosmos. All creatures, like moths to a flame, are rushing head long into your gapping jaws of death... and coming out in a changed form as a new born baby. O my God...

Part Five

RELIGION AND SCIENCE

Step Thirty...

THUS TAUGHT THE MESSIAH

"Science without religion is lame and religion without science is blind".
...Albert Einstein

The sign of the beginning of a Solar System is a Supernova. A Sun explodes and heavy material is dispatched into space to form the Cores of future planets. Ejected Cores rotate and gather material from space, in this way develop into planet.

Due to the process of differentiation (heavy material in the body of a planet falls inward towards the Core while lighter material rises), the Core of a planet grows. When the Core is equal in mass (mass can be thought of simply as weight) to the residue of the planet, the Core is ejected. In the case of Earth the ejection will take place in the Weddell Sea in the vicinity of the Antarctica. The Earth ejects its Core as a single body while certain planets, such as Jupiter eject their Cores in separate pieces over a period of time.

The satellites of planets, such as Mercury, our Moon, Phobos and Deimos of Mars etc., are the ejected Cores of planets. When a planet ejects its Core the mass of the planet is adjusted to suit the gravitational conditions which prevail in an orbit one position closer to the Sun.

The Sun is thought to derive its energy from nuclear fusion reactions occurring at its Core, what actually takes place is that Mercury and Venus are attracted into the Sun and their combined mass is converted into solar energy.

The conversion of Mercury and Venus into solar energy leaves two vacant orbits in the Solar System. The Moon moves into the Position, which was previously occupied by Mercury and Earth moves into the position, which was occupied by Venus. The Core which is ejected by Earth remains in the third orbit. Mars enters into the third orbit and this pattern is carried along the line to Pluto which moves into the position previously occupied by Neptune. The present position of the planets, commencing from the Sun and moving outwards towards Pluto is as follows: Mercury, Venus, Earth, Mars, Ceres, Jupiter, Saturn, Uranus, Neptune, and Pluto. The position of the planets after the next shift will be as follows: Moon, Earth, Mars, Ceres, Jupiter, Saturn, Uranus, Neptune, and Pluto.

Earth is the Great Mother Goddess of all religions and the Core is the Great Father God. Call the Core what you will, YHVH, Brahma, Shiva, Allah, God, you are one people of one God.

The Universe is finite, it is a mega Sun. Were you able to put your head through the periphery of the Universe you would see a system of giant planets revolving around it. The Universe, which you perceive as many star systems, is the Sun of a mega Solar System. Our home is, a mighty ball of fire.

The invigorating energy which rises from the Core enters all bodies on Earth as 'life' and consciousness. It enters into all seeds which are planted in the ground, brings healthy seeds alive and nudges them through the soil until they emerge as young plants on the surface of Earth. Both the young saprophytes of a seed plant and the human foetus are stirred into life by the same energy.

Now that you have located God at the center of Earth, you will feel immeasurably closer to Him. You cannot reach into the center of Earth and embrace God but you can embrace all the wonderful manifestations that God has produced on Earth.

From His cave in the center of the Earth God watches over His creations. When the soul of one of His creations has outgrown its body, God puts that soul into a more evolved body.

Your soul is the energy seed, which contains the potential of your future self. Just as the seed of an orange tree cannot produce an apple tree, when your present body expires your soul cannot produce a different person, it can only reproduce you.

****

With the above and hundreds of other, facts after confirming her arrival, Devi Messiah cried out and said to all the so called God-men, "Please help me. Please all you Holinesses and God-Bawas please help me. I am a mother. Try to understand my pain. It's a fun for you, unbearable pain for Mother. Their outgrown mind cannot find suitable food. They suffer from the mental diseases of Meaninglessness and Purposelessness. They are lost. They cannot find the love of a real mother for whom they can live and die. Although they know that a mother's love is unique, they cannot understand mother. They cannot live without a mother's love. You know, you are not their real mothers or fathers. You know, you are not their savior. You know you have mesmerized them to use them. Many intelligent children feel like orphans who have lost their mother for good. This is very painful for children and for a mother."

Indeed it is logical, a mother's love is incomparable. The word 'Mother' is indescribable and too wonderful for words to express, so we try by saying it means 'Ocean of Love and Care'. In the form of God, she hugs them, she cuddles them, and she feeds them when they get hungry. Her loving hand's gentle touch nourishes their minds and bodies. She loves them in the form of a daughter, a wife or a mother. When they are young, she loves them in the form of a mother. When they grow up, she loves them in the form of a wife. When they get old, she loves them as a daughter, or even as a grand daughter. She loves them in a way that they always feel cared for – an invisible support of soul and body. Similarly, she gets love from them, and she also feels loved. Every child must swim in the ocean of love.

Then she said to everyone, "I nurtured your minds through pain and suffering. Many times you complained and asked me not to give you so much pain, but I knew how much you could take and how much you could bear. I knew your strength. Whenever you became unconscious I lifted you in my arms and loved you with my gentle feelings. You did not notice but I have always been with you. Yes my children, I was always with you. You cannot breathe without me. With each and every breath you inhaled and exhaled, I was with you. I was pumping your heart so that your brain could function and grow wise to understand the miracles of Mother and Father.

Sometimes I gave you a chronic disease with constant mental and physical pain. It was essential for you to grow wiser. That was the only teacher which taught you to pray, to bow your head down to the ground, and to recognize that there is a superior force which controls your destiny. Pain and fear has taught you to become a good human being and to understand the meaning of this life. Pain has taught you to be kind and loving to others. Fear has taught you to become a decent human being; a decent wife to your husband, a decent husband to your wife, a decent parent to your children, a decent child to your parents, and a decent person to your community and to this world. Pain has taught you to understand the philosophy of Bhagwan Ram - you are in this world for a reason.

I was attentive in bringing out intelligent life that would strive for perfection, and would fulfill the needs of needy people. I sent you in human form for the unique purpose which only you could carry out in the world. When a beggar was in a desperate need for help, I needed your hands to become my hands to help him. When a confused man was wandering in the dense darkness, I needed your hands to light a candle of love, and another candle of knowledge in him. If you could save one life you could save many lives. If you could be good to one enemy, you could be good to the whole world. That was the sign of your perfection.

Your improved life and improved performance would make you a fit person to receive recognition and reward from Ardhnaareeshwar (Mother and Father in one body) of this world, explained the Messiah.

In this world many children were planning to disobey the law of the Mother as they didn't know the consequences. Devi Messiah begged those misled children to follow the law of nature, but some of them couldn't understand. Then Devi Messiah approached their mentors; Sackcloth, Prophet-Diwaree, God-Bawa, Real Diwaree and other God-leaders. In-front of their followers she said, "I am the Mother, therefore, I am telling all of you; 'You Are Not the Real Father'. Tell me if I am wrong. Tell me, now in front of your followers!!"

"But, but hhhow .... doo yuuuu... know?" frightened God-Bawa asked in a shaking voice.

The Mother replied, "Because I did not associate with you as your consort. Only I know; who their Father (God) is. I am their mother and you are not their father. Only I know it. I am their real mother, therefore; I am the true well-wisher of my loving children. I know when they should be fed and when they should have their clothes changed. You are concerned only about your fame and money, and I am concerned about their safety.

There are two kind of Satans in this Universe; 1. People like you who claim to be the Savior and steal my innocent children, misguide them to use them. You don't teach people like Mr. Harry Kingson and Politician Andrew, that there are many Anna Marios who keep praying; *"God, God, Father, Father, Mother, Mother where are you ...?"* and 2. People who have left their mother planet, living in a spaceship to steal my innocent children using their organs to replace with own perishing ones. On earth there are many human organ dealers who steal poor children's organs and sell them to rich people, but they will die on earth.

There has always been Satan in this Universe. Now, (after reading this book) my children will become wise and they shall recognize you for what you are. If you can escape from my wise children then remember this Universe too is powerful. You cannot hide yourself underground or above ground. You cannot escape from this powerful Universe. You cannot escape from your creator. You cannot escape from me. However, before the end of this time I must give you one more chance. 'For-giver' is also my name. If you surrender just before the end of your time then; I will request your father to forgive you. He is very angry with you because he loves me immensely, and he has seen my tears. He has seen the sufferings of his beloved and mine. And now, he is not happy that you have been falsely claiming to be the husband of his beloved consort.

Each day, I faced horrible pain because of your ignorant actions. My pain was his pain. He could not do anything because He was busy producing energy (life) from the distance of Earth's diameter divided by two and almost the size of the moon. I came to the surface of the Earth to protect my innocent children from the two kinds of Satan. Victimized children like Anna Mario were in great pain and praying for help. Your duty was to tell the corrupt people of the world that; 1. You cannot save them. 2. You and they shall have to stand before the Judge and await his justice. 3. You have no connection with the Judge, even if you do; the Judge is not corrupt. 4. They shall receive the consequence of their Karma and you shall receive yours."

H.H. God-Bawa said, "Mother, I know, everything you said is right. I am not their savior or father. These people were facing unbearable traumas and did not know why they were going through such suffering. These people were going crazy, thinking; there was no father and no mother who would listen to their prayers. In this situation I mesmerized them. It is true that I used them, but they were the ones who kept coming to me. When I promised them heaven, they felt relaxed. At the time I got your message, through your messenger, I was unable to understand you. I was lost in the clouds of confusion. I thought no matter what, enjoy life and make them feel relaxed. But I was not aware, that it was a sin. I was not sure what was going on."

His Holiness Pattiwala, Prophet-Diwaree, Sackcloth, Real Diwaree and many other dead prophets and religious leaders were standing with their heads down, in-front of their followers. Devi Messiah Mother was hoping that they would either surrender or apologize. Many followers fled as they could not stand and witness the insult of their God-men. Many other truth lover children were happy to face the Truth. The

Messiah said to their followers who stayed, listening to her, "Dear children, there are innumerable things about these two great forces; Mother and Father. Together they constitute the positive and negative energy required to produce life. He is like a cold Moon without Her, and She is like a barren lifeless planet without Him. He and She are self-created to love, respect and honor each other, and produce beautiful children who could sing the Almighty's glory.

Now, many of my children think that on earth there is no Divine mother to whom they could surrender, to find solace and food for the mind. They cannot live a without mother, therefore; they took recourse to drugs to forget the unbearable pain of separation from the loving mother. Their pain is my pain. A Mother is unhappy when her children are unhappy. She is unhappy when her children commit self-violence. I kept begging God-Bawa and all His Holinesses; again and again I requested them to tell their followers that the time for games was over. There has to be an end to every unreal thing. God's path is neither fun nor a game. I requested them to tell their followers that they were not the real father or savior. Their followers would definitely believe them if they would tell the truth because of their trust in them. They had the key to their followers' destiny, therefore; I requested them to tell the truth. Once again I am requesting them in front of you,

"O God agents and God-men! You have wrongfully usurped the functions of the God-father and God-mother. You have ruined their spiritual lives and they are now like a rudder-less boats in the ocean. Every brainwashed person has every confidence that your philosophy will save him or her, therefore whatever you told them they did with without question. You promised them heaven and in return they were ready to do anything for you. Using Satan's destructive powers in this highly evolved age of science they are ready to cause wave upon wave of destruction. Now it is time when scientists and religious people should turn around and facing each other, start walking together to understand each other;

Now it's time for me to tell you that real God exists. You must have proof while you are alive.

"Behold, I make all things new." Revelation, 21:5.

Behold, the days come, saith the Lord, that I will perform that good thing which I promised: I will cause a branch of righteousness to grow up. And this is the name wherewith She (SHE) shall be called, The Lord, our righteousness.

Mother and father (Core and Earth) are described in many ways.

Shiva and Shakti: energy (life) and body

Universal Mother and Father (Mother earth and Core). Lord of the body and Lord of the soul. Lord of visible world and Lord of invisible world.

Step thirty One…

UNIFIED FIELD

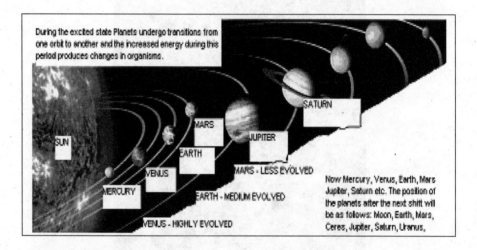

During the excited state Planets undergo transitions from one orbit to another and the increased energy during this period produces changes in organisms.

SUN

MERCURY

VENUS

EARTH

MARS

JUPITER

SATURN

MARS - LESS EVOLVED

EARTH - MEDIUM EVOLVED

VENUS - HIGHLY EVOLVED

Now Mercury, Venus, Earth, Mars Jupiter, Saturn etc. The position of the planets after the next shift will be as follows: Moon, Earth, Mars, Ceres, Jupiter, Saturn, Uranus,

… … … … … …

UNIFIED FIELD

Chapter1.
INTRODUCTION

Existing concepts of evolution have largely formed around the publication in 1859 of Charles Darwin's 'The Origin of Species'. Darwin envisaged evolution as many small transitional changes in the genetic structure of organisms and as one small change proved advantageous it was carried along the corridors of time and added to by later changes which introduced further improvements, however, all efforts to trace the origin of man are dependant upon a fossil record which is totally unable to provide an unbroken series of transitional forms.

Rather than producing an unbroken pattern of development between man and his closest relatives, the ape family, the evidence strengthens the case for 'Punctuated Equilibria', a theory put forward by Neil Eldredge and Stephen Jay Gould which proposes that evolution takes place in a series of sudden and repeat changes.

The true facts about evolution are actually an astounding marvel of organization and improvement. It is common knowledge that the processes which led to life on Earth could not have occurred in the Earths present position, a mean distance of 149 and half million km from the Sun.

The origins of the human line can be traced back to a cold orbit in the distant regions of the Solar System.

All of Earths history did not unfold in this particular orbit. Earth started out in the orbit which is presently occupied by Pluto and experienced shifts which carried the planet step by step closer to the sun. With each shift the organisms present on the Earth were changed into forms which were able to survive under the different conditions of the new orbit.

****

Chapter 2
THE TRANSMUTATION OF SPECIES

There has always been life on Earth; however, all of earth's history did not unfold in this, the third orbit from the Sun.

The Solar System is a scene of constant changes wherein long periods of equilibrium are interrupted by brief periods of excitation.

During the excited state Planets undergo transitions from one orbit to another, Earth has served terms in each of the orbits which are presently occupied by Pluto, Neptune, Uranus, Saturn, Jupiter, Ceres and Mars.

Terrestrial life is a phenomenon which originated in an outlying orbit of the solar System, where microorganisms, gathered by the convolutions of the Planet, were packed into hard-ice conditions suitable for the preservation of organic material.

From a cold, outlying orbit Earth has transported organic material across the Solar System with the raised energy level during excited states bringing about the changes as proposed by Neil Eldredge and Stephen Jay Gould in 'Punctuated Equilibria'.

Organisms do have their origin in other pre-existing types; however, differences are not due to gradual modification over successive generations.

The increased level of energy during the excited state of the Solar System causes significant changes in organs and parts, resulting in the exact degree of adaptive alteration necessary to fit organisms to the different environs of an orbit closer to the Sun.

The repeated operation of these factors produces changes in species.

****

Chapter 3
THE ELECTRON PLANET

If we think of Planets in terms of transitory electrons which have not spent millions of years in the same orbit it becomes clear that a radical departure from the concept of evolution through gradual change is needed.

The equilibrium of the Solar System is interrupted at regular intervals by brief periods of increased energy; the periods of increased energy are herein referred to as the excited state of the Solar System.

During the excited state Planets undergo transitions from one orbit to another and the increased energy during this period produces changes in organisms.

Changes are not uniform throughout organisms; those organisms trapped lower down in Plutonian Earth would be ahead in development due to direct exposure to the electrical influence of the Core of the Planet.

Different levels of development carried along the line to the terrestrial orbits sees species at various stages of development co-existing.

A further consideration is that of racial differences, such differences being due to geophysical conditions with species being adapted to both the orbit and to geographic location.

The following allocation is intended to convey the general pattern of development.

Orbits are hereafter referred to as K, L, M, N, O etc., with the K orbit being closest to the Sun.

Ceres is included with the accompanying asteroids as revolving in the O orbit.

Organic material gathered from space and rolled into the icy mass of Plutonian Earth was carried into the S orbit during a period of excitation.

During excitation the organisms underwent changes which resulted in the exact degree of adaptive alteration necessary to suit them to conditions prevailing in the S orbit.

Upon return to equilibrium the Core of the Planet provided the electrical stimulus necessary to sustain replication.

This process was repeated with the energy unleashed during each subsequent period of excitation producing further biological changes.

A built-in repair system, operated on by enzymes, ensured that the organisms were able to survive such violent changes.

This self-healing ability is an essential requirement during the period immediately following excitation.

The third shift placed Earth in the Q orbit where formation into single cell organisms commenced, culminating in a population explosion in the P orbit.

Lemuroidea, Lorisoidea and Tarsioidea are not classified as Prosimii because of the implication that they arrived ahead of Anthropoidea.

Anthropoidea herein excludes Hominidae who are placed in the N orbit.
Species exhibit both different stages of development and racial differences among species at the same level of development.

Chapter 4
QUANTA THEORY FOR CORES

The satellites of Planets, such as the Moon, Phobos and Deimos of Mars etc., are the ejected cores of planets.

When a planet makes a transition from one orbit to another the planet ejects its core and it is this action which adjusts the mass of the planet to suit the gravitational conditions prevailing in an orbit closer to the Sun.

The term 'quanta' herein applies to the ejected Cores of Planets. Mercury is included in this category (as quanta).

A terrestrial Planet retains its quanta as long as it remains in a specific orbit, however, when the Planet undergoes transition it will eject its quanta.

Locked securely within this system is the destruction of the quanta in the K orbit (Mercury) and the Planet in the L orbit (Venus) for the conversion of matter into solar energy.

The vacant spaces in orbits K and L are filled by the quanta from the M orbit (Moon) and the Planet from the M orbit (Earth) respectively.

352   OUR GOD OUR EARTH

The pattern repeats throughout the solar System with the vacant spaces in the M orbit being occupied by the ejected quanta of Earth (before Earth's transition to the L orbit).

The ejected quanta of Earth remains in the M orbit and becomes the accompanying satellite of the Planet which arrives in the M orbit from the N orbit (Mars) and so forth.

Planets and their quanta should be thought of as separate bodies experiencing equal momentum in opposite directions with the direction of motion having a bearing on the nature of the charge.

The quanta, though considerably smaller than the residue of the Planet, is made up of heavier material, therefore, the mass of the quanta can equal that of the residue of the planet.

Rotation of the quanta (Core) of earth takes place to the clockwise direction; the opposite direction of Earth, thus the charge of the quanta is equal in magnitude but opposite in sign to that of the Planet.

These two equal and opposite forces act to secure bodies to the surface of Earth.

****

Chapter 5
UNILATERAL WINDING OF MOLECULES ATTRIBUTED TO THE CLOCKWISE ROTATION OF THE CORE OF EARTH

The basic molecules of all living organisms on Earth are helical, wound to the right, this fact has led to the mistaken belief that organisms of widely differing groups have arisen from common progenitors.

The current explanation for the clockwise winding of molecules is that a few early molecules, thought to be responsible for the development of all life-forms on Earth, were coincidentally clockwise wound.

There is nothing coincidental about Nature.

Natural growth takes place upward and to the right through work done by ascending electromagnetic waves which emit from the Core of Earth.

The energy enters all bodies on the surface of Earth and winds the molecules of the bodies into right hand threaded helixes.

The winding applies tensions to the molecules of a body which is proportional to the weight of the body.

Weight can be considered to be that property of a material body by virtue of which the electromagnetism in the molecules of the body exerts a pull towards the core of Earth.

****

Step Thirty Two...

KARMA (Action/Reaction)

Karma is the law of action and reaction. An action, which takes place in this life can result in either a reaction, which takes place in this life or a reaction which is suspended and carried over to the next life.

Karma is not a system of punishment but a system of learning through experience. This experience always inflicts suffering, therefore Karma is often thought of as system of punishment. Pain is the fastest and most effective teacher, whether it be emotional or physical. The system works like this: In one life a man commits a misdeed; consequently, in his next life he is placed in a position wherein he is the recipient of misdeeds of a similar nature. The purpose of Karma is to prevent the same misdeed from being repeated in future lives and the method is simple. If in one life, through greed a man inflicts hunger on others, in his next life the greed of others will inflict hunger on him.

How can Karma be effective when a man has no recollection of the misdeeds and lessons of his past lives? What is to prevent him from making the same mistakes again? It is not necessary for a man to remember his past lives; the purpose of Karma is to improve a man's character through his natural reactions. Genes, which deal with heredity, store the lessons, which are learned in previous lives.

Genes (DNA molecules) are dealt with in a branch of biology called genetics, which deals with the heredity of attitudes. Genes are responsible for more than eye color, and so forth; genes are also responsible for perceptions, behavior and instinctual reactions (behavior arising from impulse). The information stored in the DNA molecules of individuals is gathered from unique life experiences; therefore, the instinctual reactions of individuals are unique.

Obey the laws of nature, serve God, be good to one another and when your Homo sapiens body dies you will be reborn on the morning star, Devaloka.

All who are born on the Devaloka have perfect forms, perfect minds, perfect, senses, perfect love and perfect peace. Be obedient to God and when death approaches recognize it as the means to a higher life. Approach death without fear because God's wisdom has seen fit to conceal, in the shadow of death, the brilliant light of a new life.

****

Devi Messiah said, "Now I have unified the realms of science and religion. I have been walking on earth for many decades trying to reach and teach each and every person, but now the seed is seeded in the soil. With time the Earth will grow these seeds. Whoever comprehends the miracle of Mother, it becomes his or her duty to serve all his brothers and sisters, with love and wisdom. Whoever passes this message on to others he or she will be the dearest to me.

Some of you believed that everyone will rise up at the time, when I come here. Some believed in one thing and others believed in something else, however everyone believed that there is Judgment after death. Now everyone is here to witness the truth. This earth has had more than enough capacity in her to nourish you with her milk. She fed you her flesh till this day, in the hope that all the risen souls would understand the truth. Now I have given you all the proofs that I am here to keep my word.

Heaven is my home and I will go back to my home, but you people will be able to come with me only after passing the test. In this Universe, nothing is impossible for me to gain including Heaven, which is my home. I am not bound to receive the consequence of any Karma, nor do I need to obtain anything because everything belongs to me, still I perform my duty. I serve you.

Everyday keep adding a new chapter of good Karma in your genes. Be a good human being; faithful, loyal, and trustworthy. Love the helpless people and understand that, they too are God's creation, and God himself is dwelling in them. Live to save others and die to save others, and kindle a lamp of love within every God-Made-Temple. Be honest to this earth because you owe a lot to her. Though, becoming good is a tough task even for the most intelligent person, as it is difficult to climb high yet it's the aim of life, and achieve it," thus concluded Devi Messiah.

Just before we end our journey together, my dears, now we know God's law. Whether we are scientists or religious authorities; for the sake of our world it is our responsibility to read, learn, understand, and teach the truth of science and religion, to beautify this Earth - our home. A thief can show how to stop all other thieves. A lawyer can explain the facts of law, and how to stop misuse of the law. A financial expert can reveal the secrets on how to solve the problems of a penniless man. All experts of different departments can present a gift to this mother Earth by providing facts. This is our home. We must beautify it. We must make each and every God-Made-Temple strong and glistening inside and out. The most intelligent people of the earth must also realize that; he or she also is bound by nature to beautify this world, so future generations may have more than hundreds of proofs to worship Devi Messiah as the only one Christ, Prophet, Avatar, incarnation of God or a Messenger of God.

They will have dozens of proofs such as;

1. She was the one who explained the miracles of DNA and Karma, soul and natural instinct.
2. She was the one who explained why DNAs are moving clockwise.
3. She was the one who explained why the Core is moving clockwise and the Earth counterclockwise, and what is gravity.
4. She was the one who explained about primitive life on Mars while the people of this Earth didn't even know that life exists there. And, we were from there.

5.   She was the one, long ago, who explained a supernova as the origin of the solar system, and how later planets were formed along-with their cores, and amazing facts of gravity.

6.   She was the only one who knew all the secrets of nature including the secrets of the craters on moon, volcanoes, larva, Mercury and the secrets of all the planets and evolution.

7.   She was the one who explained the consequences of 'Time Travel'.

8.   She was the one who explained the secrets of the Savior or how God comes to Earth in the form of a human being.

They may have hundreds of proof that she lived a more difficult and a truthful life than any other Prophet, Christ, Avatar or Messiah and they might even find out that she did not live for money. They may have no proof of any other God's messenger who had revealed the secrets of DNA also may not agree that DNA existed in those days. The new question will be if DNA existed those days then why did they not speak about them, or if they did then why could not interpreters of this time match the reality of this world and the original language of scriptures. Misinterpretation is likely possible as translators of eighteenth century didn't have a clue about DNA, Internet, time travel and many other realities of the present time; but now someone should interpret them properly and match the two realities. Everyone must be just and fair in this case because it's God's path - our destiny.

Above all every human being is gifted with a unique intellect, and the history of religion provides evidences that 'good' and 'bad' has always been the two parts of this worldly life and there has always been a struggle in the name of religion. Everyone is always being inspired by the 'inner scripture' to do good things, and after walking a few steps with a priest, the inspiring voice may be louder. Therefore I trust; there will be lights in many God-Made-Temples. This humble servant of yours has a gift to present to the world, and now you know your responsibilities.

****

Devi Messiah said: One earth of another Solar System had a real struggle with her disobedient children. As I told you this body is like a uniform that one has to take off to put on a new one. She was about to take all her children to heaven. A few of the rich children became disobedient and they wanted to runaway from death, they started arguing with the Mother.

The Mother explained to them, while trying to take off their uniforms, saying, "This is the law. You cannot preserve the flesh of this body in heaven. In heaven the temperature is different than what it is here on earth. A heavenly body is very different from an earthly body. Everyone who had gone there had to discard this body here. A fish cannot walk like a human being in downtown Manhattan. If that fish wants to enjoy walking in downtown Manhattan, it will have to, do some good things, leave that body and enter into the womb of a human mother who has one full cell of 23 chromosomes from the mother and 23 chromosomes from the father. After developing in the mother's womb and taking birth properly, it will have to learn walking as human beings. It will be known as Mr. Thomas ... ... or whatever ... ... Then his dream will come true. He will have much more understanding than he could imagine while living under water. Then, he will be able to understand the difference between life under water and life in Manhattan. Therefore, come on my child, leave this body behind. Now it's time to move to heaven. I am here to explain the law to you."

The disobedient child ran away into the space on a spaceship and thus he remained in that body while the earth was moving to the second orbit. He didn't get a new body in heaven. Eventually, when his old organs started decaying in space, he suffered terribly. Having no choice, he started landing on other planets where he started replacing his organs with the body parts removed from the young children of those planets. That was the terrible sin. Innocent newborn children of that planet didn't know what was going on because those newborn babies were of a very tender age. They were very God-fearing and innocent, and couldn't even think of such scientific criminals.

But the obedient children were blessed. The silky smoothness of their new bodies brought a wonderful smile to their faces. Their vision became strong and with the new evolved brain immediately they recognized the Mother. They said, "Oh Mother, our wonderful Mother!" They bowed down to her and kissed the Mother Earth. Then, they took Her soil in their hands and applied it to their foreheads and smiled with tears of love. They looked at each other and said, "God, how wonderful it is!!!"

The sons said, "Mother we could not even imagine one percent of these wonders of yours, while we were in a homosapiens body." Again, they bowed down. Their foreheads were touching the soil and again they kissed Her.

They said, "Mother."

"Yes, my beloved sons," said the loving Mother.

"We were afraid of death, but it was nice to sleep in your lap. We didn't know that this amazing life was just one step ahead in the onward journey of the soul," said the sons.

The Mother said, "Dear children, now you know, what is right and what to do. Now you are wise. Here, I don't need to tell you anything as now there are no questions in your mind but only answers. I have brought you up to here. You can now imagine how hard it was for me to bring you up. It is not easy to be a Mother. This is Sabbath (the day of rest) for you, but for me there is no such thing called 'rest'."

My beloveds keep helping others tirelessly as life is meant to love and help others, as you know it now. Life is for seeding good seeds by loving and serving others. My beloveds, helping has no end; keep going on and on.

Again she continued, "Now I have one more painful thing to endure. Your younger brother has run away from me while I was bringing him here to give him a new body. He was totally confused by Satanic Philosophy. He screamed and started yelling at me and finally ran away. At that time I had told him, the consequences of running away from the Mother, but due to his fear of death he could not understand.' I explained to him, those who do not listen to the Mother, they get no place in this world. Merciful mother's mercy is limited to her domain only. He never listened to me and now he is suffering and committing big sins. Eventually, he will have to die. When he finally leaves that body, there will be no mother to protect him. At that time, he will be the sufferer. His pain is my pain … …My obedient and loving sons now you know, this body is to help others. Help as much as you can," That mother said.

The children started thinking, "Mother, we know, our disobedient brothers are suffering badly, we want to help them but now we know it's not easy to do. We have to get a similar body to speak to them in their language. Even if, we do all those things the problem is that they are terribly ignorant, stubborn, and they will not listen to us. They don't know that they don't know. They don't know that they are ignorant. They don't know you and your wonders. They are blind to your laws and miracles; every truth is invisible to them. But, still we will try to help them…" thus Devi Messiah explained their story.

After completing the story God cried and said, "O! Mr. Pattiwala, I wish you had made a better use of your money. I gave you that money, because I trusted you not to betray me. Once, when you were a poor beggar like Anna Mario you prayed to me from the bottom of your heart saying, *"My God, one day if you give me power, I will do whatever you want, I will serve your poor children with that money to spread the practical chapters of love and humanity. I will not use your gift for my own name and fame."* I trusted you and gave you enormous power, but you opted for your personal lavish comforts and fame. God-Bawa - when he was just about to die of poverty, promised me that after dense clouds of confusions and ignorance all over the world, the holy soul will appear and he will welcome Her (the incarnation of the Holy Spirit) but he forgot his promise in this very life. Many children have betrayed me like that.

Mr. Pattiwala, today there are many Anna Marios on Earth. You can see them. There is a reason for them becoming like that. Mr. Pattiwala, nothing is here without a reason. Some people are sowing to reap in future, and some are reaping what they had sown in the past, but … Again God cried ………

"God, why are you crying?" asked Mr. Pattiwala.

"I cannot bear the pain of poor Mario," God said.

After sometime God said, "I cannot stop crying because the President of the nation is acting on your instructions... and major events in the world are taking place at your command. The law of this world needs to be changed, so that I can light the lamps of love and wisdom in my shrines. My poor children... Their wailing is cutting right through my heart. They are suffering not because of their sins, but because of your greed, your ignorance. I loved them, as it is natural for a mother to love her children. Their kind hearts were ready to welcome the light but I need your help. They are broken, and I need to repair my broken shrines, as it is not easy for anyone to live in broken houses. For how long must they suffer?" God asked wiping off her tears.

****

Step Thirty Three…

BEING THANKFUL

The Monk, Singh Messenger, Priest and the Farmer were bowing down before Devi Messiah saying, "Thank You, Devi Messiah! Thank you for visiting our planet. We shall be obedient to you."

Charles Darwin was looking from a hundred and fifty years in the past. Darwin had mixed expressions of guilt and happiness on his face. Bruno was smiling with tears from miles behind. Behind, there were many great souls including Mahatma Gandhi, Asaph Hall, Simon Marius, Galileo Galilei, Saint Thiruvalluvar, Saint Benedetto, Kung-foo-Whing, Alexander Graham Bell, Saint Miguel De Unamuno, Alfred North Whitehead, Sadhu T. L. Vaswani, George Stephenson, George E. Moor, Nicolas Copernicus, Swami Ramanand, Raja Ram Mohan Roy, Keshav Chandra Sen, Ramkrishna Paramhansa, St. Thomas, Father Damien, Thomas Edison, Sant Tulasidas, Varah Mihir, Sant Kabeer, Albert Einstein, Bohr, Heisenberg, Mother Teresa, Bhag Chand, and Tom were among them. There were hundreds and hundreds of other unknown saints. They all had different appearances but the same expressions with tears of love. They all were looking at Devi Messiah with tearful eyes and praying, "Thank you Devi Messiah, thank you, our Lord eventually … we knew you would come." Again God said;

Paritraanaaya Hi Saadhunaam, Vinaashaaya Cha Dushkritaam.
Dharma Sansthaapanaarthaaya, Sambhavaami Yuge Yuge.

For the protection of the good, and for the destruction of the wicked, and for the establishment of righteousness, I am born in every era. …Gita.

"And, you are constantly being watched because I love you. I have everyone's daily Karma diary," God said to everyone. **

Some people were shocked to know that the end is a real phenomenon. They knew that the journey of soul is much more important than the journey of life. They learned that the journey of the soul will be decided according to the Karma they perform during the journey of life. They learned that snakes will always exist in this world, but if they returned poison-less genes to this mother earth, God will grant them a poison-less planet. They knew that there is no way to get out of this world of horror except through perfection. They made a list of all essential and nonessential items. They packed up all the essential things for the journey, and left all the unnecessary things out of their lives. They learned that God's law is much more powerful then the law of this world, therefore they resolved all problems which could become stumbling blocks on the path to their ultimate destination.

They became wise enough to recognize the good and bad effects of belongings, and became strong enough to commence with the proceedings. The moment they made up their minds to do so, God helped them in moving ahead. Their dream will come true as they kept working properly while dreaming. They kept working sincerely and each day they received a compliment from their inner heart. Their complete transformation had helped them to look at the world with a saint's vision. They saw the world was perfect, because their mind and vision was perfect. They, naturally, became well-wishers of self and everyone. They understood the meaning,

Aatmaiva Hyaatmano Bandhuraatmaiva Ripuraatmanah || Gita

One's own self is one's best friend, and one's own self is one's own worst enemy.

After wandering all around, they returned within and found that the main light of love was blazing in the core of their hearts. They worked hard to maintain the amazing flash light through which they started looking into the depths of this world, and understood the power of the main core of all reasons. They understood how much this Mother Nature loves them. They communicated with her mountains, rivers, deserts, oceans, and with their motherland. They started communicating with the Father. They were happy to recognize the Loving Father and the Loving Mother.

Through the power of Inner Scripture they understood the aim of their life. They understood many other wonderful things.

One of the best things was they understood the meaning of "God has sent man on earth to build a Shrine", therefore many of them adopted one or more broken churches of God, and when they fed Anna Mario with love and food it lit his inner candle, and he thanked God. Though it was too late to light the bright wisdom candle in Anna Mario-temple, but the love candle was his need and he got that. He was very happy. His happiness couldn't be compared with anything, and Mother Earth was very happy with his happiness. Their improved life brought improvement in others. May be one day a rich righteous king will adopt a poor country. Many temples needed candles of forgiveness which they got, and thanked God. Many people understood that this is our beautiful earth, which should be made a beautiful place to live, as in future we may have to live here again if we don't go to heaven, and if we go to heaven whoever occupies this place, he and she shall be thankful for this performance. That became another long story… Those good people made history.

My God, please bless those good people. We need few more of them.

Thank you for walking with me these thirty three steps. There are a couple more steps, but for now you have to walk on your own. I wish you good luck and success on the journey. May God bless you.

Goodbye.

Mahesh Shastri, Priest

****

Credit and thanks:

All Hubble Images of stars, planets, galaxies, and solar system - with courtesy of STScI NASA and Wikimedia. Credit: STScI, and NASA.

All images of evolution, DNA and planet are with the courtesy of Wikimedia.

Page 21: "Jeep ...100 Crores," Credits: Tehelka.com'

Page 94 "Around the world... put to sea." Credit: Wikimedia.

Page 188: "If there are different ...and requirement." Credit: Swami Shivanand.

Page 274: "What is not ... it completely." GITA: Courtesy, The Living Gita by Sri Swami Satchidananda excerpted by permission from Integral Yoga Publications.

Page 276: "Justin Martyr... Chuang Tzu 23" Courtesy, Ernest Valea email@comparativereligion.com Used with permission.

Page 279: "The Soul Passes Into Another Body At Death" Artwork courtesy of The Bhaktivedanta Book Trust International, Inc. www.krishna.com. Used with permission."

Page 310: "A person of... those of others." Credit: Swami Ramsukhdas.

Pages 310 & 280: Image stages of Evolution. Courtesy: Laurence D Smart, Unmasking Evolution, Canberra, Australia. Laurence Smart laurence@unmaskingevolution.com Used with permission

Page 330. Photo "collecting fossil bones & skeleton". Courtesy: Richard Buckley, Director, University of Leicester, Archaeological Services. Used with permission

Page 311: "Seek Him in the smile ...are but him alone." Credit: Swami Chimayanand.

Special thank to: Poonam & Pramod Raghav

Cover Images NASA Hubble, Unmasking evolution, Wikimedia

Author's photo: Jay Seth

Cover designe: Paul Glantzman